A Transplant

A Transplanted Chicago

Race, Place and
the Press in Iowa City

ROBERT E. GUTSCHE, JR.

McFarland & Company, Inc., Publishers
Jefferson, North Carolina

LIBRARY OF CONGRESS CATALOGUING-IN-PUBLICATION DATA

Gutsche, Robert E., 1980–
  A transplanted Chicago : race, place and the press
in Iowa City / Robert E. Gutsche, Jr.
      p.   cm.
  Includes bibliographical references and index.

    ISBN 978-0-7864-7367-0 (softcover : acid free paper) ∞
    ISBN 978-1-4766-1628-5 (ebook)

  1. African Americans—Iowa—Iowa City—History.
2. African Americans—Illinois—Chicago—History.
3. Migration, Internal—United States—History. 4. Chicago
(Ill.)—Emigration and immigration. 5. Iowa City (Iowa)—
Emigration and immigration. 6. African Americans—Press
coverage—Iowa—Iowa City—History. 7. Journalism—Social
aspects—Iowa—Iowa City—History. 8. African American
neighborhoods—Iowa—Iowa City—History. 9. Community
life—Iowa—Iowa City—History. 10. Iowa City (Iowa)—Race
relations. I. Title.

F629.I6G87 2014
305.896'0730777655—dc23   2014015888

BRITISH LIBRARY CATALOGUING DATA ARE AVAILABLE

On the cover: Low-income apartments, home to many new black
arrivals to Southeast Side, Iowa City, Iowa, are synonymous in local
press coverage to urban ghettos of Chicago.

Printed in the United States of America

*McFarland & Company, Inc., Publishers
  Box 611, Jefferson, North Carolina 28640
  www.mcfarlandpub.com*

To my wife

Contents

Acknowledgments

I wish to thank my wife, Bridget, for her guidance and support for this project. Without her love, nothing matters. A big thanks also goes out to my dissertation committee, from which much of this book emerges—Dan Berkowitz, Mary Campbell, Frank Durham, Judy Polumbaum, and Phil Round. Andre Brock deserves thanks for his answering of my constant questions and attempting to cure my constant fears of failure. I couldn't have done this project without the continued support of Julie Andsager, Bill Casey, Carol Casey, Mary Fisher, Kelly Giese, Scott McKenzie, Erin O'Gara, Teresa Ponte, Nick Yanes, Dad, and Ma. My graduate research assistants at FIU, Maria Rosa Collazo and Bianca Morrison, read and re-read the chapters and maintained a production schedule. Their analytical skills, conceptualizations, and challenges to initial drafts made this book possible. I also thank the two peer reviewers for their comments and suggestions, which were applied to strengthen the book's focus.

Finally, I would be remiss if I did not thank the faculty and staff at Florida International University who provided funds and time that helped bring this project to completion.

Photographs and some of the political maps used to locate parts of Iowa City, as indicated, were supplied with permission and at no cost from the very talented Andre Brock, Alicia Kramme, Adam Sullivan, and Tyler Johnson. To be sure, their visuals have added a dynamic to this project that I could not have done on my own. Thank you, also, to the Urban Communication Foundation and the Journalism Studies Division of the International Communication Association, which awarded the dissertation upon which much of the project relies with the Gene Burd Urban Journalism Research Prize in 2013. I also thank Gene Burd, himself.

Finally, I wish to thank those who shared their stories for this book. Without their bravery, their stories would have been lost. Or even worse, their stories would be misunderstood.

Preface

It's three p.m. downtown, a confluence of businesses, bars, restaurants, and university buildings in Iowa City, Iowa. It's overrun by students and professors, panhandlers and homeless. The daily churning of people in one space adds a bit to the charm of a city that comes out of nowhere in rural America, plopped amid farmland, with its city limits that curve along blurred lines of city and country.

Buses gurgle and cough outside the Old Capitol Town Center, a shopping mall that until the late 1990s was a bustling mecca, a sign of a community trying to save notions of America's Main Street by keeping business, residents, and life in a central city space. When a new shopping mall opened in the neighboring city of Coralville in 1998, the downtown mall sat nearly empty. For close to a decade, storefronts were closed and gated. Though the second-floor movie theater was abandoned, escalators ran continuously, hauling next to no one to a lone health store left open upstairs.

The mall scene changed in the mid–2000s when the University of Iowa, around which much of the city is built, slowly moved offices into the Town Center's empty stores and massive hallways. By 2013, the university occupied some 70 percent of the mall with its classrooms, offices, bookstores and conference rooms. A few stores and restaurants have since gained traction. Upstairs, a local newspaper has opened up shop. On the main floor, with its thick clusters of tables and chairs, an otherwise dull space is filled with activity—college students study, flirt, arrive and leave in a flurry.

But it's outside the mall where the real action happens.

There, each weekday afternoon, smack dab on the border of private enterprise and higher education, public bus lines from across the city converge. Seemingly at once. Within a few minutes, intersections and curbs fill with

THE BUS STOP. Iowa City's downtown public bus hub signifies how traditionally white parts of the city are increasingly being shared with new black arrivals from elsewhere. Photograph by Alicia Kramme.

massive people movers. Chaos ensues. Riders of all types swerve and merge. College students head to their dorms. Those who hold prized positions in the city—working for the university and its hospital—stand, ear buds plugged in. Fast food and warehouse workers, homeless, and business owners, stand their ground as pedestrians pass through. In other parts of the country, this scene may not be special; it's Afternoon in America. In this downtown, though, and only for these few minutes each day, the space resembles someplace other than Iowa.

For the past 20 years, for many who live and work in Iowa City, the bus stop has signified symptoms of larger racial and cultural problems throughout the city. More specifically, through a portion of this scene, a particular population that stands out among the afternoon frenzy, represents decades of cultural change and challenges here: Gaggles of black high school students clustered at the curbside.

In Iowa, state law mandates that schools are not responsible for busing students if they live within three miles of their school, yet most of these students are picked up from City High School on the East Side and dumped at the bus stop downtown where they are told to wait—for as long as an hour—

to catch a bus home from school, just because their neighborhood falls inside the three-mile limit (Sullivan, 2012).

After waiting in the sun or snow, depending on the season, students finally board their buses home, all hailing the same street names—Broadway, Cross Park, Lakeside—streets in Southeastern Iowa City, the black neighborhoods, the "Southeast Side." If these children's families had cars, a ride from school to doorstep would take 10 minutes. Instead, a route from school to home, passing through the downtown, takes more than an hour.

Home to a mixture of white townies and new, black arrivals from Chicago, St. Louis, and other metro regions in the Upper Midwest, the Southeast Side is known—mythically—as a bastion of affordable housing, black families, and stories of devious behaviors (Gutsche, 2011). Still, it's cheap living in the Southeast Side. Apartments go for $600 to $800 a month. With Section 8 housing—a federal affordable housing program that assists qualified people to help make ends meet—out-of-pocket rent for these same places could be as low as $100. There, you can find a duplex to rent and even small houses to buy—an amazingly different housing market than many of these residents are used to.

Indeed, housing is a complicated business everywhere, whether they be projects in the cities, or in the suburbs, where cheap apartments are harder to find, massive McMansions so expensive that several families need to fill one house to make the rent. Kneebone and Berube (2013) write about how these polarized options—the broken ghetto or the burbs—are increasingly becoming the norm across the country. "Nationally, by the end of the 2000s one in three poor Americans lived in the suburbs, making them home to the largest and fastest-growing poor population in the country" (Chapter 2, Location 512). By 2010, for instance, "more than one in four suburban residents were poor or 'near-poor'" (Chapter 2, Location 515). In Chicago, for example, roughly two-thirds of residents live in the city's suburbs; 51 percent of them are considered poor. Iowa City, then, provides some promise in making a home.

There's no clear estimate of how many residents from urban pockets throughout the Midwest have sought Iowa as a new home, but some numbers give at least some indication: By 2007, 14 percent of the families using the voucher system as reduced rent assistance within Johnson County (in which Iowa City is located) were from Illinois and one-third of the 1,500 families on waiting lists for affordable housing in Iowa City were from the Chicago area (Bailey, Law, Mason and Phillips, 2011; Keene, Padilla and Geronimus, 2010; Spence, Lawson and Visser, 2010).

Still, there are no hard numbers that accurately measure this migration. Many families tend to move back to Chicago—or to somewhere else—within the first few months to find better work, more affordable housing (even when these things are lacking "back home" [Hu, 2013]) or to live closer to family. Local governments and agencies, then, have a difficult task in tracking who is coming and going.

But for local Iowans, the real question is: "Why are 'they' coming here?"

That's a question that emerges when people want to complain about new arrivals, and it's asked as though the answers are beyond reason—and as though the question deserves a response, that people need to or must justify themselves for where they choose to live. But the answers, for the most part, are quite simple. Yet, they do little to squelch local voyeurism: People move to Iowa for safe streets, for education, and to find work.

Indeed, it's quite common for new arrivals to Iowa City to find a job the same day they moved. They are fairly good jobs, where working on a register at McDonald's, loading freight at a warehouse, or cleaning at the university provides consistent employment, with good pay that *starts* at minimum wage. Combined with a fairly low cost of living, these jobs can pay the bills and might leave some set aside for savings.

But there's another added cost to living in Iowa for many of these new residents: Dealing with the daily hate. While most of the racial hatred towards blacks in Iowa is subtle—and is explicated throughout this book—a few times a year, the distain for new arrivals makes itself known, often exposing itself through discourse in local news.

In 2010, the city's local newspaper—*The Iowa City Press-Citizen*—decided to publish an opinion piece about tensions surrounding an influx of residents to the city from Chicago and other "urban" places. It was this story that seemed to sum up the fears about this migration among long-time Iowans. The editors' headline to a story written by Maria Houser Conzemius, a resident who was part of the paper's select "Writer's Group," told the whole story of Iowa City's changing culture in bold, black letters: "Perpetrators of urban decay" (Conzemius, 2010). Throughout the article (which is discussed in more depth in Chapter 4), the author describes single mothers, their druggie boyfriends, and dangerous "inner-city refugees" as contributing to Iowa City crime and the deterioration of wholesome, Midwestern (read *white*) living.

The article's tone and language painted a very different picture of the Southeast Side than what those living there would say about it, and journalists legitimized these stereotypes of the Southeast Side as a ghetto through a concept this book refers to as *news place-making*, in which journalists—through rhetoric and sourcing—contribute to dominant characteristics of geography based upon long-standing narratives about race, place, and people. In this case, the news characterized the Southeast Side as a rural ghetto.

Journalists chose this particular article, for instance, because it served a purpose that was more than just presenting a personal opinion. Using a pseudo-journalist who was sanctioned by the newspaper to articulate hateful language and stories about the Southeast Side, professional journalists released themselves from approaching these ideas themselves and presenting them as though they were ideas of the newspaper staff. If the newspaper had taken this same position under the guide of the *Press-Citizen* rather than under the veil of being an opinion—albeit a validated one because of the author's connection to the paper—the professional staff would have risked political and financial backlash from readers who may have been offended. Instead, the newspaper presented itself as being a forum for community discussion, allowing its Writer's Group member to say what the paper couldn't.

But the paper's journalists shouldn't get off so easily. They still have a responsibility for the discourse that appears in their pages. Here's why: First, editors chose to run the article in the first place as legitimate and verified information from a writer the paper had presented as a preeminent community member. Second, editors selected a headline (reporters and columnists rarely write their own) that furthered what some considered hate speech, categorizing and marginalizing a fairly vulnerable group of people. In effect, the headline served not just to present the story itself, but educated the public about what was considered "accurate" and acceptable news related to the community.

Furthermore, in addition to rhetoric that removed these residents from the larger community by referring to them as deviant ("perpetrators") and "other" ("refugees"), the article's cultural authority, having been approved and published by the newspaper, furthered divisive, destructive, and ambiguous discourse about real changes amid real people and real issues that Iowa City faced while trying to adapt to its growing community. This article mirrors dominant characteristics of how local news media has covered the Southeast Side. Just as the article casts its residents as assailants driven to attack the community and calls the Southeast Side "Little Chicago," other news articles presented the same stories of this rural ghetto, calling it a "No Go Zone," and "Fight Central," place-naming that identified public boundaries of its community.

The Southeast Side (and its pseudonyms), then, became someplace other than Iowa City, namely the places of Chicago believed to be ghettoized by residents who do drugs, who seek mischief, who have low motivation to work, and who have no aspirations for a "better life." In this way, Conzemius and the *Press-Citizen* hit the nail on the head about the dominant meanings assigned to the Southeast Side—and its black residents. In turn, local press achieved its goal of creating dialogue, not debate, about the Southeast Side and those who live there. Indeed, the article described above must have resonated with the community, because very few people seemed pissed off by the publication and the story only encouraged more talk about what the Southeast Side was—or, what they *thought* it was.

Setting aside the idea that people just might not read their local newspaper, little to no public outrage about racist discourse surrounding the Southeast Side is quite troubling, but, sadly, not shocking. By the time of the above article's publication in 2010, the Southeast Side had become a mythical place, and the people from there—including black high school students who boarded downtown buses for Southeastern streets—had become an extension of the Southeast Side.

The presence of Southeast Side blacks in the downtown (and anywhere outside of their neighborhood) came to resemble the fears of most white Americans and signs of urban America that don't belong in downtown Anyplace, Iowa—an encroachment of *others* into *our* spaces. Rhetoric about Iowa City's Southeast Side, then, provided a foundation for public explanations of high schoolers' antics in the city's downtown bus hub. In fact, the students' loud and physical after-school play, their experiencing freedom after being cooped-up in classrooms, were ostensibly so disruptive between three p.m. and six p.m. on weekdays between August 2011 and the end of March 2012 that police responded to eight "juveniles-related calls" there (Sullivan, 2012). (Apparently, in Iowa City, eight calls to anything seems to signify a crisis, because just "responding to calls" wasn't enough action for the community.)

Starting in 2011, city leaders and businesses took further action. They instituted rules and deployed security guards to corral the kids. Over night, security guards arrived to pounce on students who broke posted rules that no one stand within 10 feet of the mall exit to the bus stop. City buses reissued their own warnings via posted rules for what it would take for riders to get kicked off the buses themselves, including having a loud voice, cursing, and physical play. Then, the big guns came in. Every day for weeks, it seemed, armed police officers stood, arms crossed, around these clusters of black youth, their squad cars parked haphazardly in the streets, lights flashing.

It became a common scene to see white folk weave through this crowd of kids and past straight-faced cops, arms sometimes on their hips, their guns protruding from their physiques. And, finally there was the press presence. Television stations and newspapers from in and around Iowa City swarmed to tell stories of out-of-control black kids infesting an otherwise pleasant city. As one television station reported in 2012:

> Large crowds of junior high and high school students who congregate there after school are making it one of the noisiest [downtown intersections].
> "We were just called down there last night for loud, rowdy kids," said Iowa City Police Sergeant Denise Brotherton.
> And it's not only noise but large crowds near the Old Capitol Mall.

"It's hard to get in the doors sometimes because the doors will be blocked cause they'll be too many kids around," said Bill Johnson who boards the bus everyday on the busy street. "You have to squeeze your way through."

Police say the crowds and the rowdiness have led to several fights in the area. So, they're keeping close watch [KGAN, 2012].

However, neither the police—nor the students at the bus stop—could define exactly what "fights" meant, and it soon became clear to me, at least, that the real concern wasn't the pending doom emanating from clusters of kids. Instead, people's concerns about the scene of black youth who just appeared to be standing around was used as a catalyst for explaining social conditions in the Southeast Side, the influx of blacks to the city, debate about the "true intents" of new people moving to Iowa City in the first place, and to keep asking how their arrival will change the city.

Couple these concerns with the fact that high school students were using publically funded buses to make their way from the Southeast Side into *our schools* and *our downtown*, and we have a better understanding of why the larger community, apparently, came to accept how their public officials (and the press) responded to new Southeast Siders—not with public resources and sympathy for kids trying to get home from school, but with police, surveillance, and forms of subtle racism that appeared in hushed conversations and daily press coverage (for example, see Hines, 2013).

The bus stop's pocket of black youth was the first thing I noticed when I first visited Iowa City in the 1990s and then again in 2009 when I moved to Iowa City to begin my doctoral studies. The scene just seemed out of place in a state in which whites make up more than 90 percent of the population. During my first few weeks in Iowa City in 2009 especially, the bus stop seemed to be the one place in the city where issues of race came to light. The curbside stop seemed to be a clear juxtaposition of how blacks and whites live in two different worlds in the same city, a glaring indication of segregation and inequality that ultimately was veiled in public rhetoric, news coverage, whiteness, and notions of post-race America.

I wasn't alone in these initial impressions. Regan, a doctoral student in English who moved to Iowa City from Oakland, California, in 2007, said that she, too, was struck by what the mall's bus stop resembled when she first arrived. "I would go there to catch the bus after class," she says, "which was usually after 3:30, and closer to 3:30 the worse the situation was."

Regan said that when the youth started speaking loudly and playing around, the response to their behavior got worse, too. "It felt like weekly, the bus drivers would get mad at the kids and call police," Regan says, "and more than three police cars would come and park. It was ridiculous. It just looked ridiculous. It looked like the kind of police response I would see in a really dangerous and risky situation. But this dealt with high school students and buses."

Independently to us (Regan and I didn't meet until late 2011), the bus stop became a sign of a subtle and yet complicated scene that needed to be parsed out. There was a lot going on there, particularly in terms of the ways in which the city began to address the "issues at the bus stop" with police posturing, threats of small business moving out of the downtown unless the scene changed, and claims by vocal residents that the "kids downtown" were causing mini riots with their "behavior" of "speaking" and "playing around."

The more people I talked to—including the kids at the stop—saw the space as a site of control and oppression, an example of how "public space" had become controlled by those in power, those who determine who can spend time there, what people can do in that space, and who can implement systems to monitor and scold scores of black students through public enterprise—particularly city, police, and university officials.[1]

Even in 2013, Regan said the downtown setting continued to represent larger racial issues in the community that's rooted in the power dynamics and systems of a traditionally white community. The struggle, she says, is among those coming to terms with how to share their community with others—or to find ways to keep them out.

"The divide," Regan says, "is between people who are home here and people who aren't. People who are comfortable here expect people to do a lot of fucking work to make themselves feel more comfortable, fucking work that people who are comfortable here don't need to do. There is no sense of 'what I have to do to change.'"

I faced dealing with the mythical power of the Southeast Side head-on when my wife, Bridget, who was born and raised in Iowa City, told me that she wouldn't consider buying a home in the Southeast Side.

"I want to live someplace where I feel safe," Bridget told me. "Especially if I have to take the dog out at night."

We also wanted to live in an area where our property value would remain stable and grow and where we could easily walk to coffee shops. The Southeast Side has none of these traits.

On one hand, I bought that reasoning. She was right, of course, about my nightly groaning and avoidance of the dog's needs. She was also right that she needed to feel safe where she lived.

Bridget and I ended up buying a home near the North Side, but what continues to bother me about this scenario is how Bridget's perception of the Southeast Side wasn't rooted in any personal experiences that she'd had there. She had no reason to fear that neighborhood's people and places. There were no spikes in violence there. No widespread reports of rape, burglary, assault.

Bridget—like most of the city—had only heard stories. Stories of what, I wasn't sure, but scary ones that kept people out of the Southeast Side. When I asked Bridget and others about why people were concerned about the Southeast Side, I only got the same answer over and over: "It's not safe."

It's troubling how easily I bought people's stories about the Southeast Side. I knew the Southeast Side was considered the city's black neighborhood. I knew police patrolled there constantly. I felt a sense that there seemed to be impending danger lurking in its streets. Had we moved into the Southeast Side, there's little to suggest we would have made a difference. Where I ended up living, I only cleaned some storm drains once during a flood, and I mowed our lawn, but I don't even remember the names of our neighbors, nor did I participate in local associations or shovel other people's sidewalks. So maybe I wouldn't really have had much of an impact living in the Southeast Side after all.

Still, it was at the moment when I bought those Southeast Side stories at face-value and when we decided to live somewhere else that we became part of the problem. By not living in the Southeast Side, we made a conscious choice to disinvest in the community and, in so doing, we started telling and validating rationales for why we avoided the Southeast Side.

Add ours to the list of stories about the Southeast Side.

Maybe this book can help tell an alternative tale.

After months of journalism students, local activists and artisans, public officials, and residents haranguing City Hall and the School Board to do something about the "unsightly scene" outside the bus stop in 2012, school and city leaders compromised in 2013 to provide buses for Southeast Side students, though only after a decade of ignoring what should have been a simple commute and of blaming the problem on the kids themselves. It's unclear how long this change will last, and certainly, as of this book's printing, nothing has been done to squelch the stigma assigned to these students' skin color, the Southeast Side, and the acceptance of these stigmas by the public—and the press.

In fact, a March 2013 *Press-Citizen* article about possible plans for a Casey's gas station to be built in the Southeast Side was headlined "Crime alarms Casey's lawyer" and subtitled "But is still 'interested' in southeast side" (Bannow, 2013). This article continued subtle chimes in local press that cast the Southeast Side as a foreboding ghetto, its subtleness a perfect example of racialized news discourses that are loaded with innuendo and lack evidence to support the veracity of their claims.

The story provides what the headline promises—a chronological account of interactions about the possible development between the gas station company, its legal counsel, city planners, police, and select Southeast Side residents. The most important interaction? Casey's lawyer, who was said to be "wary about crime" and who had "met multiple times at length with local law enforcement officials about crime in the area." Along with police and city officials, the lawyer had "carefully reviewed the neighborhood's crime statistics and said officers have asked Casey's not to build shrubbery that people potentially could hide in or that would obstruct officers' view of the site."

Besides several more paragraphs about the process of rezoning and construction, quotes from city planners and a near-to-Southeast Side resident (who also happens to chair the city's Zoning Commission), and concerns via a resident's letter to the Zoning Commission that the gas station would "increase crime, traffic and noise in the area," the article stops at innuendo in its description of the neighborhood and its "problems."

Most troubling was how the article resembled previous local reporting about the Southeast Side in that journalists failed to include crime statistics to support assertions that the Southeast Side was in any way dangerous. Indeed, there were no assessments of what types of crime may occur in the neighborhood, no mention of whether there had been an increase or decrease in recent crime (it had decreased), and no comparison of crime rates between the Southeast Side and the rest of Iowa City. Had journalists made such a comparison, they would have shown that downtown was more dangerous. In the end, very little evidence supported the lawyer's hysteria other than the same "stories of crime" that had kept me from living there.

The gas station report represents a common way in which local press has covered the Southeast Side—focusing on like-minded public and business officials to determine the dominant characterizations of the neighborhood. As in most Southeast Side coverage, no resident appeared in the story other than an official (a zoning commissioner who said she would buy pizza for her kids, if the gas station were built, because she lives nearby) and a complainant from the neighborhood resident who just didn't want the gas station and wrote as much to city officials. But what about other residents in the neighborhoods? Do any of them want a gas station? Does it matter? These reporting problems could have easily been fixed had the reporter talked to more people than the usual suspects, had editors required more voices in neighborhood news, and had readers demanded equal coverage of people in the Southeast Side.

More than anything else, however, press coverage of the Southeast Side— as this book will show and the gas station story exemplifies—characterized and racialized the Southeast Side and its people by keeping the story too simple: The bus stop is full of bad black kids. People from Chicago are ruining Iowa City. The Southeast Side is a bad place to build a business. In terms of the gas station coverage that tends to show the neighborhood in a negative light, the news story lacked the potential positive contributions the business might have for the local economy. While not great jobs, the service industry would likely provide *some work* for those in and around the Southeast Side that they could get to easily, that would be close to home, and that is in close proximity to their children's schools.

If journalists wanted to be critical, watchdog reporters, they could have also evaluated the potential challenges to the neighborhood other than "crime," especially since this challenge wasn't supported by any evidence. Potential challenges from a gas station could include increased traffic and poor food options, for example. Gas stations and urban groceries, generally, don't offer quality food at reasonable prices; they do, however, provide fast and expensive junk food rather than healthy options, contributing to rising numbers of heart disease and diabetes among minorities.[2] That could have been a great story.

Lastly, the newspaper could have discussed the role police have in developing city environments (for example, see *Press-Citizen*, 2013; Schmidt, 2013). The news article already quotes police as wanting to limit foliage in which assailants could "hide." But instead of exploring the ability the police have in influencing what and how private and public developments look, the story uses the concerns from police to cast the space as a war zone and seems to limit any efforts of beautification that a business (albeit a gas station) can make in a neighborhood. (As an aside, it's hard to ignore the irony in how limiting the numbers of bushes and trees from new development in the Southeast Side only reinforces settings of a real-life concrete jungle—the very thing Iowa City residents seem to be against.)

This book is not about an Iowa City bus stop. Or a gas station. It's also not about evaluating the journalistic style of local press in and around Iowa City. But this project begins with these scenes and these players in part because they illustrate characterizations of the Southeast Side as being the city's "bad side of town." I begin this project with these scenes because I wish readers to remember them throughout the book. Indeed, these subtleties are at the focus of my arguments of how rhetoric in the press further notions of white supremacy and social control. By their very nature, subtleties are overlooked and explained away, but it's within these movements that dangerous ideologies thrive.

Second, these cases help set a foundation for this project, in which I wish to implicate the press and its power as major players in establishing and furthering racialized discourse and decision-making surrounding people and place. This project, therefore, attempts to undermine the discourse surrounding the Southeast Side and its people by addressing head-on, and with some personal venom, the rhetorical and ideological attacks during a time of urban migration to a place that is supposed to be welcoming and supportive.

I have tried to be aware of the potential audiences for this book, first by grounding it in a conceptual framework with which to explicate and explain the otherwise veiled racial acts occurring in news media, public discourse, and policy. More specifically, I am interested in capturing a snapshot of historical change in the Midwest—specifically, how one community—Iowa City—is dealing with a slow, but sustained influx of black residents, which is why much of this project is based between 2008 and 2012. Just enough time has passed since then, perhaps, that one can look back in recent history for a deeper explanation of events. Let's hope so.

The front end of this project provides the conceptual work that then is applied to the news place-making of Iowa City's Southeast Side and, to some extent, other places in the country in the book's second half. In this respect, this book is meant for communications scholars and students. This project is also aimed at and for Iowa City's diverse communities. It is my hope that this book bridges both scholarly and popular audiences and can be used to discuss the role of power in place. More specifically, I wish to acknowledge the power of those in Iowa City who have shared their stories about being marginalized. In the end, these residents have experienced Iowa City in ways different than most, and those experiences deserve to be accepted.

To some people, this project may feel personal—particularly to those who have dedicated their lives to making Iowa a better place. For that I apologize. Many Iowans are likely aware of a piece written by a journalism professor at the University of Iowa and published on the *Atlantic*'s website in 2011. In that piece, the professor made perverse generalizations about the state. He called Iowa a "schizophrenic, economically-depressed, and some say, culturally-challenged state" in one part (Bloom, 2011), while another section of his article garnered the most local and national attention:

> Those who stay in rural Iowa are often the elderly waiting to die, those too timid (or lacking in education) to peer around the bend for better opportunities, an assortment of wastetoids and meth addicts with pale skin and rotted teeth...

Throughout the shit-storm that followed this article and an embarrassing NBC interview in which the author took on the wittier Willie Geist, it was hard for Iowans to recognize any of the article's truths: Iowa's rural parts do struggle with development; it is hard to attract—and keep—young people in the state's smaller communities; drugs, such as meth, continue to be a problem among rural communities that, under the radar, produce and sell, in part because it's cheap; and, there are rural stretches that work to maintain their own sense of identity as its people age and move and die.

Any benefit that could come from an analysis such as that which appeared on the *Atlantic*'s website was overshadowed by small and simply constructed descriptions. The article's attacks were too personal and they were made against those who may not have the power to overcome local economic challenges, who might already have been seen by outsiders as culturally inferior, who might be seen as living in a "fly-over state." In the end, it's simply not right to strike at those who are already down and out, and coming out from under that attack would make anyone weary of another project about Iowa.

The main difference between this project and the *Atlantic* piece is that this book addresses the stories of Iowans who are on the bottom, placed and kept there by inequality that reaches back generations, but that is instilled and maintained by the more powerful. To some extent, I am going after the same groups that the *Atlantic* author did, its white residents who are already down and out. My intent, however, is to place blame on the powerful—not those who can't defend themselves.

This is also not to be a book that bashes journalists (though I know many may feel it is) by ignoring the good that they can do and that they, sometimes, identify the problems of the world. In late 2013, local Iowa newspapers, including *The* (Cedar Rapids) *Gazette* published a series about racial inequalities in the state (Gruber-Miller, 2013; Gruber-Miller and Hennigan, 2013; Gruber-Miller and Hennigan, 2013a; Gruber-Miller and Pigee, 2013; Gruber-Miller and Sutter, 2013). The series focused on disparities by presenting data which included numbers that showed, among other things, that home ownership for whites was around 74 percent, 51 percent for Latinos, and 31 percent for blacks; that black families earn "less than half" of whites in the state; that blacks rank high among those who commit crime and low among those who graduate high school. The coverage, however, wasn't without its subtle racism. The introductory article, for instance, ended with a quote from a local community college official who acknowledged the difficulty inherent in being a new immigrant to Iowa but who couldn't help but say that new arrivals are simply better off by being here: "It may be difficult," the official said, "but it would have been worse if they would have stayed where they were from" (Gruber-Miller, 2013).

Another story presented racial bias in a more overt manner (Gruber-Miller and Pigee, 2013). That story focused on racial disparities among those who are jailed in Iowa—specifically that while blacks made up 3.2 percent of the state's population, black offenders in the system increased from 15.6 percent to 17.4 percent 2008 and 2012, while whites dropped from 76.6 percent to 74.5 percent. To personalize the story, journalists turned to the tale of a drug-user-turned-pastor who talked about pulling himself out of a blackened stupor that blacks seem to face and that lead to these folk simply making "bad decisions" (Gruber-Miller and Pigee, 2013). None of the reporting provided a complex analysis of racial disparities that are rooted in pure hatred and fear of blacks that continues to permeate society. That story might be too unkind for Iowans to hear.

Iowa conjures up nostalgic imagery of one-room schoolhouses, farms, and Sunday family dinners—the glorified constructions that build notions of America's "Heartland" (Fry, 2003). Iowa is, after all, the place of Grant Wood's *American Gothic*, an image that resounds throughout American culture as a symbol of, among other things, a Midwestern "Protestant work ethic." In fact, a two-story-tall version of this image stands in downtown Dubuque, Iowa, as a constant reminder of that painting—and of dominant culture and power-brokers.

Dredging up our nation's failed ancient and current history of racial integration to assign alternative meanings to what some define as "progress," as

TRADITION. Giant statues resembling Grant Wood's *American Gothic*, which was set in Iowa, lord over downtown Dubuque, Iowa. This "American Gothic" is a reminder of the state's traditional—and racialized—history; as late as the 1990s, Dubuque was the scene of Ku Klux Klan demonstrations, cross burnings, and racial violence in the city schools. Author's photograph.

this project does, must put both ourselves and our ancestors in an uncomfortable light. Consider it growing pains. Or constructive criticism. The great fact that Iowa was a Free State (it did not allow for slavery), for instance, must also include discussion that its people burned crosses in Dubuque as late as 1990s (Chaichian, 2006), that Waterloo has two high schools that were built with the intent of separate but equal and that still straddle the Cedar River, set in two heavily segregated neighborhoods. These past moments never go away; they become wrapped in collective memories and applied to new settings, with new characters, and new conflicts.

To some extent, I'll be asked—and maybe rightfully so—just who *I am* to write about such things. If it's not already clear, I'm a white guy. I'm not from Iowa. Nor do I live there anymore. So to this question, I don't have a great answer, but I'll tell you that I've approached this topic with the best of intentions.

As last notes to this Preface, the reader should know that many of the names in this book have been changed to protect the innocent, vulnerable, and angry. I complied with all requests to change names, and the reader will recognize a name change when I only mention a first name. Full names are used in particular cases when the individual has sought public attention, such as writing a newspaper editorial, or gave express permission for her or his name to be used. Finally, in the interest of full disclosure, the publisher of *The Daily Iowan*, Bill Casey, is my father-in-law. If anything, this relationship has afforded me a closer look at the news outlet's operations and provided me with contacts at the newspaper with whom I spoke regularly.

In the end, this is a book of stories told to me by people who have a hell of a lot more invested in Iowa City than I do at this point in my life; therefore, any royalties that come from its sale will be donated to the Community Foundation of Johnson County to further invest in the children (and other new arrivals) in Iowa City.

Introduction

Welcome to the Rural Ghetto: "Southeast Side" as "Little Chicago"

John Versypt wanted to hang a "No Smoking" sign. It was one of several improvements he hoped to make that October weekend in 2009 to help keep his tenants' homes clean and welcoming. Versypt, who owned several apartments in the Broadway Condominiums on Broadway Street in Iowa City, Iowa, had also planned during his visit to talk with apartment managers about what could be done about a rise in crime and vandalism there (Keppler, 2009).

In previous months, police had been called to these apartments more than 200 times for cases of domestic violence, drugs, weapons charges, and a string of other incidents. Versypt and others thought something needed to change. Even though he lived hours away, he tried not to be a neglectful landlord. Conversations with these managers and residents, Versypt said, would help him stay attuned with local vibes in a place where he considered himself another neighbor.

The meeting never happened.

Police found Versypt dead on the floor inside his apartment building on October 8. The 64-year-old father and sheet metal worker from Cordova, Illinois, about 30 minutes northeast of the Quad Cities, had been shot in the head, his body found next to the sign he planned to hang, a screwdriver, and the handgun that killed him. Versypt's murder left a stain on the community, but few in the city were surprised. People had expected this kind of thing to go down soon, especially in the Southeast Side, a place that seemed to become more like the ghetto each day. The October killing was the end of a summer of violence in the neighborhood, where gangs were said to be in the midst of battle, people told stories of droves of drug-runners dealing in apartments, and mobs took to the streets with guns, baseball bats, and fists (Keppler, 2009). But murder wasn't as scary as the thought of who might have been the killer.

Months later, local police charged a 17-year-old black man who, in 2008, had moved to Iowa City from Holland, Michigan, with Versypt's murder. Police say the gun went off during an attempted robbery. Versypt is thought to have grabbed the gun when a single bullet shot through his hand and into his head.[1] At the time, police suspected several black youth of being involved in the crime, and it was these details of race—that the alleged shooters were black, Versypt, white—that jarred the city the most and catapulted it into a frenzy of fear. A white property "owner" being shot and killed by a black "subject" represented white Americans' worst fear—a black uprising.

Concerns about the city's changing culture and its future were targeted at blacks said to have moved to Iowa City from Chicago and other cities to prey on white Iowans. These people, popular discourse maintained, continued to move to the state to steal Iowans' social welfare and to destroy their public schools. For the next few years, local news stories about the Southeast Side focused on perceptions of its social decline and destruction.

Images of the Southeast Side in local media showed a rural ghetto (Gutsche, 2011): bushes overtaking tiny duplexes, weed-ridden lawns lining the block, plywood patches covering apartment windows, dumpsters overflowing with used furniture, trash and empty cardboard boxes. Also in these images—Southeast Side residents who are almost always black, wandering the streets or loitering at crime scenes.

To those outside of America's inner cities, such stories and scenes of Iowa City's Southeast Side may seem to have been pulled from somewhere else—Detroit, Chicago, St. Louis. Anywhere but Iowa. Crumbling and boarded-up brick apartment buildings resemble scenes of the low rises in HBO's *The Wire*, a drama based in the urban ghettos of Baltimore—after all, yellow police tape surrounding shell casings on the pavement are more Chicago and Compton than the middle of the Midwest.

And despite the Southeast Side's expansive parks, soccer fields, community gardens, school yards, and tree-lined streets, the neighborhood is constantly talked about and shown by local press as a bad neighborhood that's found itself in the middle of a migration of blacks from urban areas to smaller cities deeper into the Midwest.

In the text ahead, I introduce Iowa City as a rural ghetto through the lens of crime news in 2009 and 2010, coverage that often hinged on stories of crime, "failing" schools, and narratives of urban and black "culture" that's ghettoized America's Heartland—turning one mythical place that's based on traditional American living into another, one which represents the dangers of inner-city living. I begin with a background on this new Midwestern migration, placing it in a context of urban decline and change. I then discuss the issues of the Southeast Side specifically and conclude with an outline for the rest of the book.

Migration to the Rural Ghetto

At nearly 70,000 people, Iowa City itself really isn't rural. Its local culture, though, is largely influenced by the rest of a predominantly rural state that's a couple hundred miles from major urban hubs, deep within God's Country. The city's location in the region keeps the people's connection to the fields, to long stretches of dirt roads, and to the hard work of a Midwestern way of life. It's common for people in Iowa City and its surrounding communities to have grown up on a farm or in a small town. If not, they likely know someone who has. These tight relationships and small towns are framed through a sense of nostalgia that paints a picture of Iowa City as a place of friendly, hardworking patriots who uphold traditional values in a world that's spinning out of control.

Iowa, then, and its slower pace of life, looks like a dream. It's the promise of this mythical new life that's contributing to a growing population of low-income city dwellers that continue to move from America's urban centers to the country's cornfields.

Increasingly, Iowa City is just one of several cities across the country's middle states that are gathering concentrations of poor minorities who continue to flee urban cores (Chaichian, 2006; Fry and Liaw, 2005; Goetz, 2003; 2013; Hunt, Hunt and Falk, 2012). Cities such as Iowa City, Iowa; Madison, Wisconsin; Bloomington, Indiana; and smaller, suburban neighborhoods around Chicago are gaining pockets of inner-city residents abandoned by governmental housing practices to house the poor in city slums (Kneebone and Berube, 2013).

The migration comes from urban neighborhoods in which many of these residents had lived inside publically funded housing projects and with the help other forms of public assistance, who then were forced out of their homes when these projects came down over the course of the last decade (Goetz, 2013). Leaving these areas, residents took with them their housing assistance in the form of federal vouchers that allow for people to shop within the private marketplace for housing that's based on their income (for review, see Fraser, Burns, Bazuin and Oakley, 2013).

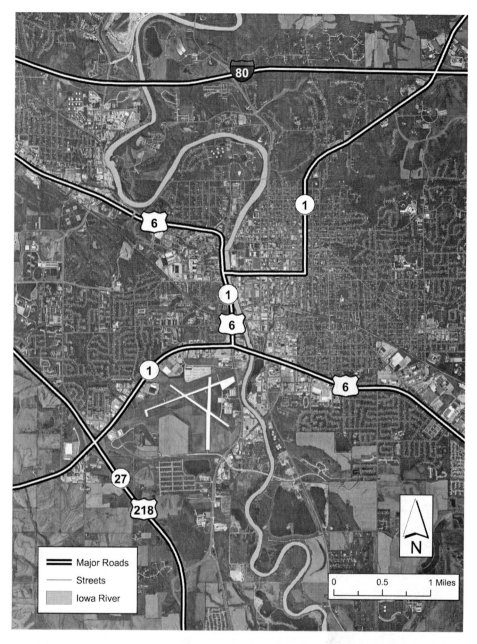

MAP I.1. IOWA CITY, IOWA, 2012. Iowa City's dominant geographic features include
the winding Iowa River that cuts through the center of the city and major highways
and an interstate at the city's North and South. The city's downtown and the University
of Iowa neighbor the Iowa River alongside Highway 1/6. Map by Tyler Johnson.

The voucher system, which merged with other forms of Section 8 housing assistance in the 1980s, was meant to disperse the high concentrations of poor and allow users to find homes that were closer to pockets of employment (Goetz, 2003). But this system has become yet another strategy of placing the burden of finding affordable and safe housing not on federal and local governments, but on the people themselves. Often, the apartments, rooms, and houses that accept Section 8 are in majority minority neighborhoods and developments that were constructed solely to house the poor.

A system that relies on such levels of social and cultural competencies of the voucher-holder requires one to navigate a complex structure of policies and neighborhood rules and norms. Indeed, the mobility of housing vouchers has created what Andrew Greenlee, an assistant professor in the Department of Urban and Regional Planning at University of Illinois, Urbana-Champaign, who studies the mobility of vouchers, calls *the third ghetto.* "A major rationale for the voucher is that it allows households to be mobile, meaning that it cannot only provide affordable housing but can also deconcentrate poverty," Greenlee told me. But mobility and the deconcentration of the poor, Greenlee says, "has become another means to not deal with some of the more structural root causes of the issues related to poverty."

With groups of poor moving across regions, away from each other and

MAP. I.2. INTERSTATE MOBILITY. The U.S. Interstate Highway System, along with mobile housing vouchers, increases the ability of urban populations to move throughout the Midwest. Map by Alicia Kramme.

cultures and social structures with which they are familiar, residents become individuals who are fully responsible for their conditions, not part of a larger population with shared experiences and the ability to voice their challenges, concerns, and the consequences of failed public policies. The effect of this dispersion, then, is a diluted sense of poverty, its causes, and notions of who's responsible. "Deconcentrating poverty does not necessarily solve it," Greenlee says, "but rather makes it more invisible than it was when it was in one place (and, in the case of public housing) in one type of very visible housing."

The "first ghetto" emerged after the great migrations of black folk from the South to industrialized urban centers in the North in the early 1900s and then to other parts of the country after World War II. Millions of blacks were led to find work and new lives away from their geographic connection to slavery. Influxes of new arrivals to these city centers—namely Detroit, New York, Chicago—allowed private business to construct massive housing projects that took advantage of desperate people needing safe homes, who wanted to make a better life for themselves, but didn't have enough to avoid being swindled (Beauregard, 2003; Katz, 2012).

Decades later, government officials identified a 30-year period of government policies starting in the 1930s that created "the second ghetto," one built around dense urban housing, constructed and funded through federal housing policies in America's big cities (Hirsch, 1998). High-rise projects included Chicago's infamous Robert Taylor Homes, and Cabrini-Green and Pruitt-Igoe in St. Louis were home to dozens of buildings each. Stout towers peppered acres of low-rise apartment buildings at each location and became places where generations of families were born, lived, and died.

At one time, 30,000 people were said to have lived in the Robert Taylor Homes alone, though it had been built for a third of that number. Yet most population estimates for these projects still don't account for the countless squatters who lived there illegally and the homeless who sought refuge in these "vertical ghettos" (Goetz, 2013; Hirsch, 1998; Katz, 2012). For decades, the projects served as landscapes for murder, drug use, and the setting for mythical constructions of inner-city/ghetto/black culture. Even from the beginning, activists, residents, and governmental leaders called for an end to this kind of warehousing of the poor (English, 2011; Kotlowitz, 1992; Massey and Denton, 1993; Venkatesh, 2000; 2006).

The popular movement of urban renewal, the drive of private business to pounce on opportunities for low interest rate loans, and governments who were generous with their tax incentives for developers well before the economic bust of 2007 fed the mobility associated with the voucher system (Kneebone and Berube, 2013). Quickly, people without homes in the urban cores—or those who wished to move into newer developments with their safer schools, open green spaces, and proximity to employment—were able to find better places to live.

But the problems with vouchers, which are complex and many, have led Greenlee to consider this movement, that of "the third ghetto," as a dispersed population dependent on the fluctuation of the "private market" that dictates rents, that creates social tensions between users and neighbors and landlords who question the character of those on welfare, and that still tend to result in users crowding the same neighborhoods for the added benefit of close and cheap childcare and other forms of informal support.

In these ways, the voucher system—despite its possibilities, such as its ability to provide users with "choices" about where to live—still represents society's interest in marginalizing poor blacks. "We need to move away from the assumption that we can solve the problems of poor people via mobility" and the racialized narratives of welfare and its users, Greenlee says. "Clearly there is a history around black and brown bodies to make it easier to justify these narratives, but to me this is as much a question about citizenship, about who has the right to access certain spaces and take advantage of whatever they perceive to be opportunity."

The opportunity of living in Iowa City—and really many of the places in the Midwest where voucher-holders have settled, often after years of moving and waiting to qualify for local assistance—comes with its own challenges. This migration has challenged communities that are new to welcoming people from outside and that tend to implement fairly straightforward social rules and norms regarding language, work, use of welfare, and educational achievements that these new people need to "abide by" in order to survive. Not following the "rules" will certainly lead to social pressures to move out of Iowa City, a place, some say, these folk don't belong to begin with. As Kneebone and Berube (2013) write:

> Place intersects with core policy issues central to the long-term health and stability of metropolitan areas and to the economic success of individuals and families—things like housing, transportation, economic and workforce development, and the provision of education, health, and other basic services [Chapter 7, Location 222].

More specifically to the people in these new places, scholarship has also identified histories of public, mediated racial narratives that have appeared in the press about social welfare, users, and their neighborhoods. Katz (1989), for instance, provides a rhetorical distinction between the *deserving* and *undeserving poor*. The deserving poor, Katz writes, are those who have, by no fault of their own, found themselves in poverty. These people, who may suffer from illness, layoffs, or general misfortune, tend to be cast as deserving sympathy and public resources to help them to survive and to attempt to climb out of their situation.

The undeserving poor, on the other hand, are seen to have made choices that led them to poverty: maybe they live beyond their means, they spend their money unwisely, they are too lazy to work, struggle with addictions, or simply want to loaf on government "hand-outs." For these people—whose racial discrimination tends to be ignored or explained away—their mental illness viewed as non-existing, and/or their personal cycles of poverty seen to be of their own creation, not created and maintained by larger society—don't deserve public help or compassion. They are left to fix their own problems themselves.

Many of the new residents associated with the Southeast Side discussed in this book have been classified in news texts and in public discourses as being "undeserving" of public aid, of compassion, and of having their experiences legitimatized by placing them within a larger social and cultural context. Conversation about Iowa City's "declining" community has turned—as it often does—to notions of "personal responsibility," a fundamentally conservative approach to persuading the public to ignore the needs of subordinate groups.

Instead of holding landlords to task for discriminatory practices, holding police accountable for disproportionate targeting of minorities, and holding the general public accountable for supporting or remaining silent about policies that maintain the power and financial position of the elite, the "undeserving poor" are expected to magically persevere through hardships that would cause most of us to fail. Placing the blame and the sole responsibility of solving the problems of the poor *on the poor* in Iowa City has resulted in even more mobility as people search for more affordable and accessible communities.

While limitations have been placed on how many landlords can accept Section 8 assistance as a means to curb clustering of low-income households, little has been done to address social stigma related to living in the Southeast Side. Little has been done to address issues of adequate transportation, education, and work for these residents—many who have been forced to move into neighboring Coralville and North Liberty. The latter city is a 20-minute interstate drive North of Iowa City, and both cities hold even fewer options for affordable busing and social services than the Southeast Side.

In each of these new places, the struggles to adapt—or, as some may see it, assimilate—are different, set by local culture, but are maintained in similar ways—policing, educational, and other social policies that makes adapting nearly impossible. After all, black residents will remain black in majority white neighborhoods, and that difference alone makes them easy targets and perpetuate what Goetz (2013) describes as a pathological movement of the poor through public policies and local politics.

"For the most part," Goetz writes, "these families are moved from one high-poverty, segregated environment to other high-poverty and racially segregated neighborhoods" (p. 19). Benefits of moving out of projects, however, are "inconsistent," Goetz writes, which include "an increased sense of safety and reductions in visible signs of social disorder, but "there have been no overall benefits in terms of economic self-sufficiency, physical health, or in terms of education outcomes..." (pp. 19–20).

The irony of moving from one place to another just to experience many of the same challenges—and new ones—as those places one wished to escape also rears its head in terms of social structures and rules that ostracize, imprison, or accost. Beckett and Herbert (2009) refer to these types of social pressures as a process called *banishment*, a form of social control within public spaces that set the standards for what—and who—is accepted in society.

Banishment includes both overt and covert uses of force and control. Overt applications can include the use of armed, uniformed police who "are marshaled to enforce and often delineate" public spaces and "use their powers to monitor and arrest in an attempt to clear the streets of those considered unsightly or 'disorderly'" (p. 8), while covert methods include the implementation of "zero tolerance" policies that, on paper, enforce dominant perceptions of what's acceptable in public behaviors. Beckett and Herbert use the example of how New York City police in the 1990s applied pressure and "zero tolerance" against even the most minimal of crimes, as a show of force to oppress and institute order. At the time Beckett and Herbert write, "[t]hat meant that all street-level misdemeanors—including the infamous squeegeeing of car windshields by sidewalk entrepreneurs—would generate a strong police response" (p. 33).

Banishment also appears in media rhetoric. News about "new arrivals" to Iowa City from "the inner-city," for instance, reduces public investment in neighborhoods, normalizes the use of force and surveillance upon the already marginalized, and empowers the dominant storytellers and spatial definers to maintain physical distance between the dominant community and the "others."

Banishment that this particular project reveals within the press operates with purposes and vigor similar to banishment identified by Beckett and Herbert in several ways. First, such banishment via press discourse was meant to exclude the less desirable among us, those who challenge dominant explanations of everyday life, and who complicate the otherwise-simple stories of how people should experience the American Dream. Second, press-related banishment also punished those who operated outside of dominant ideology through ridicule and marginalization as a means to force these members of a community to submit to the dominant system and as a means to encourage the masses to act according to the dominant norms. Third, this process of banishment through the press removed from individuals their right to participate in the community as full members who could both contribute to and benefit from social cohesion. Finally, banishment formed particular geographies within which the banished were restricted, creating a divide between dominant and subordinate communities.

Through this lens, the stories of people's experiences in Iowa City discussed throughout this project reveal the ideological depth to the otherwise veiled racialized news coverage about the mythical and localized Southeast Side-as-ghetto. Constructions that determined what resources were made available to those in the Southeast Side, how rigorous such aid should be, and the explanations for social conditions there are rooted in a deep sense of who owns local neighborhoods and who has the right to challenge dominant characterizations of people and places.

The Rise of the "Southeast Side"

Iowa City's longtime residents and the established press have long said that those who move to Iowa City in search of assistance place additional strains on the community's social services, including transportation, health care, schools and police—and that these services are first and foremost for those who *are from Iowa*. In 2007, for instance, 14 percent of housing assistance—both vouchers and public housing units provided through the Iowa City Housing Authority—was used by families from Illinois; those from Illinois accounted for 30 percent of those on the waiting list.

By 2010, the number of Illinois residents on the waiting list grew to 50 percent (Keene, Padilla and Geronimus, 2010). Because of residency requirements that maintain voucher recipients must live in Iowa City in order to receive assistance, those from outside of the region continued to apply to receive aid after moving to the city and sat patiently on the waiting list.[2]

In addition to the public housing provided by the Iowa City Housing Authority, local non-profit groups such as the Housing Fellowship, the Johnson County Housing Trust Fund, Habitat for Humanity, and the Hawkeye Area Community Action Program all provided various forms of housing assistance for low-income and impoverished families. By providing aid, Iowa City appeared open and welcome to people—both locally and not—who wanted to call the city home. But a common misconception in Iowa City that's often told with distain—that black families from Chicago hog the community's affordable housing—shows how closed the community really is to people in need.

MAP I.3. IOWA CITY'S "SOUTHEAST SIDE," 2012. Map by Tyler Johnson.

Ironically, the reality has been that the majority of the city's housing choice vouchers are utilized by elderly, disabled white women, and that while some new arrivals had moved from somewhere else to Iowa City and utilize city and county social services and those of local non-profit groups, they account for only a small portion of those who seek assistance (Spence, Lawson and Visser, 2010). Furthermore, data gathered by Greenlee—the one who argues for the "third ghetto"—suggests more people take their vouchers from Chicago to elsewhere in Illinois than to Iowa City.

But who these new arrivals are—or who they are thought to be—and where they tend to settle in Iowa City has formed an ideological foundation for how to talk about poverty and race in the region. After all, families still have to rent houses and apartments they can afford, and many of those fall within the same neighborhoods south of Iowa City's Highway 6—a four-lane highway that serves both as a main artery into the city and as a physical boundary that divides many of the city's new black residents. In recent years, parts of Iowa City's Southeast Side have grown six times faster than other areas of the community since 2000. The Southeastern Broadway and Grant Wood neighborhoods, for instance, have expanded by as much as 25 percent, and the population of the Southeast Side increased by more than 19 percent between 1990 and 2000 (Bailey, Law, Mason and Phillips, 2011).

Seeing Iowa City's Southeast Side as an extension of Chicago's ghetto

THE ENCLAVE. Iowa City's Dolphin Lake Point Enclave in the Southeast Side resemble inner city projects of Chicago, Baltimore, and St. Louis. These and other low-income apartments are home to many new black arrivals to the city. Author's photograph.

has been a long time in the making. Since the 1960s, this southeastern space has been home to first-time home-buyers, the elderly who are on a fixed income, and the poor of all races. More recently, however, the neighborhood has attracted those with even less social capital and finances to fight being crammed into run-down apartments and rental homes, removed from the rest of the city.

Southeast Side apartment buildings are full, but the parking lots sit virtually empty. Few can afford a car—clunker or no—a common sign among both urban and suburban poor (Kneebone and Berube, 2013), and while college students pay thousands of dollars for rickety homes throughout the city—wearing their status as "poor college students" as a badge—poor and black new arrivals who live in disrepair in the Southeast Side are stigmatized and segregated.

By 2010, black families came to represent 2.9 percent of the state's population (and 3.2 percent by 2012), up from 1.4 percent in 1980 (Gruber-Miller and Pigee, 2013; State Data Center, 2012), an increase that becomes quite visible—especially at the local level. As of 2009, the number of racial minorities (predominantly black and Latino) in Iowa City's southeastern neighborhoods was double the city average. While nearly all focus is on the racial tension caused by African Americans "from Chicago," Asian Americans have quickly come to represent the city's largest minority population, accounting for 5.8 percent of the city's residents in 2009, compared to African Americans, who represented 3.9 percent (Bailey, Law, Mason and Phillips, 2011).

Still, few news stories discuss the Asian American population—many who, by local guesses, work or study at the University of Iowa and tend to live downtown, in university housing, or in Western suburbs. Regardless, it's the Southeast Side that attracts the most attention, simply because of perceptions of who lives there.

Cut off from the rest of the city by Highway 6 and within walking distance of only big box retail and junk food stores, Southeast Side residents rely on public transportation to access the rest of the city. These are the same buses that for at least a decade have forced City High School students from the Southeast Side to travel for more than an hour, transferring downtown for a trip that takes less than 10 minutes by car, which this book's Preface discussed in great detail.

Today, Southeast Side students and residents continue to be bused on schedules that start too late for first-shift factory workers, that end their service early in the evening, that have limited access on Saturdays, that don't run on Sundays, and that require multiple transfers to get from one side of the city to the other.

Higher concentrations of affordable housing and students eligible for free and reduced lunch—a program to provide more affordable meals in schools for those who qualify—in the Southeast Side have not just contributed to the image of the neighborhood as a poor place, but as another world filled with a dense number of people who struggle to be integrated with the rest of the city.

By 2010, the number of students eligible for free and reduced lunch had nearly doubled since the 2001–2002 school year. In the elementary schools on Iowa City's Southeast Side, more than half of the students are minorities and more than 60 percent of students have qualified for the program in recent years. (More on this topic is discussed in Chapter Eight). Yet, few of these details—such as who receives forms of welfare and the complex reasons why—have appeared in news coverage of the Southeast Side, replaced instead with dominant explanations based in blaming "black" and "ghetto" culture that all started on Mother's Day 2009.

The Mother's Day Riots

On the same day that many families were celebrating their moms, some 60 residents on Mother's Day 2009—including entire families—armed themselves with knives and baseball bats on the streets of the Southeast Side. Thirty more people clogged the streets during another melee just a couple of days later; this time young men were accused of wielding baseball bats and entering a home in the neighborhood to end a feud between two families. Those cited by police and press to be involved in the melee were 12- to 15-year-old black "men." These were called the "Mother's Day Riots" and the stories of violent crowds of black families rumbling in the Southeast Side launched a summer of racialized news coverage related to local violence.

In July of that year, a plain-clothed sheriff's deputy in Iowa City shot and killed John Deng, a 26-year-old Sudanese man who had been living in the city's homeless shelter. The deputy approached Deng and drew his service weapon after Deng allegedly stabbed a man with whom he was fighting. Deng—thought to be one of the "Lost Boys of Sudan," a group of 20,000 youth who fled civil war there before 2005 and were scattered across the globe (Corbett, 2001; Eggers, 2007; Hermiston, 2009)—spoke broken English. There was yelling and movement and in a moment of confusion, Deng, who was said to have tried to stab the man again, was shot once and killed (*Daily Iowan*, 2009).

After several news reports about the shooting, a vigil to remember Deng, and an investigation that cleared the deputy of wrongdoing, the story left the news pages, but remained in the city's collective memory. Deng's death at the hands of a police officer attracted the attention of local activists who claimed that skin color played a role in the shooting. The deputy was white, and Deng—for all intents and purposes—was black. But while the Deng story died out, stories about the "Mother's Day Riot" continued for weeks throughout the summer as police continued to arrest more residents suspected in the melee.

At the same time, public debate was brewing about pending changes to the local school system that would alter what schools elementary students would be attending to better disperse racial and socioeconomic inequalities in classrooms—a process called *redistricting*. Hidden in a conversation of redistricting was the concern of many white Iowa City parents that they soon could be sending their students to school with those from the Southeast Side—a debate that continued through 2013 (Hines, 2013a) and into 2014.

To calm fears about Southeast Side violence (and as a precursor to addressing concerns about the desegregation of Iowa City's elementary schools) the City Council in 2009 voted to start a nightly curfew to rein in Southeast Side youth. The curfew started in March 2010 and required 16- and 17-year-olds to be off of the streets by midnight. Younger youth had earlier deadlines.

However, while the curfew was intended to cover the entire city, it was clear to some of us that police were really targeting those in the Southeast

CONTAINMENT. The city's only police substation that was built after the "Mother's Day Riots" on the Southeast Side is more about containing blacks in the neighborhood than keeping the peace. Photograph by Alicia Kramme.

Side. It turned out that we were right to worry; of the 40 contacts police officers made in Iowa City in the curfew's first months, a disproportionate number of the youth contacted by police regarding the curfew—more than 50 percent—were minorities (Hennigan, 2010).

Then in 2010, the police department opened its only substation—on the city's Southeast Side (Earnest, 2011). Police quickly moved into a strip mall at the corner of the infamous Broadway Street and Highway 6, bolted a large, illuminated sign announcing their presence on the top of the building, and parked a single squad car parallel to the mall's sidewalk to make the station's presence even more obvious.

Open weekdays between 8 a.m. and 5 p.m., the substation hosted community meetings and a sole officer sat in his office behind what looks like bulletproof glass several yards from the front door. Computers lined the walls where residents could look for jobs, access the city's library databases, and surf the web—all under the officer's watchful eyes. But the police presence was more a signal of safety to the rest of the community than to the Southeast Side itself. That next summer, a community activist would tell me, the police chief told her the department's plan to "keep calm in the Southeast Side" would include citing residents for petty violations such as littering, loitering, and jaywalking.

"We're going to ticket the thugs back to Chicago," she says the chief told her, a believable story based on the status quo for dealing with Iowa City's dark-skinned population. By 2013, the detention rate for black youth in Johnson County (in which Iowa City is the county seat) hit about 19 percent, while rates for white youth sat at roughly 12 percent (Miller, 2013). School suspension rates are stacked against black youth, as well, with blacks in each of the three academic terms in the 2011–2012 school year equaling nearly 17 percent of all enrollments, but between 47 and 55 percent of suspensions, according to district records.

But concerns about the Southeast Side have extended beyond murder, violence, and gangs. Instead, it's been about "black culture" infiltrating a white community. It's about American and Western ideology (racist ideology) that puts people with white—or light—skin above people with dark—or black—skin. Such belief systems don't start or stop at the Iowa border. There has been a long history of black-white-Hispanic tensions in the U.S. (Telles, Sawyer and Rivera-Salgado, 2011) and unequal treatment based upon skin tone among American blacks (Robinson, 2010).

In the Midwest, the meanings of skin color go deeper than pure racism or intolerance. What fuels this conflict is a fear that traditional American values are being challenged and crushed. In response, many Midwestern cities have taken to local businesses and governments to report specifics about their growing "diversity" and to propose how to respond. It's partially these "official" reports that fuel the local news cycles and shape media narratives about their changing communities. Frequently, these narratives focus on shortcomings of the new arrivals as individuals, not on the abilities or interests of the communities themselves to change. In 2008, the Galesburg (Illinois) Area Chamber of Commerce, for instance, published "A Call to Action: Poverty in Knox County, Illinois" that said new arrivals from Chicago (read, black) had contributed to "[s]ignificant medical and legal problems," and are "unprepared to handle standard class work at their grade level," having come from "different cultural norms and expectations to the school environment" (Galesburg, 2008, pp. 4–5).

Little of the report focuses on the problems local medical and legal services had in understanding the particular needs and concerns of new arrivals, of businesses in providing fair and affordable prices for their products and housing stock, and of teachers and administrators in applying appropriate, progressive pedagogies in the classroom to engage with new students at their level. While it may be true that students from somewhere-other-than-Galesburg may struggle with understanding their new surroundings, the following is also true: urban schools continue to be sites of immense racial and educational and geographic segregation that affects learning (Kozol, 1991; 2005; Noguera, 2008; Payne, 2008; Rich, 2012). Furthermore, it's more likely that mythical narratives of the urban ghetto and city living and black culture that are retold in rural communities make local education even more complicated than just the people who are moving there, as educators blame children for "inattentiveness," "disruption," and "poor home life."

These narratives allow the power elite to ignore the effects of local, cultural and structural influences that may make their environments unwelcoming or, at the very least, difficult for newcomers to rural schools and neighborhoods. It's just easier to claim that local strains are coming merely from population change and to assign blame for new "challenges" to an urban migration (Burgess, 1985; Gutsche, 2011; 2012; Parisi, 1998; Wilson, 2009). It is these narratives that I hope to undermine in this book.

In this Introduction, I have attempted to discuss the emptying of urban cores, such as the projects of Chicago, and set Iowa City in a larger landscape of changing communities across the country. Combined with a federal voucher system that allows people to transfer public housing assistance funds virtually anywhere, the federally-funded interstate system in the Upper Midwest has provided a new way to pay for transporting and housing the poor with public dollars (Kneebone and Berube, 2013). Given the changing communities and cultures that emerge with the introduction of newcomers (a phenomena shared across cultures and centuries), I argue that the contested nature of the Southeast Side of Iowa City becomes a case study for a closer look at how notions of the "ghetto" and fear of minorities were populated throughout news coverage to perpetuate racist ideologies.

The rest of this book takes on this dominant, mediatized construction of place through a study of how the press, their official sources, and Southeast Side residents experienced Iowa City and its Southeastern neighborhoods. Beyond describing a portion of the recent migration of urban blacks from the inner cities further into the rural Midwest—and the ghettoization of them and their new homes—I hope to contribute the notion of *news place-making*, "in which geography is selected as the ideological focus of journalistic forms of social construction" (Gutsche, in press). The following section details the discussion that appears in the chapters ahead.

Outline of Book

Chapter One presents an analysis of how news operates as a form and function of ideology. More specifically, I discuss the various levels of how journalists operate as individuals, as a collective, and as cultural storytellers to embed into news moral meanings of life. Because this project deals with how news shaped notions of the Southeast Side as both a geography and as a mythical place, I introduce previous work on how journalists cover physical environments, from the "Heartland" to "The Inner City." Furthermore, by visiting research on journalism as a social and cultural institution, I implicate news media as an ideological tool that explored issues of Iowa City's Southeast Side through beliefs of dominant cultural and social power brokers. Through this lens, this chapter sets the scene for interrogating the construction of the Southeast Side via the news as a tool for interpreting events, people, and places for the audience, thereby rejecting the normative claim of an "objective" press.

In Chapter Two, I move further into explicating the concepts of space and place to solidify this project's focus on constructing the notion of news place-making as an ideological power function of the press. The work of major human and critical geographers that is presented here contributes to a theoretical discussion of how the Southeast Side was characterized in the news. This chapter also provides a practical understanding of how one may look at and experience geography. Rather than a mere concept, our environments are things to which we assign meaning that then hold power to transform not just our own experiences, but the types of people who are categorized along with that environment, the activities we allow to occur there, the degrees of access assigned to both insiders and outsiders, and the social resources we as a society make available to particular places.

Chapter Three outlines the methodological approach to the reading of news texts about the Southeast Side used in this study. In addition to articulating the process of qualitative textual analysis as applied to this study, I deepen the understanding of what goes into a cultural reading of texts. Here, I present a supplemental conceptual set—that of white supremacy and race in the press—through a cultural history of how the press have operated as social and cultural forces in the United States, particularly in terms of covering race relations during the Civil Rights movement and school desegregation. In this chapter, I use the term "black news" to represent the historical and mainstream treatment of news as related to America's blacks. I argue that black news—stories about crime, welfare, church, fashion, entertainment, education, and drugs—holds and assigns particular meanings to news coverage of a single "community." And while I don't subscribe to the idea of a single "black community," I do argue that news coverage of blacks in the U.S. forms the idea, unfortunately, that such a singular community exists (Robinson, 2010).

Lastly, because I argue that journalists operate as a collective *interpretive community* in covering Iowa City's Southeast Side, this institutional background of how media have operated in terms of setting the national agenda on racial issues is an important background that needs to be understood in order to surmise as to the explanations for how and why media covered the Southeast Side in particular ways. This discussion, once conceptualized with analysis in future chapters, helps to identify Southeast Side news coverage as a rhetorical device that connects today's blacks in Iowa to those from Chicago's "ghettos" and then to (all of our) ancestors in Africa.

Chapter Four reveals how the term "Southeast Side" became a racialized social construction, an *ideograph* (McGee, 1980) rooted in rhetoric and a rich history of racial inequality that allowed journalists to characterize those neighborhoods and people as operating separately from the larger Iowa City community. In this discussion of control and space via news, this chapter reveals the ideological work that the dominant community of Iowa City performed to ostracize and generalize newcomers.

Chapter Five explores the dominant, mediatized news characterizations of the Southeast Side. It does so through a form of triangulation among interviews with journalists, their official sources, and Southeast Side residents that show how they characterize the Southeast Side and a textual analysis of news coverage. This chapter presents the methodological approaches—and initial findings—related to notions of news place-making in this case that furthers conceptual arguments about how place is made through the press.

Chapter Six highlights personal narratives of new arrivals to the Southeast Side and examines the challenges of limited mobility once they reach rural America. This chapter revolves around the irony in residents' stories of wanting out of Chicago, where they said that they largely felt isolated because of street violence, to become equally dismayed in Iowa, strapped to their homes by a lack of transportation and overt racial discrimination. Residents talk about increasing police surveillance, deteriorating housing, and problems with schools. In this chapter, the reader explores the mental maps produced by participants and is introduced to the particular place-making processes that are revealed in the comparisons among journalists and officials as dominant place-makers and residents as the "experts" of their neighborhood that are excluded from the news. In the end, this chapter suggests the degree to which journalists extended their authority to like-minded, socially connected, and culturally legitimate sources, creating a second level of the journalistic interpretive community.

Chapter Seven focuses on the ideological power of news place-making. Here, I apply news place-making as a concept through further explication of the findings from the main portion of this study—the mental mapping of the Southeast Side. Also, I conduct further analysis of news place-making around the Southeast Side by exploring news coverage of the city's southeastern neighborhoods and mobile home parks that were found in 2010 to be home to dilapidated and dangerous environments that garnered state-wide attention. In this analysis, I suggest how news place-making presented the causes of social conditions in the mobile home parks—which house mainly white residents—to be based on financial, governmental, and legal problems while the problems of the Southeast Side were blamed on "black" or "ghetto" culture of that space. This analysis, then, articulates how journalism operates to explain social conditions by descriptions of environment and geography as much as by describing the people themselves.

Chapter Eight revolves around news coverage specific to Iowa City schools, since this debate was a popular (yet veiled) topic in news coverage about the Southeast Side in 2009 and 2010. Through a detailed discussion, this chapter argues that news coverage of schools that focused on official data and explanations for unequal distributions of socioeconomic status and race among the city's elementary schools served as an opportunity to discuss the "damage" caused to the community by an influx of inner-city blacks. Conceptually, I discuss in this chapter the notion of how schools have become "pipelines to prison" in that they construct highly policed and authoritarian environments that disproportionly target minorities. Efforts such as zero tolerance and truancy policies are increasingly becoming a function of the Alexander's (2010) New Jim Crow and appeared as acceptable, non-challenged means by which to address Iowa City's changing (read darkening) classrooms. This chapter concludes by discussing the degree to which news discussions about schools substitute (or supplement) more overt discussions about neighborhoods.

The book's Conclusion serves as a summary of the role the press played in characterizing Iowa City's Southeast Side the way it did, thereby solidifying the position of the press and journalists' official sources as part of a shared interpretive community. Here, I also address efforts in more recent years to create calm and inclusion in Iowa City, such as work in local theatre and film to focus on sharing the stories that compete with dominant, mediatized narratives of the Southeast Side. Such efforts connect to concepts of agency and resistance as an element of how change can be created, but also highlight the realities of cultural barriers to equality and representation in the rural ghetto. I also use the Conclusion to articulate this study's shortcomings as avenues for future research on diaspora, about place-making in the news, and to identify ideological functions of elite press.

Lastly, the book's Epilogue steps away from Iowa City and its Southeast Side to apply news place-making to a historically black city in the Midwest— Cairo, Illinois. Throughout this book, I will argue for engaged research into the process of news place-making among journalists rather than merely exploring the representations of place in news; however, in this final chapter, I present a case in which journalists are once again operating within a second level of interpretive community. My hope for this exercise is to show the power of place that's rooted in its cultural history, its current-day use as an ideological representation of dominant cultural meanings, and the power of news place-making to marginalize based upon these characteristics.

ONE

How News Explains
Everyday Life

In 2001, Houston, Texas, housewife Andrea Yates drowned her five children in a bathtub (Barnett, 2006). She told police that she did it to save them from Satan. Information later emerged that Yates had been struggling with, among other things, postpartum depression. Even though Yates' actions were anything but rare—some 13,500 children in the United States were murdered in the two decades before 1999 (more than half by their parents)—news media presented this story of infanticide as "rare and spectacular" and as "especially newsworthy" (Barnett, 2006, p. 413).

More than that, newsworkers came to treat infanticide—particularly in cases when mothers commit the murder—as *especially* heinous. Barnett argues that the storylines surrounding these women cast them not just as killers but also as failed mothers. Instead of presenting the cases of infanticide in context—that mothers are women who face challenges and social pressures related to carrying and raising children—news stories tended to characterize the mothers as "evil, deceptive, and callous" (Barnett, 2006, p. 416). The news stories, then, weren't as much about the murders and murderesses as they were social commentary about motherhood itself.

Barnett doesn't argue that people should be allowed to kill their children—or anyone else. Instead, she suggests that the news media's focus on failed motherhood through interviews with medical doctors, lawyers, family experts, and other mothers reinforced a pervasive ideology that women should *want* to be mothers. Barnett writes that media portrayals of motherly challenges (the worst of which that led to murder) present women as automatons "guided by 'natural' feminine instincts that confer an angelic temperament and make them instantly loving" towards their children (Barnett, 2006, p. 411).

There are real results when news coverage doesn't explore complexities of everyday life—in this case challenges of motherhood and womanhood. As news articles cast Yates and other women as crazy and as "bad mothers" in discussions of postpartum depression, they denied the reality of mental health issues related to having children. Few media outlets explored the demands placed on women in U.S. society to marry and produce and care for children of their own. And, little discussion focused on risks women take with their careers, sexual freedoms, and notions of womanhood surrounding whether or not to have children.

Such news coverage that follows a familiar storyline (all women *can* and *should* be mothers, for instance) manufactures evidence that standardizes and normalizes what women should be. Moreover, these standards are used to marginalize women if they don't follow the status quo—not just in terms of whether or not they are homicidal, but if women choose to go to college, work in powerful careers, remain unmarried, exude financial and sexual freedom, or not have children. News carries powerful lessons about life.

Barnett's work on news coverage of infanticide illustrates the cultural work of news (Berkowitz, 2011), the role of the press to maintain dominant social and cultural norms. Looking at news coverage of mothers who kill their children through a cultural lens allows one to examine news as texts that hold lessons of what the story "really means" in addition to the news story's role of transmitting information (Bird and Dardenne, 1997; Lule, 2001; Schudson, 2005).

In this chapter, I present a conceptual discussion about how news operates as both a platform for presenting information and as an institution that reifies dominant beliefs and behaviors. Specifically, I present various levels of understanding journalism, from the individual newsworker, to that of the news industry, and to the cultural values that appear in news production and reception. In doing so, I describe how news is a powerful cultural tool that's aligned with dominant values and ideologies rather than merely a source of "truth" and "information." This discussion aids a deeper exploration of how the mythical construction of the Southeast Side in the news became a tool to oppress one Iowa City community while affirming another's position of power.

Concepts of Journalism: News, Narrative and Geography

Muckraker William F. Storey once said, "It is a newspaper's duty to print the news and raise hell." In the most traditional and lasting conceptions of journalism, there's a sense of truth, of objectivity, of purpose to report on the ills of business, government, and the cruel. Not much has changed since Storey shared this thought in 1861; today journalism as "duty" continues to be the foremost explanation for its existence by journalists who see their jobs as serving "the public good" (Gans, 2004; 2011; Kovach and Rosenstiel, 2007). To many journalists, their work is a "calling" in which reporters find and report the news by collecting facts, placing them in context, and distributing information to the public (Robinson and DeShano, 2011).

The journalism field requires each of its members to be socialized to shared values, standards, and expectations that influence their newswork and come to make journalists' use of news judgment, language, and storytelling second nature (Bantz, McCorkle and Baade, 1980; Berkowitz, 1997; Gravengaard and Rimestad, 2012; Riegert and Olsson, 2007; Skovsgaard, Albæ, Bro and de Vreese, 2013). Debate still exists, though, about whether journalists simply tell the news—or if they make it. By and large, journalists tend to argue that they determine what they cover by measuring information against set standards of "newsworthiness" and an event's or issue's "timeliness, proximity, prominence, consequence, rarity, and human interest" (Hough, 1994). With these standards, journalists say, they construct stories that resemble a sense of consistency and standards across the profession.

By telling stories through sources rather than through their own opinions, for example, journalists distance themselves from directly commenting on what they deem to be the news. Sources—not the scribes—provide descriptions and interpretations of events. Combined with other standards such as accuracy and verification, journalists argue that they provide an objective representation of reality (Gutsche and Salkin, 2011; Tuchman, 1973; Zelizer, 1993).

Set with agreed-upon standards and practices, journalists hold to single, normative descriptions of their trade—that they are out to find a good story, there to protect the public (Singer, 2007). As Kovach and Rosenstiel suggest in *Elements of Journalism: What Newspeople Should Know and the Public Should Expect*, "The primary purpose of journalism is to provide citizens with the information they need to be free and self-governing ... [N]ews media serve as a watchdog, push people beyond complacency and offer a voice to the forgotten" (p. 12). Still, these explanations of news don't answer everything about how "the news" comes to be.

Media scholarship complicates definitions of news as both process and product by viewing news as a cultural text through which dominant beliefs about everyday life are presented as information (for review, see Berkowitz, 1997; 2011). In this sense, news audiences receive information that's embedded with cultural meanings used to explain events and issues of the day (Hall, 1980). Journalists do this through narratives, telling familiar stories of the human condition (Lule, 2001). In this understanding, Tuchman (1973)—and a line of scholars after her—propose that journalists "make" the news. With this perspective, Tuchman argues that journalists may still work with what they consider "facts," but that they are led to these facts through cultural and social pressures. Journalists, Tuchman writes, interpret news "moment to moment" and present news as information and meaning that's been "defined and redefined" based upon society's needs (p. 184).

To make these meanings salient for themselves and audiences, journalists share social and cultural power with other institutional players, including business, law enforcement, and government. Therefore, messages that journalists spread are shaped by dominant ideologies that serve elite groups (Carey, 2009; Herman and Chomsky, 2008; McChesney, 2013). By viewing news as a social institution and as a cultural entity, rather than as an accurate reflection of community or a "single reality," one can uncover how journalists explain everyday life through cultural interpretations of multiple "facts" and multiple "realities." These stories are often referred to as *narratives*—established histories, myths and fairytales that journalists use to tell stories that introduce and maintain dominant beliefs about how to interpret the world (Ettema, 2005; Gutsche and Salkin, 2013; Lule, 2001).

But news doesn't just shape the world at a global or national level. News operates in similar ways at the local level, particularly in guiding residents in how to interpret a city and its neighborhoods (Harvey, 2003; 2009; Soja, 2010; Wallace, 2008). Yanich (2005), for instance, suggests that city news becomes demonized for broadcasts in the suburbs, ultimately arguing that television reporters are more likely to reference crime within a city based on its rough geographic location rather than at an exact address as a means to present the "city" as an ambiguous space that carries a singular meaning.

Journalists rely on geography to shape their stories and to bolster their storytelling authority in two major ways (Zelizer, 1993). First, journalists gain social authority by "being there" to cover the news. Often cast in metaphors and modifiers that assign meaning to their work during this mode, such as terms like "watchdog" and "eyewitness," news reminds audiences that journalists are authorities because "they were there," watching with their own eyes, thereby validating their take on events.

Reporters need not always be at the scene of the news to maintain positions of social power, however. Journalists also gain authority by presenting the news as a "recollection" of moments in history that relate to today's news event, an act of *collective memory*—shared ways of remembering the past in order to explain today's world (Cecil, 2002; Neiger, Meyers and Zandberg, 2011). Even if particular journalists weren't around for past histories, collective memory allows journalists to tap into dominant understandings of past occurrences and rearticulate and reappropriate them within the context of current events.

A political journalist of today who may comment on news coverage of past political scandals, such as Watergate, for instance, positions herself as an authority on all political drama, even if she hadn't yet been born in the 1970s. Through interpretation of dominant explanations that were set and maintained by previous journalists and power elites, reports today can span time and geography by connecting a news event from one place to something similar somewhere else. Journalists, then, become authorities on the stories they tell and the meanings—and "life lessons"—that they assign to the news.

Journalism and Ideology: Presenting Levels of Analysis

To get to the point where we can understand how journalists influence interpretations of daily life, it's helpful to identify and explain the negotiations involved in reporting and presenting the news (Carlson, 2006; Robinson, 2007; Zelizer, 1993). There's a large body of scholarship on how journalists work (for review, see Berkowitz, 1997; 2011) that includes ways to explore news at different levels, from the individual journalist and her organization to the role journalism plays as a social institution and cultural force (Shoemaker and Reese, 1996; Shoemaker and Vos, 2009).

These levels of understanding newsmaking and the news don't operate separately, but they work together as a complex ideological process (Zelizer, 2004: Berkowitz, 2011; Reese, 2001). While each level provides its own explanations and avenues for interrogation, it's crucial to explore news as a process and function of culture through multiple layers of meaning.

"The Journalistic Self": The Individual Level of Analysis

As individuals, journalists carry their habits, beliefs, personality traits, and career goals that shape how they approach telling the news (Deuze, 2005; Schultz, 2007; White, 1950). I refer to this level of analysis of exploring that of the *journalistic self*—a compilation of a journalist's personal values, experiences, and biases that shape her view of the world and of what is and what isn't news. These influences help journalists sort information through categories of personal biases and perceptions of societal expectations as a means to determine how the information should be used (Stocking and Gross, 1989).

Not surprisingly, journalists use individual "gut feelings" to determine what topics or events fit definitions of newsworthiness (Schultz, 2007). Heider

(2000), for example, writes that journalists must balance their personal perceptions of race with their ideas of racial and ethnic communities in their own communities and dominant cultural values about how race should be covered in news. Exploring news at the individual level, then, demands inquiry not only about the journalist and her individual background and experiences but also how her cultural awareness and journalistic methods operate within a larger context.

"Professionalism" and Organization: Analyzing Socialization and Standards

"Journalistic professionalism" belongs in quotation marks simply because journalism isn't a profession; it's a trade.[1] Still, looking at journalism as a quasi-profession allows researchers to address the work of journalism through a lens of sociology, which has a history of exploring work and workplaces in terms of socialization. In addition to a particular newsroom's norms, values, codes, objectives, and methods (Breed, 1955; Gans, 2004; Kieran, 1997; Tuchman, 1973), journalists are socialized to a broader professional ideology that provides newsworkers with a sense of purpose and identity (Donohue, Olien and Tichenor, 1989; Ettema, Whitney and Wackman, 1987; Robinson and DeShano, 2011).

At this level we see how journalists are socialized to use, among other tools, the *source* as a means to explain the news through someone else's experience, reducing the journalist from an omnipresent voice to a storyteller of local communities and meanings. Sources not only provide journalists information, verification, and visuals, but they help journalists distance themselves from overtly interpreting events on their own, thereby maintaining the claim to objectivity (Manning, 2001; Reich, 2011; Tuchman, 1973).

And, just as journalists come to learn how to integrate sources into presenting the dominant meanings of news instead of inserting their own opinions, journalists work to maintain these shared standards across the industry, forming journalism as a broader organization of common values.

Journalistic Structures: Analysis of Organizations

Exploring journalism at a third level, that of the journalistic organization, reveals how journalists follow traditional journalistic objectives and standards, including objectivity and accuracy in what scholars call *journalistic paradigm* (Carlson, 2012; Hindman, 2003; Reese, 1990). More specifically, organizational studies explain what happens when a journalist breaks this paradigm by operating too much as an individual (sharing her own opinion when she ought to be objective) or failing to meet the standards outlined by the industry (being inaccurate or tardy). In a seminal work, Breed (1955) referred to the social pressures to comply with journalistic standards as a form of social control.

Here, demands of the daily job (deadlines, financial costs, competition, the desire for fame and glory) influence journalistic decision-making and how tenants of verification, objectivity, competition, and deadlines shape how reporters view and define news. Journalists who fail to adhere to the paradigm weaken the argument for news as an objective representation of reality (Handley, 2008).

If the journalistic paradigm is violated or gets "broken," the media's credibility and authority are at stake (Frank, 2003). As a journalist, for instance, I might create working habits that reflect my organization's requirements and journalistic standards: I will turn in my stories on deadline so I do not get fired. In this act, I am complying with institutional standards set by my news organization and likely accepted by a larger community of journalists.

There's incentive, then, in maintaining the journalistic status quo in that if the journalistic authority of some is questioned, the entire field falls under scrutiny. In hopes of repairing the journalistic paradigm, journalists speak out against "bad journalism" and attempt to bolster how others within the journalistic community maintain the agreed-upon practices (Soloski, 1989).

Yet what journalists are upholding during paradigm repair is just as much about the ideological messages that they spread as it is the ways in which they do it. To lose the faith of other ideological players—businesses, governments, educators, police—would be to damage journalists' reputation as a trusted source of ideological power and an institutional force.

JOURNALISTIC CAPITALISM: JOURNALISM AS INSTITUTION

A fourth level of analysis for exploring journalism is that of the societal or extra-media, which consists of interactions among and between "ownership, press freedom, and financial arrangements" (Berkowitz, 2011, p. xviii) of the press. Viewing journalism as an institution reveals how news operates with social authority (Reese, 2001; Schudson, 2005). Media share social authority alongside governments, militaries, and business (Herman and Chomsky, 2008), and its close proximity to other institutions—both geographically and ideologically—influences how journalists select sources and tell stories (Bantz, 1985; Berkowitz and TerKeurst, 1999; Coleman, 1995; Durham, 2008; Frank, 2003; Hindman, 2003).

This proximity positions journalism as its own institution in which journalists become "officials" alongside police, governors, and business leaders, providing information about the world, but also interpreting the news in ways similar to other power houses. Aligning themselves with other official institutions' explanations for daily events performs a function of maintenance at an institutional level. Such cohesion ensures that the news resonates not just with the public audience, but with fellow officials, and strengthens both the newsworkers' positions in society and the cultural meanings of their stories.

JOURNALISTIC IDEOLOGY: JOURNALISM AS CULTURAL PRODUCT

A final level of analysis, that of the ideological function of the press, helps one identify how media work with a cultural cachet (Barnett, 2006; Carey, 2009; Filak and Pritchard, 2007; Gutsche, 2013). As Bird and Dardenne (1997) write:

> [R]eaders learn from news. However, much of what they learn may have little to do with the "facts," "names," and "figures" that journalists try to present so accurately. These details—both significant and insignificant—all contribute to the larger symbolic system of news. The facts, names, and details change almost daily, but the framework into which they fit—the symbolic system—is more enduring [p. 335].

Like other forms of story, such as literature, news rarely explicitly reveals its deeper cultural meanings (Edy and Dardanova, 2006; Ettema, 2005; Lule, 2001). Durham (2008), for instance, suggests that news coverage of dramatic scenes of disaster and inequalities in the response (or lack thereof) by the U.S. federal government to Hurricane Katrina in 2005 served as political commentary on governmental failure. Through its reporting, journalists "found a newly de-centered form of media ritual as they appealed directly to the people in the voice of the people, but in a way that was also intended to get the attention of the absentee government" (p. 112).

While news about Katrina focused on the physical and emotional destruction done to New Orleans, journalism also publically scolded governmental leaders for ignoring the needs of citizens. These moral and cultural messages are embedded in larger, salient stories about everyday life that make the news an understandable *narrative*. Narrative storytelling in news presents factual information as approachable as fiction, embedding cultural messages in news that is presented in a familiar form, where reality reads like fiction.

And, like our favorite novels, journalists deploy a facet of literary devices to tell the news, using introductions (leads), quotes (dialogue), transitions, drama, irony, and conflict to present information as narrative (Gutsche, 2013; Schudson, 2005). Such was the case as the U.S. ramped-up for war in the early

2000s. Lule (2004), for example, argues that national and cable news stations turned to metaphor as a literary device to rally for the 2003 U.S.-led Iraq war, thereby ignoring or simplifying the positions of opponents to the war.

Lule selected the NBC Nightly News as a representative news outlet to explore how television news used phrases such as "timetable for war" to present violence as inevitable. Lule pays specific attention to how news stories presented "actors (or agents), settings (or scenes), actions (or acts), chronology (or temporal relations), and causal relations (or motives)" (p. 182) as an approach to reveal the "narrative elements" of the news and to show how journalists work together to tell the same story as a shared community, with similar ideological beginnings, middles, and ends.

Conclusion

From the above, we have come to understand that journalists operate within organizations and relationships among themselves and fellow institutions such as local government, police, and businesses. These relationships between journalists and power structures that give meaning to news have been defined as an *interpretive community*, a "cultural site where meanings are constructed, shared, and reconstructed by members of social groups in the course of everyday life" (Berkowitz and TerKeurst, 1999, p. 125).

The notion of the interpretive community exists in the fields of communication studies, anthropology, and literary studies, and despite the differences in definitions, each field views interpretive community as a group of people with shared ideologies (Coyle and Lindlof, 1988; Degh, 1972; Fish, 1980; Hymes, 1980; Mitra, 2010). Scholars use the understanding of interpretive community to explore the many negotiations of social and cultural authority and legitimacy with other institutions. The levels of analysis discussed above explain how journalists act as their own interpretive community.

More specific to this project is past research on how journalists' routines and values operate within particular ideological paradigms and boundaries (Frank, 2003; Hindman, 2003). Seeing journalists as an interpretive community also helped me understand how and why I seemed to see the same types of stories about urban spaces—including Iowa City's Southeast Side—in mainstream media across the country.

When I first learned of the Southeast Side, it sounded like other urban cities, cultures and communities I had heard about as a child. While working as a journalist, I had covered "urban" (read, black) street crime, school issues, and community policing in city neighborhoods, and I had lived in several cities with places deemed "ghettos." I thought for sure I was prepared to deal with the Southeast Side, since I'd seen and been to places like it before. But I was wrong. Something didn't seem right in how the press constructed the Southeast Side.

For some reason—maybe because I was finally feeling like part of a community in Iowa City, not just as though I was reporting on it—I watched news coverage of events in the ominous Southeast Side with much interest and with the intent of undermining mythical constructions of the ghetto. To do so, I found out, it wasn't enough for me to *do journalism*, something I had been doing for more than a decade as a way to understand the world.

By the time I reached Iowa City, I realized that I was too involved with journalism's daily practices and functions to interrogate it critically. I needed to step outside of myself—and my community. Like readers of this book, I needed to understand the layered meanings of how news operates. In the following chapter, I continue to build a conceptual framework for exploring the Southeast Side as an ideological construction, a place that's rooted in news rhetoric and racialized news narratives.

Two

Place and Its Purpose

Imagine a United States where Philadelphia is its own state and Iowa has been replaced by Colorado, Wisconsin, and North Dakota. In this version of the U.S., there is no Nebraska, New York is the size of New England, and half of the Southwest is called "Indian Territory." This is a New Yorker's map of the country drawn in the 1930s by artist Daniel Wallingford whose satire highlights the exaggerated views of East Coasters' self-importance. In 2011, the website Funny or Die published an updated version of this map. Atlanta is its own state. There's a space below Chicago (also its own state) that's labeled "This might be Nebraska." A state next to that shares the same name. Another Nebraska.

An even more famous map of New Yorkers' view appeared in 1976 on the cover of *The New Yorker*. The drawing shows Ninth and Tenth Avenues and the Hudson River before jumping over a couple of buttes by Kansas City to the Pacific Ocean. In the far distance: mountains that represent China, Japan, and Russia.

These maps may be considered many things. Maybe they're art. Maybe just humor. Maybe both. Few people, however, would likely consider them accurate portrayals of the U.S. or as guides to get from "point A" to "point B." In that sense, these aren't "real" maps. Instead, they are drawings of how self-centered city slickers (and Americans) may view the rest of the country (and the world). Such maps belong, in part, to the field of *human geography*, the study of how people construct beliefs about space and place (Gould and White, 1974; Soja, 2010; Wood, 2010), and these are called *mental maps*—drawings by which we express how we imagine space and place based upon our experiences, memories, and values (Gould and White, 1974). Mental maps are intangible, found within each person's stories of how they see the world—

and what they see in it; they become expressions that help us see where we are and where we think we belong in the world.

Stories of people's position in their environments have fascinated geographers since the 1970s, when the study of humans' environmental perception explored the constructions of where we live—our cities, the countryside, regions, and nations. The examples of mental maps above, whether the cartographers knew it or not at the time, are perfect examples of human geography's ability to interrogate lived experiences of place. Wallingford's construction of the U.S. from the perspective of New Yorkers, for instance, provides commentary on how local values and perceptions can shape perspectives of entire regions of space, where urban areas may be seen as accomplished and important and the countryside as empty and simple.

Cultural theorist Raymond Williams (1976), for instance, examines how perceptions of rural lands are generally seen as traditional, wholesome, kind, and feminine; whereas, urban spaces are advanced, masculine, and harsh. Descriptions of geography—that the city is the future, the country is home to tradition—shape how people think not just about those areas, but also about the people who live there.

That's not to say there aren't real cultural differences between some of these places, however. Plop a person from Boston in a room with individuals from New Orleans, Seattle, Miami, and Hope, Minnesota, and you'll see some differences. But in this book, I'm less concerned about local culture than how narratives about place are propagated and applied to a locale by people outside of that location.

I'm also interested in how people *within* those spaces form understandings of their environments and how those constructions compare to outsiders' perspectives—particularly those in the news media. To do so, I turn to a form of mapping, a tool which has a history of revealing how news media influence neighborhood storytelling. This isn't completely new. Matei, Ball-Rokeach, and Qiu (2001), for instance, conducted a spatial-statistical analysis of 215 maps made by media users in seven neighborhoods in Los Angeles to show how news coverage of crime influenced their perceptions of fear throughout the city.[1]

Participants were asked to use markers to mark neighborhoods on their provided maps to reveal their level of perceived safety, with different colors representing different levels of comfort (or discomfort). Participants' maps were then coded into a computer program and compared to maps of higher crime areas in the city. Results showed how the mapmakers felt less safe based on perceptions of racial makeup of the neighborhoods than the level of crime that occurred there. The findings complicated understandings of how residents respond to notions of fear as presented in the news when they are living in those areas.

"This comfort bias toward high crime areas is at least in part a consequence of the fact that our respondents live proximate to the central area of
the city, where crime is more likely to occur," the study authors write (p. 452).
The authors also explain some rationale for how these perceptions of neighborhoods and space/place are formed. "People tend to perceive their own community as more secure while constantly projecting fear into the neighbor's
backyard," they write, "especially where people of another ethnicity live."

In this chapter, I present a conceptual foundation from the field of critical
studies and human geography that will be used in my analysis of how media
characterized Iowa City's Southeast Side as a particular type of environment
through which the press embedded cultural meanings about the people living
there. This conceptual set will help explore how, through the news, one city
space is presented as safer and better than another despite data that suggests
otherwise. I begin the chapter with a brief overview of major narratives used
to discuss urban areas. I then present a discussion of how place-making occurs
in everyday life and functions as an ideological device that individuals use
to make everyday choices about where to go, where to avoid, and what to
think about people in different parts of the world. The chapter concludes by
placing the Southeast Side in a geographic context that's formed by discourse
and how journalists have historically shaped meanings of geography in the
news.

Spaces, Places and the City

When talking about everyday life—especially in cities—geography
becomes a concept to explore. We read so much about cities in the news that
tales about their environments merge with other narratives about the people
living there. We become confused as to what stories about the city to listen to
and which to believe. Stories of drug dealing, rape, and assault fueled our fan-
tasies of urban ghettos in the U.S. throughout much of the 20th century, for
instance. Riots of the 1960s, the Black Liberation movement, and scenes of
Compton and Watts ablaze in the early 1990s continue to reappear on television news reports today (Abu-Lughod, 2007; Entman and Rojecki, 2001).

Politics of the 1970s and 1980s formed an era of personal responsibility
to explain media depictions of crime and the decline of the American way of
life in U.S. cities. In 1976, for instance, soon-to-be President Ronald Reagan
referred to the "Welfare Queen" as an example of how urban America has run
amok (Omi and Winant, 1994). This "Queen"—an archetype that appeared
prominently in narratives of Iowa City's Southeast Side that's discussed
in much more detail later in this book—has become the national icon for

mythical poor blacks who "exploit" our nation's welfare system and fuels America's fascination and speculation about danger and decline in the "ghetto."

Indeed, when I first moved to Iowa City, its Southeast Side, its gangs, gangstas, and Queens sounded like the inner-city places and the people I had heard about as a child. As a kid who spent much of my summers in Milwaukee, I had heard similar stories about black crime there and in other "big cities" across the country. I saw the stories unfold on the *COPS* television show and then read about them in college sociology, criminal justice, and anthropology classes. As a journalist, I had covered "urban" (read *black*) street crime, school issues, and community policing in city neighborhoods. In Madison, Wisconsin, for instance, the street name "Allied Drive" in the early 2000s represented a street in a predominantly black and Latino neighborhood, purportedly where most of the city's violent crime occurred (Hall and Mosiman, 2005).

By the time I made it to Iowa City, then, I thought I was ready to hear all about the Southeast Side and its ghetto-ways. At first, because of the stories I had heard—and written—about urban black culture, I didn't question these stories and descriptions of black violence. On the surface, these stories of urban blacks moving to Iowa and bringing violence, drugs, and "culture" with them sounded familiar, believable enough, but when things sound simple, they usually aren't. Therefore, exploring Iowa City's Southeast Side as a geography and unpacking meanings of its characterizations in the media requires understanding more about how people talk about geography and environments through the notions of *space* and *place*.

The Meanings of Space

Though often used interchangeably, there are substantial differences between the ideas of space and place. For the purposes of this project, the term *space* refers to a particular geography to which people assign purpose or meaning, such as a city, a building, or a park (Lefebvre, 1991; Soja, 2010). Space transforms the meanings of geography as people assign social practices and purposes to particular locations. Meanings assigned to an empty building, for instance, would change if it opened as an elementary school.

Human behavior and socialization begin to interact with the location and its dominant meanings. In this new school, for example, teachers, administrators, staff members, and students are assigned specific roles. Social control (punishment, shame, etc.) may come to shape one's behavior in this space, as the space itself is constructed to uphold organized and agreed-upon expectations. After all, the teacher's desk is placed at the front of the room or posters stuck to the walls to dictate rules for "respectful" behavior.

We also interact with space based on where we live and how we travel. If we despise large groups of people, we might make choices to avoid big cities or shopping malls, but if we like them we might be more likely to live in a busy neighborhood, spend more time at clubs, or be less annoyed by street parties or protests. Harvey (2003) identifies how one shapes his or her relationship with space as *spatial consciousness* or through their *geographical imagination*. Because individuals experience space in their own unique ways, such as through personal memories and values, meanings of spaces are often contested in the public sphere—and spaces considered public are especially so.

In these places—city downtowns, parks, streets, and even schools—so many people with so many backgrounds and conflicting values and experiences wrangle to construct dominant interpretations of space. In the end, those who win set the standards for how to read a particular space—and how to control it.

The Meanings of Place

The concept of *place*, on the other hand, refers to when meanings are assigned to a specific space. While these meanings may be formed as a response to a location-as-space, meanings of place are also set by dominant society and shared throughout culture (Harvey, 2009; Round, 2008). For instance, a school is transformed from a space to a place the more one interacts with it both physically and ideologically. These interactions then shape how one explains events that have happened or will happen within the place.

In other words, if I remember being bullied on a school playground or stifled by teachers, I may regard the school as a dreadful place. I may describe the place as oppressive or even boring. I may further associate that place—and its negative connotations—with its people: brutally strict teachers, pesky and impudent students, and bossy administrators.

More examples of dominant constructions of place are discussed below, but it's first important to see these constructions as an ideological function, a process, designed to place us and others in familiar territory. As Entrikin (1991) writes, "We see place not only as the context for our actions, but also as an important component of our sense of identity" (p. 14). Place-making is a product of both individual and larger cultural influences, he writes, "that we as individuals create to connect ourselves to the world and in the narratives that bind us together into groups and communities."

To explore the operation of *news place-making* around which this project focuses, then, I turn to how place serves a cultural purpose within the news via the study of human geography (Gould and White, 1974; Harvey, 2009; Soja, 2010; Wood, 2010).

Place-Making, Culture and the News

Dominant meanings of place rely on "appropriate" interpretations of history, our interactions with the geography itself, and our purposes for the future (Cloke, et al., 2004). Understanding that what we understand, collectively, about the world's places depends on ideological constructions of social and cultural elites. When discussing colonialism and the long-standing, mythical *Orient*, for instance, Said (1979) writes that instead of representing a physical location, "the Orient is an idea that has a history and a tradition of thought, imagery, and vocabulary that have given it reality and presence in and for the West," what Said refers to as the *Occident*. "The two geographical entities," he writes, "thus support and to an extent reflect each other" (p. 5). Such notions of places—such as the Orient, the West, and the Southeast Side—fuel ideologies upon which societies decide how to operate militarily, economically, and socially (Gutsche, 2013).

Beyond constructions formed in part by governments and global business, media serve as a dominant definer of place. Hallin's (1986) work is especially helpful in understanding how news media tell stories of place by identifying five categories of how elite media covered world politics following the Cold War. First, Hallin writes about place as *authority*, in which journalists report from a location and share with that space their social and cultural authority to explain events and characterize the location in which they occurred. Such a notion resonates with Zelizer's (1993) thoughts on how journalists use geography as a means to enhance their cultural authority and legitimacy, as discussed in Chapter 1. Being in a place while reporting on it, then, presents journalists as official sources of information about that place.

Hallin also considers place to be *actionable information*, in which news focuses on events or issues occurring within a given geography; a *social connection*, such as when journalists discuss geography to create a sense of community that unites space with common ideologies; a *setting* in which journalists overtly describe geography as means to tell a story about an event or issue, even if the setting is abstract or stereotyped; and, as a *subject*, such as when reporters cover particular locations as a dominant focus of the news story.

Types of Places in the News

The various modes of identifying, describing, and using place to present the news and dominant ideology then result in place-characterizations and constructions that appear in the news.

The Other World

Lule's (2001) work on "The Other World" demonstrates how journalists ascribe notions of "the other"—social subordinates, often seen as different and culturally primitive—to geography. Lule's study on U.S. news media's post–Cold War coverage of Haiti at a time of great domestic political and cultural changes there suggests that when journalists fail to understand cultural context of a community or space, reporting tends to cast a community and its people as operating outside the journalist's own dominant culture.

In terms of Haiti—and other spaces home to dense populations of ethnic and racial minorities in the United States—journalists characterized the place as primitive, savage, "feared," and to be "avoided." But these "other" geographies aren't limited just to places considered to be other countries, or on another continent oceans away, as is shown in news coverage of "The Inner City" (Burgess, 1985).

The Inner City

Presenting place or a people as being "other" allows the storyteller to distance a particular geography—and its inhabitants—from dominant society and culture. Casting the others' positions, actions, or geographies as counter—or as threatening—to the storyteller's dominant ideology releases her from having to explain or explore alternative explanations that may undermine the dominant position. Burgess (1985), for example, identifies the concept of "The Inner City" as an urban environment characterized as an "alien place, separate and isolated, located outside the white, middle-class values and environments" (p. 193).

Specifically, Burgess attributes this notion of the inner city to British news coverage of street violence there in the 1980s. In doing so, she argues that news media (1) described the environments in which the violence occurred, (2) described people in those spaces based on race and class positions, and (3) applied language all to characterize the culture of those involved in street violence as deviant.

By identifying the riots as taking place in an "inner city"—a rough, poor, crime-invested area—and having been sparked by its residents who are subject to their neighborhoods' pathologies, Burgess argues, newsworkers ignored the root causes of the riots, which she suggests were grounded in economic and racial strife. More importantly, Burgess writes, labels of racialized hatred were placed on those from the "inner city" from the outside—private business, governmental policies, and public disgust for city life.

Campbell (1995) also reveals how historical archetypes of racial and ethnic minorities—particularly blacks—have been characterized in U.S. news media as primitives, savage and dangerous. Racial minorities, Campbell argues, are often cast as urban criminals, aggressive athletes, and as dependent on others as a means to avoid reporting on more widespread and complicated social problems. These archetypes reduce and marginalize alternative explanations that would go against society's status quo and are presented to the public through literary devices that mask the overt meanings embedded in news.

The Inner City: Part II

Ideas about space and place—particularly of the city—become embedded through storytelling. Beyond any literary devices used, Parisi (1998) writes, journalists tell news through "literary constructions that are yet profoundly aligned with viewpoints and values of particular social and economic structures" (p. 240) but that are hidden in stories of spaces and places, not just in the people themselves. In some of his work, Parisi argues that *New York Times* reporters, in a series titled "One Block in Harlem" in the 1990s, used personification to tap cultural narratives about urban blacks and the inner city as being dangerous, devious, and troubled. Vignettes of poor blacks, Parisi writes, spoke to national beliefs about urban life and black culture in that "the mythic, aestheticizing, personalized techniques with which the series creates an air of compassion and dignity actually represent an extension into print journalism of 'modern racism'" (p. 238). But stories about space and place that embed meanings related to those living there aren't limited just to cities.

Small-Town Pastoralism

America's rural parts receive similar attention. Sociologist Herbert Gans (2004) presents small-town pastoralism as a place-making device that journalists use to describe and explain rural space. In this perspective, the small town is slow-paced and wholesome, traditional, and nostalgic. Rural America's "romantic" (p. 49) qualities are used as a benchmark to measure technological advancement and news that challenges the nation's roots in big cities.

In "the small town," Gans writes, "[t]radition is valued because it is known, predictable, and therefore orderly ... and order is a major enduring news value" (p. 50). Williams (1976) also writes of the "the country" in a country/city dynamic. Here, rural lands are generally represented as sensitive, simple, and feminine, while the city tends to be viewed as aggressive, advanced, and masculine. Williams questions these simple constructions of the city and country, arguing that popular ideology informs literature, politics, and mass media to maintain dominant ideologies of place and power rather than to validate one's possibly alternative personal experiences.

The Heartland

Fry's (2003) work on national television news coverage of flooding in the Midwest during the 1990s builds off some notions presented by Gans and Williams when she constructed the concept of "The Heartland." Fry suggests that mythical constructions of the Midwest as the nation's Heartland portrayed floodwaters as threatening Midwestern values of work ethic, community, and heritage as much as describing how the waters could destroy infrastructure and human lives. News of flooding, then, became more salient for a wider audience as news stories cast the disaster as threatening America's core, not just small towns along the Mississippi River. Rightfully, Fry warns, such constructions detour both the press and audience from exploring or recognizing deeper meanings and social conditions within nature and the news.

Who Owns Place?

While the above examples discuss *place representations*—how media discuss and shape place—what's even more important is unpacking the social and cultural power within these places and representations by moving beyond asking how a particular place is defined to exploring who is allowed to define place and who benefits from those definitions. Below, I discuss the power of place by expanding notions of "rights" to access spaces and places to the "right" of forming dominant definitions of those places. I also further the notion of news place-making as a concept to further ideological studies of news that places cultural and critical studies of geography and place-making as a focus of exploring the power of news.

The City and Its Rights

Since the late 1960s, human geographers have discussed the "right to the city," the idea that urban space should encapsulate the needs, desires, and objectives of its inhabitants rather than the demands of social institutions, authorities, and industry (Lefebvre, 1991). The "right to the city" has a focus on identifying issues of power and evaluating people's "rights to housing, rights against police abuse, rights to public participation in urban design, rights against established property laws, or rights to a communal good like aesthetics, as necessarily connected" (Attoh, 2011, p. 675).

Who (or what) has "the right to the city" is often determined through the politicization of a city's built environment, perceptions of citizenship, and

HIGHWAY 6. The four-lane Highway 6 that borders Iowa City's Southeast Side serves as both a physical and an ideological boundary. Some Southeast Side residents say the highway stops them from integrating with the rest of the city. Photograph by Alicia Kramme.

individuals' access to shared public space (Harvey, 2009; Soja, 2010). Though the definition of rights "remains both vague and radically open," (Attoh, 2011, p. 670) what constitutes a "right" generally revolves around identifying—and attempting to resolve—inequalities in geography. Who—and what outlets—can help create and share a city's or neighborhood's dominant story has also been identified as a "right" (Ball-Rokeach, Kim and Matei, 2001).

Soja's (2010) exploration of *socio-spatial dialectic* disassembles space to identify elements of inequality in how space is constructed and manipulated by the powerful to maintain order. More specifically, Soja provides a critical perspective of built environment, specifically in how environment can be "abused" by political, economic, and social interests. His analysis of spatial inequality includes evaluating: (1) where communities place hospitals and grocery stores, (2) community members' access to transportation, (3) availability and use of "public" space, and (4) by comparing neighborhoods' racial and economic backgrounds and density.

Movements to identify and encourage diverse "rights" to the city can also encourage collective action through which residents can demand and enact changes that increase access to transportation and financial capital, apply pressure to control police brutality, and define place (Harvey, 2009). Discussions of the "right to the city" generally include identifying these issues of power and evaluating people's rights to fair and adequate housing, access to local government, and a say in how to use city spaces (Attoh, 2011).

PLACE OWNERSHIP AND NEWS PLACE-MAKING

Throughout this project, I argue that news place-making—as both a function of news media and as a process by which dominant, mediated geography is defined through the press—is among the "rights to the city" (Lefebvre, 1991). While I consider the rest of this study to be an example of news place-making, a short example of how geography appears as an ideological device in the press might help better formulate the argument going forward.

Therefore, sticking with the case at hand—the construction of Iowa City's Southeast Side—consider how the press in May 2011 covered (or didn't) the Broadway Street Neighborhood Center's second annual 319 Music Fest, an event that residents had started to "reclaim" the first Mother's Day following the 2009 "Mother's Day Riots."[2]

Designed as an event for the entire community to enjoy local bands, meet new neighbors, and draw people into the Southeast Side, its second year drew more than 2,000 people; yet, here is what the local press covered that weekend:

- *The Iowa City Press-Citizen* wrote about 1,000 walkers in City Park on Iowa City's Northwest Side as part of an effort to raise cash for heart research, an event that was connected to the American Heart Association. The Sunday story of Saturday's walk featured a nice photograph of a lot of white people and peppy quotes about how we all—including sorority members at the University of Iowa—can stop bad things that happen to hearts.
- *The* (Cedar Rapids) *Gazette* reported several news stories on Sunday from over the weekend, but none of them related to the largely black Southeast Side of Iowa City as they did during the "riots" of 2009.
- *The Daily Iowan* at the University of Iowa, which does not publish on the weekends, still didn't mention on Monday that thousands of people had flocked to the concert at the Southeast Side's Wetherby Park on Saturday. Monday's front page, though, did focus on the non-news of how police are enjoying a quieter downtown amidst large crowds of sometimes drunk and unruly white college kids.

People at the music concert that day told me that no press or photographers had shown up—even though there had been food, games, music, sunshine, and families, things that make for great community news. Did the press need to choose between both events? No. Was it "wrong" to cover the walk to fight heart disease? Of course not. But what does it mean when one event gets covered and the other doesn't?[3] What influence may the page-one coverage of active white people doing good have on the community? What if that story was of a diverse crowd in a stigmatized part of town, enjoying the weather, music, and each other—despite their differences? What's geography got to do with any of this?

In all fairness, local news media do a fair job of promoting community events; both the *Press-Citizen* and *Daily Iowan* had published briefs to announce the 319 event in advance. But my guess is that skin color didn't just influence the coverage: walkers apparently raised $95,000, while the community concert was on "the other side of town" and was more about building community than raising cash. In the end, the Southeast Side couldn't offer the same kinds of benefits to the community as a whole; the potential peace that could come from a community event in Southeastern neighborhoods was apparently worth less than the cash raised on the city's North Side.

Conclusion

In this chapter, I have approached place-making as a communicative process, one that relies on voices of power (in this case, news media) to establish and maintain definitions of local community and to award power to particular voices. Specifically, this lens allows one to view Iowa City's Southeast Side through issues of access and people's rights to interact with public space. It also highlights the needs, desires, and objectives of its inhabitants rather than the demands of social institutions, law enforcement, and industry. Therefore, I position journalists at the center of place-making and as working among other social power structures to construct dominant community identities that influence decisions about how resources are distributed to its people.

More specifically, I argue that local journalists operated as an interpretive community (Berkowitz and TerKeurst, 1999; Zelizer, 1993) and awarded power to sources who explained social conditions in the Southeast Side as being derived from "The Inner City" (Burgess, 1985) rather than presenting alternate, complex and sometimes contrary explanations for social conditions. In doing so, official sources, such as police and city workers, were awarded the authority and legitimacy from journalists to shape dominant stories about the Southeast Side as place, while residents—and their stories—were marginalized.

In the following chapter, I prepare for a reading of the Southeast Side through the concepts of whiteness, culture, and critical geography as a means of presenting place-making via news as an ideological project of the powerful.

THREE

Building the Ghetto

Reading News as Cultural Mortar

Flames soar behind the Milwaukee television reporter. His tight, white collar and black coat stand as a sharp contrast to the disorder of a factory explosion in the city's Menomonee Valley. It's December 2006 when this forgotten industrial bed of factories scourged by demolition and change loses yet another factory. An 8 a.m. explosion had ripped through a Falk Corporation mechanical plant (Borowski, 2006). A plume of smoke lasted for hours.

In his live stand-up, the journalist's signal bouncing from the satellite truck up to the sky and down to the television station just blocks away, he reports that three men are suspected dead in the early morning fire as Milwaukee wakes up asking, "What's the Valley?" After all, the news media rarely report from this part of the city.

If this area of Milwaukee were built now, it would be called an "industrial park," but there is little chance the city would take waterfront property to build more factories. The area surrounding the factories, the homes on the surrounding highlands, have suffered the most over time. Nothing and no one here is a special story—an ironic testament to its history of racialized oppression and the agency of those wanting to end it.

But in more recent years, nothing here really happens. Until today.

"So, how are you?" the reporter asks a woman from the neighborhood. It takes her a second to answer.

"I just don't know," she says. "We are planning to move out of here anyway. My kids don't know why they can't go outside at night to play, and it is just time to move."

The camera pans back to the reporter, cutting the resident out of the shot. Not knowing this area of the city, he seemingly misunderstands what the resident meant.

"As you see," he starts, "this explosion has scared some people enough to move away for good."

The Valley has long been a swath of land known for both its industrial prowess and as being a boundary of strong racial divides in the city. Indeed, this is where Civil Rights leader Father James Groppi led marches across what was then called the 16th Street Viaduct and was later renamed in his honor (Bialek, 2007). "Groppi's Army"—as he and his marching colleagues were called by *Time* magazine in September 1967—applied pressure on Milwaukee, its leaders, and citizenry to protest segregation in local housing policies (Balousek, 1995). *Time* reported the Milwaukee situation this way:

> Milwaukee's Negroes constitute only one-tenth of the city's population and— partly for that reason—have yet to mount a major rebellion on the scale of Watts or Detroit. Yet, like other ghetto dwellers, they have their grievances. In the Inner Core, as Milwaukee's Negro slum is called, unemployment is more than twice as high as in the historically German and Polish districts that surround it... [*Time*, 1967].

Milwaukee had rioted earlier in 1967, but it was quickly squelched, and Groppi took to the streets to keep the story of the city's ghettos alive. He turned to the Valley as a border of racial and class divide. But while histories of the popular event have remained strong over time, the history of the Valley has been lost. Just as in the coverage of Iowa City's Southeast Side, with its own past and current complex troubles, journalists in Milwaukee seemed unfamiliar with the Valley as a space and as a community the day it exploded.

The people of the Menomonee Valley who wanted to move away didn't make that decision just because of the Falk explosion. Houses surrounding the Valley are rundown cinder boxes that sit just blocks away from former mansions that have been converted to low-income and, as a result, poorly maintained apartments. Life on the edge of the Valley is seemingly much harder than in the high rises of downtown's East Side and the suburbs from which the morning news is often reported.

Such focus on Milwaukee's business districts, the wealth of the city's surrounding counties and cities, and visits to its underwhelming areas only during times of crisis contribute to constructions of space and place that are largely formed by absence. In other words, a lack of coverage around a particular location is just as powerful as if the space was covered each day. As the phrase goes: "Out of sight, out of mind."

Throughout this chapter, I discuss news as a text that can be analyzed and interpreted in systematic ways with the goal of understanding culture (Carey, 2009). I do so to unpack the meanings in news about urban centers, such as Milwaukee, Chicago, and the extension of those places via the migration of urban populations to Iowa City's Southeast Side, and the institutionalization of news as a communicator of oppressive discourse.

The discussion below includes an introduction to studies on whiteness and white supremacy as a dominant ideology in the United States and in its press. Next, I present a brief history of press coverage of racial issues that inform institutionalized norms for covering the news as a means to set the scene for my analysis of news place-making in Iowa City's Southeast Side. I conclude the chapter with a methodological explanation for how I selected and read news stories for this study.[1]

Power of Race: White Supremacy, Color Blindness and Institutions

I first learned about *whiteness* when I heard Jane Elliott speak at a small college in Wisconsin in 2001, when I was in my early 20s. Elliott is known mostly for an exercise with her third-grade students in Riceville, Iowa, following the Rev. Martin Luther King, Jr.'s assassination. All of her students had wondered aloud why "that King" had been killed. Living in a white community, Elliott asked what they knew about blacks in America. Students responded with what they had heard from others and what they had seen in books, films, and on television—blacks were lazy and dumb.

Elliott then assigned those same stereotypes to her students who had brown eyes. She opened a floodgate of emotion once brown-eyed students were treated poorly, wearing armbands to set them apart from the rest of the class, restricted from access to time at lunch and recess, and berated in front of the entire class for being less intelligent when they answered questions incorrectly.

Blue-eyed students took to laughing at brown-eyed students. They called them names. The blue-eyed students thrived at feeling good about themselves, because now they had someone close to them—former friends, former equals—over whom to lord. The next day, Elliott said she had been wrong about the "better" blue-eyed students. *They*, in fact, weren't as smart. *They* were bad. Blue-eyed people, Elliott told her students, needed to wear armbands, have shorter recesses. This reversal worked: hate was spewed the other way.

Finally, Elliott told the students that it was all an exercise. She wanted them to see and to feel how easily hatred and distrust is formulated, especially when it is taught to them by someone they trust and respect.

From this exercise, Elliott became one of the early teachers of white privilege who traveled the country to replicate this exercise, including with adults.

Jane Elliott. Jane Elliott, a former elementary school teacher from Northeastern Iowa, became famous for her "Blue-eyed/Brown-eyed" exercise she conducted with her white students following the murder of Martin Luther King, Jr. The exercise ostracized her from the rest of the community and strengthened her resilience to teach about whiteness. Author's photograph.

Her efforts revealed, nearly each time, how easy it is for one person to diminish another, regardless of race, and helped her audiences to get a first-hand look at the hatred whites apply against those who threaten their positions in the world.

Not all people have welcomed such thoughts, though.

In small-town Iowa, for instance, Elliott's exercise has caused her family much grief and pain.

No one would sell Elliott a home in the city in which she worked. She also got death threats.

Elliott had become a race-traitor, and even today, decades after "blue-eyed/brown-eyed" was televised by ABC News and she appeared on television shows such as *Oprah* and has spoken to tens of thousands on issues of racism, sexism, and LGBTQ rights, Elliott's still not welcome in many communities near where she lives in Osage, Iowa.

Short, with white hair and large glasses, Elliott at first appears (as she has for decades now) as a kind, old grandmother. But it's that false first impression with which she uses to strike.

"Black people don't cause racism," she would end up telling me when I visited with her the weekend after I defended my dissertation at the University of Iowa. "White people, ignorant white people, are the reason we have what is called racism."

That's the Jane Elliott I had come to hear.

Elliott lives in what looks like a small farmhouse outside the towns where she had taught and where she had been denied the ability to buy a home.

The farmhouse sits next to a church that she and her family bought and renovated for guests and family get-togethers. It was in the church where she spoke with me and two undergraduates armed with cameras and questions.

When we all sat down, with Elliott wearing a sweatshirt that said, "Prejudice is an emotional commitment to ignorance"—a line credited to author and educator Nathan Rutstein—I knew a bit about what to expect. This was going to be wild.

Elliott was, after all, the first white person I heard say that whites were the cause for black oppression. That white supremacy was alive and well. That *I* could do something about it.

I knew, that autumn morning, that Elliott was going to give us an honest assessment about race relations in the U.S.—and that meant she might not be kind about it. My students, on the other hand, who had called to set up the appointment—interrupting Elliott at home as she baked a cake—were in for a surprise.

"Now because of the election of a black president," Elliott started, "instead of that making us more determined to go forward to make things better, white people who are concerned about losing their numerical majority in the United States of America ... now we have taken drastic steps backward."

She had started easy on them, but then, she ramped it up.

"White people are afraid of losing their numerical majority," Elliott said, "and they are concerned that if people of color get power they are going to want to do to us what we have done to them. It isn't about skin color, it's about the fear of the loss of power."

Just the thing white people don't want to hear—that we have power and that we *want to keep it.*

To some, Elliott represents the worst that emerged from a time of "political correctness" in America. Her words evoke both disdain and fear. Easily dismissed as a liberal, white-hating feminist, Elliott is often challenged by other white people for her comments on race, especially in places, she says, "where there's no racism, where people say to me, 'Why do you say those things here? We don't have any racism in this county, in this city, in this town. We don't have any niggers.'"

She continued: "And that's what they said to me in Riceville: 'Why are you doing that exercise in Riceville? There's no racism in Riceville. We don't have any niggers' and [they] didn't see that as a racist statement."

But Elliott's decades of messages that most places are racist and that we choose not to see it has resonated with me nearly each day since I first heard her speak more than a dozen years ago. She's likely one of the catalysts for this very project. But Elliott's not alone in her study of whiteness and racism.

Below, I present several important elements that help to further develop understandings of how white supremacy has become institutionalized in culture and society as a means to place whites in safe positions of power, a perspective that serves as an ideological foundation for this study.

Whiteness and Its Institutional Supremacy

At its most basic level, *white supremacy* is defined as an ideology perpetrated throughout culture that places the needs and interests of white and light-skinned members of society above those of a darker skin (Alexander, 2010; Bonilla-Silva, 2010; Lipsitz, 2006; Zuberi and Bonilla-Silva, 2008). In this project, *whiteness* is a term I use to identify the privilege and ideology that operates within white supremacy. The term *white* includes those of Anglo descent, though it can be extended in more racially heterogeneous communities and based on who is in power to people outside of Anglo groups to people of lighter skin tones.

Some of the most important elements of white studies are the rhetorical claims assumed and possessed in discourse about power and ideology that benefit the established power system. While white studies has received a growing amount of attention in recent decades, though it emerged more than a century ago (for example, see Du Bois, 1903), I wish to explore just a few of the many veins that are most pertinent to this study. I intentionally quote scholarship at length as a means to present the clearest articulation of these concepts.

First, it seems important to acknowledge that white supremacy is an intentional, methodical ideology that serves as *the* dominant ideology (at least in the United States) that institutions and individuals use to interpret everyday life and to set social policies (Lipsitz, 2006). As Zuberi and Bonilla-Silva (2008) write in *White Logic, White Methods*:

> White logic assumes a historical posture that grants external objectivity to the views of elite Whites and condemns the views of non–Whites to perpetual subjectivity; it is the anchor of the Western imagination, which grants centrality to the knowledge, history, science, and culture of White men and classifies "others" as people without knowledge, history, or science, as people with folklore but not culture [p. 17].

Lipsitz (2006) refers to the formulation and maintenance of whiteness and white supremacy as *possession* that

> connect[s] attitudes to interests, to demonstrate that white supremacy is usually less a matter of direct, referential, and snarling contempt and more a system for protecting the privileges of whites by denying communities of color opportunities for asset accumulation and upward mobility [p. viii].

Especially problematic is that the more engrained an ideology, the longer it takes to undo (Thompson, 1990; Williams, 1976)—especially when the ideology informs every facet of social life. Indeed, not only does whiteness function "through intersections of race, gender, class, and sexuality" (Lipsitz, 2006, p. 73), but is maintained through Christianity as a dominant world religion: its "white" Christ also appears alongside popular promotions of America's white heroes as an additional "Founding Father" who sacrificed to launch American Exceptionalism (and despite the fact that the first man to die in America's rebellion against Britain was black).

Yet, many whites would not only baulk at this example, but would disregard white supremacy as a "real thing." Alexander (2010), for instance, argues that public denial about white supremacy reveals itself in discussions about the incarceration of blacks, particularly when people suggest blacks "deserve" to be jailed in disproportionate numbers to whites, in part because blacks just commit more of the crimes. "Denial," Alexander writes, "is facilitated by persistent racial segregation in housing and schools, by political demagoguery, by racialized media imagery, and by the ease of changing one's perception of reality simply by changing television channels" (p. 177).

Arguments that one type of person is predisposed to violence or commits more crimes than another *despite* evidence suggesting otherwise is a rhetorical function of dominant culture to explain away other, more complex—and maybe incriminating—reasons. Another function of dominant culture to misdirect people from understanding the power and institutionalization of white supremacy in everyday life is the notion of *color blindness*—the argument that all people of all races are alike and that only identifying a person by their color creates discrimination (Alexander, 2010; Bonilla-Silva, 2010). Color blindness is explicated further below through notions of the New Jim Crow (Alexander, 2010).

Color Blindness and the New Jim Crow

America's Jim Crow era—the overt oppression of segregation in the South—set the standard for how the country's racism "should look," particularly that racism is best exemplified when it appears in signs that limit water fountains or lunch counters to whites or blacks and that only physical manifestations of outright rules and words constitute racism (Berger, 2011). When "official" Jim Crow "ended" with desegregation of much of the South, white ideology hailed itself successful in being able to show its openness and to dispute ideas that its ideology was, in the end, racist. Color blindness, then, became a rhetorical device used to promote notions of equality across races and skin colors.

Popular phrases such as "we are all one people," "I don't see color," "there is only one race—the human race" were designed to propagate the idea that "color doesn't matter" while in the background popular culture and public policy was being designed to shift the country's racism to a more covert state. "Much as Jim Crow racism served as the glue for defending a brutal and overt system of racial oppression in the pre–Civil Rights era," writes Bonilla-Silva (2010, p. 3), "color-blind racism serves today as the ideological armor for a covert and institutionalized system in the post–Civil Rights era." He continues: "And the beauty of this new ideology is that it aids in the maintenance of white privilege without fanfare, without naming those who it subjects and those who it rewards" (pp. 3–4).

Zuberi and Bonilla-Silva (2008) argue that institutions charged with educating the masses about our society's dominant ideologies set white males as the norm and minorities as the alternative, creating a *White gaze* through which we view the world. The authors write:

> African Americans and other people of color have been historically central to disciplines such as sociology for this reason exclusively: they have served, alongside women and workers, as the "abnormal," "deviants," and "problem people"; they have served as the "object of study" as well as subjects for practicing social engineering and "reforms" of all sorts [pp. 329–30].

These histories and treatments of "others" have constructed what Gallagher (2008) calls "White lies," sayings that tend to be shared among whites when they are questioned about their racial attitudes. Among others, these lies include: "There is NO White privilege," "Racism is always in the past tense," and "A color-blind United States allows you to choose your destiny" (pp. 177–78).

Because many in our society continue to tell themselves—and each other—these lies, many more people are allowed to ignore the presence and prevalence of white supremacy as a dominant ideology. In the end, that these lies have seeped into our daily practices, needs, and desires makes this new form of racism just as deadly as previous ones. As Touré (2011) writes, "Racism doesn't often come with a machete these days but the death of your self-esteem by a thousand cuts can still lead to the murder of your soul" (p. 76).

News as a White Institution

Perhaps the hardest connection for audiences to make is how we are all part of white supremacy; to some degree, each of us act in conjunction with it through the material we consume, and produce, and the cultural norms we promote through media. Commitment to dominant narratives that support white power appear consistently in news coverage presented from the position of how the issues affect whites. For instance, American media still continue to focus on issues of drugs in urban slums as being the result of city culture rather than the result of suburban policing of white neighborhoods early in the "war on drugs" (Alexander, 2010; Katz, 2012).

Media in recent years have also covered the decriminalization of drugs such as marijuana in an effort that seems to benefit liberal and progressive whites and those with health insurance who can afford medical versions of the drug. At the same time, however, stories seem to ignore police tactics that target minorities for minor drug offenses related to recreational or off-the-books medical uses of marijuana and using penalties that threaten their public aid and freedoms.

News and other public discourses about our nation's schools also debate the role of public education and educational "success" from the position of white, suburban taxpayers. With an increasing amount of Americans seemingly tired of paying for what they consider "failing schools" that service minorities in America's inner-cities, news media follow the status quo of its users, subscribers, and advertisers by evoking racialized discourses about urban minorities. Such discourses are formed, in part, through the close working relationships between the press, local governments, and police.

"The media, in an uneasy duet with police, make decisions about which victims count as victims...," Stabile (2006) writes in her book *White Victims, Black Villains.* "The media play a pivotal role in the processes of criminalization and are often the first to publicize a new category of crime, as in the case of 'carjacking,' a new social category of crime that first entered the media vocabulary in 1986" (p. 3). These deep ideological connections between reporters and official sources make it hard for one to deny not only the work of the press to further the dominant ideology of a culture, but that the dominant ideology the press propagate is that of white supremacy.

Indeed, news media fall into the racialized intuitional structure described by Schram, Fording, and Soss (2011) in what they consider as a form of public management. Practices of social control through racialized policies of societal institutions, they write, "extend beyond the state itself to the full array of non-governmental actors who are integrated into policy processes ... as collaborators in hybridized systems under 'the new public management'" (p. 131). This "new management" has been constructed over generations of racial tension, with news media at its center.

Indeed, over time the practices of white supremacy as a dominant ideology in the U.S. have been tailored to appear natural through journalistic practices that support their notion of "objectivity." Governmental public policy—and news coverage of policy—are often presented as serving the "public good," further muddying the racialized objectives of a host of social policies that affect housing, education, and the criminal justice system. Certainly, tension between maintaining journalistic objectivity and meeting the demands of maintaining dominant ideology appeared in coverage of the Civil Rights movement in the U.S., the fight against Jim Crow that has led to what Americans consider today to be a "post-racial" America. In fact, one of the main concerns leading up to Jim Crow—and that remains today—is the degree to which society allows blacks to be part of the news aside from only speaking as "black leaders" or about "black perspective." In fact, even the staple for black expression—black press—has been under attack.

Curry (2013) makes the case quite well for exploring the current state of the black press—and the treatment of blacks by mainstream press—in cases from both today and in the past. A philosophy professor who also studies issues of race, Curry writes about the importance of today's black press—and about the concern of mainstream (white) press as being the main source of information about issues related to the black community.

"[T]he Black press has not only offered critical commentaries and political critiques of the sempiternal racism of the modern world," Curry writes,

> but correctives as to how white newspapers, opinionmakers, legislators, and most importantly the white public sought to justify their complacency towards and support for anti–Black racism and the sexual brutalization of Black men, women, and children.

Curry is particularly concerned about "the deradicalization of Black news and the complacency of the Black journalistic endeavor" that's "preventing the Black public from engaging the concrete American condition confronting Blacks, immigrants, and the poor." With these concerns in mind as a means to understand how mainstream press operate as purveyors of explaining race-based news—building consensus about today's issues—I discuss below a brief history of the journalism related to the "black press," "black news," and news "about blacks."

Press Coverage as Racial Oppression

Press coverage of race—and the ideological work of the press to maintain racial oppression—has a history that reaches deep into America's past and crossed the North-South divide. Despite the South's own popular and prevalent mainstream news media, Northern press—namely *The New York Times* and evening television broadcast news programs—furthered a divide between the practices and traditions of the North and the South, often marginalizing blacks and the Civil Rights Movement by ignoring causes or failing to look below the surface of complex social and cultural issues.

SOUTHERN NEWS VIA NORTHERN PRESS

The 1930s saw no major national news organization with a Southern bureau, yet *The New York Times* would cover—mostly on the inside of the newspaper—issues of anti-segregationists from the perspective of white civic and political leaders (Goodman, 1994). These perspectives, which ignored black voices, but also the voices of traditional Southerners opposed to integration, were muted in the *Times* coverage. This coverage of racial tensions by outsiders (Northern press) of insiders (Southern residents) in the early part of the 1900s was perceived by the South as a limited, idealized, and liberal view that cast a shadow over whatever future coverage Northern media would provide.

Actions of the Northern press, through intervening into the news and cultural affairs of the South, presented a hypocritical notion that the North had solved its racial tensions in terms of maintaining Northern slums, ghettos, and economic equality (Collins and Coleman, 2008; MacLeod, 1995; Massey, Rothwell and Domina, 2009) and that it was time for the South to move into contemporary times. Whereas the North had—and would have—its own tensions about how to better integrate schools, residential neighborhoods, and the workplace (Wilson, 1997; 2009), Southern movements towards integration represented a larger ideological shift due to the region's history of slavery and hyper-local tradition (Eckstein, 2006; Graham, 1967). Such an exploration of press coverage of social change provides insights into the regional tensions within the U.S. and the inner sociological and cultural understandings of newswork (Berkowitz, 1997; 2011).

The ways in which news media maintained the power structure through its news judgments and practices involves a much more complex scenario than a North-South divide. News media played a role of being instigators of crimes against blacks and editorial voices to maintain separation between whites and blacks in social, cultural, economic, and educational venues.

When Richard Lloyd Jones moved to Tulsa, Oklahoma, in 1919 to take over the *Democrat* (renaming it the *Tribune*), for example, the editorial page became a space by which to argue against opening the bustling West to the "Negro," their primitive ways, and their dangerous nature that called not just to stop blacks from moving to the West, but to rid populations of them—even through violence (Hirsch, 2002). Indeed, the riot of 1921 in Tulsa was sparked by news reports of an assault against a young, African American girl. The headline ordered the public to "NAB NEGRO FOR ATTACKING GIRL IN ELEVATOR" (Hirsch, 2002, p. 79, capitalization in original).

During the Civil Rights movement, newspaper editors in the South maintained the traditions of Southern freedom and carried with them tales from places like Tulsa and other cities that had previously experienced race riots to voice concerns for providing blacks even more integration than they already had. In doing so, these newspapers provided respectable voices to declare freedom from Northern incursion into Southern practices, and they turned to news judgments that would make the social role of African blacks within the U.S. clear—by ignoring blacks altogether.

Another important starting point for this exploration into the ways in which mainstream press have viewed the news of blacks is to explore how blacks themselves are characterized as members of society. It's well argued that even today's coverage of blacks in mainstream U.S. press is limited to crime, deviance, and poverty (see Deggans, 2012; English, 2011; Lule, 2001; Noguera, 2008; Parisi, 1998). Media practices that frame blacks as a subculture and a subclass within the U.S.—similar to what occurred in covering Iowa City's Southeast Side—harkens back to days of slavery and overt racial oppression through the types of stories journalists choose to tell about black neighborhoods, "culture," and individuals.

BLACK NEWS IN WHITE CONTEXT

U.S. news coverage of blacks up until, perhaps, the last decades of the 1900s, ignored black affairs, issues, culture, and activities that existed outside of deviant topics of alleged rape, murder, lynching, and misdeeds (Hirsch, 2002; Roberts and Klibanoff, 2006). Yet, presenting black news and editorials about black freedoms was a tricky activity—even among black newsworkers. In the early 1930s, for example, Oscar Adams of the black *Birmingham Reporter* may not have made overt statements about the innocence or the punishment of the Scottsboro Boys, nine young men who were accused of raping two white women on a train in Alabama in 1931, but he did turn to placing stories in his paper—sometimes in juxtaposition to his editorials—that provided a biased insight into his belief that the young men may have been unfairly tried (Goodman, 1994). Adams' covert expression of his opinion—a common task of black editors—reveals the difficulty of discussing issues of race and rights during such a time of social strife.

Today, racial tension continues within newsrooms and communities in terms of how journalists approach and present the news about blacks. For example, Heider (2000) reveals that in some cases, black television broadcasters present "black news," even if the news has been written and reported by white producers. It would be hard to argue that such a covert practice (similar to what I have seen myself during my newspaper career) is not cultural commentary on the state of our communities and that racial relations in the U.S. are strikingly similar to some forms of press actions of the past.

In the Jim Crow South, the mainstream press enforced the hegemonic ideology of the nation that maintained blacks to be separate but equal. Southern tradition held true to the notion of independence from Northern (read: Jewish, elitist, etc.) pressures for economic and social change in the South (Goodman, 1994). Racial tensions that erupted within cities across the U.S. in the early to mid–1900s had resulted in state and federal military and legal intervention (Fairclough, 2008), and influence from the North to calm the South was perceived by those outside the North as an offensive upon Southern states' freedoms to conduct their own affairs.

Therefore, in order to maintain distance from a military and federal presence in the South, Jim Crow laws provided the controlled culture of separate but equal (for history, see Maly, 2005). Many journalists who would end up writing about the Civil Rights movement in the 1950s and 1960s had been socialized to believe that Jim Crow was a "good" solution to tensions that otherwise would result in violence and Northern force (Davies, 2001; Kneebone, 1985). The naturalization of such cultural and social orders among whites and blacks contributed to the "common sense" of excluding blacks from general news coverage.

The exclusion of some voices within the news and the acceptance of other viewpoints as valid perspectives on the state of Southern affairs represented the ability of Southern newsworkers to be legitimate, authoritative voices of proper ideology. However, Southern editorial voices varied in their acceptance of Jim Crow and of providing further emancipation for blacks (Davies, 2001; Fairclough, 2008; Graham, 1967; Kneebone, 1985; Roberts and Klibanoff, 2006).

NEWS AS COUNTERING OR CONTINUING JIM CROW?

While the press may have operated as an interpretive community with shared ideological approaches to producing news based on sources and for the "public good" of their local communities during the Civil Rights movement, the positions that various groups within the press took were quite different. Percy Greene, with his black paper, the *Jackson Advocate*, provides an interesting example of the diverse journalistic approach to issues of covering Jim Crow (Davies, 2001).

Greene, a black editor, walked a thin line between supporting white racism and black emancipation. Greene advocated for restrained freedom for blacks in a Booker T. Washington approach by which blacks should work within institutionalized racism in order to, one day, achieve equality. Greene limited his coverage of black oppressions through his refusal to publish mixed marriages, and his editorials ignored the murders of blacks by whites, lynching, and the closing of voter registration for blacks. His approach to easing racial strife supported a slow, respected work with the white power structure and was charged by fellow blacks as a traitor to their collective cause (Davies, 2001).

Selling Ideology Alongside Ads

Because the news business is, after all, a business—one that deals in selling advertisements as much as it sells dominant ideology, alienating advertisers through news coverage and editorials is just as deadly to a news outlet as reporting upon issues that are counter to those supported by elites and powerbrokers. Indeed, Greene himself defended his decisions for supporting slow racial integration as being one driven, in part, by business. Along this fine line of editorial and ideological decision-making, Southern journalists found themselves among one of two camps—conservatives who felt Southern tradition should remain as is, or among liberals who saw potential economic, social, and political value in further integration.

But let us be clear: even this distinction of "conservative" and "liberal" among the journalists' public presentation of editorial bias is not clean-cut. With his paper, the *McComb Enterprise-Journal* in conservative McComb, Mississippi, in the early 1960s, J. Oliver Emmerich earned the mark of being a "moderate" in his views who turned to "objective journalism" in the coverage of Civil Rights issues (Davies, 2001). Emmerich ran KKK stories and advertisements in his newspaper, but as a state's rights advocate, he lobbied for restraint in the public's actions to maintain racism, believing that a Northern invasion was imminent if racism grew violent. Emmerich's desire for "objectivity" emerged in his tailored and tempered reporting of bombings and overt racism in instances of violence by turning to officials (read, white law enforcement) to frame news. Yet, the *Enterprise-Journal* was not committed to one ideological perspective that shaped its coverage; the newspaper also chose to cover "racial turmoil" when other Southern newspapers chose to ignore it (Davies, 2001, p. 134).

The motivations behind supporters of integration—perhaps viewed as liberal—were divided among views of what integration could mean: (1) that it would provide more political players to support white politicians or white-controlled black politicians, (2) that integration could be a sign to the North of Southern hospitality, a move to stave off Northern political, military, economic, and social sanctions, and (3) that desegregation of public space was inescapable because of Northern economic and political pressures; therefore, integration should begin—but slowly.

Ira Harkey and the *Pascagoula Chronicle* provide an example of how political and personal "conservative" and "liberal" positions on racial integration were further confused as they began to adopt religious overtones (Davies, 2001). Harkey, a white man, decried Mississippi's actions against blacks as making the state look foolish in the eyes of the greater nation. His adoption of the "sinful" nature of segregation and racism attempted to tap into the religiousness and righteousness of the population to sway opinions on Jim Crow, whereas white counterparts at other publications, such as Richard Lloyd Jones in Tulsa (Hirsch, 2002), relied on the beliefs that blacks, themselves, were sinful and cursed.

Newsworkers became intermediaries during this initial shift from Jim Crow to social integration. Their words in editorials and news stories—however overt or not—became seen as social messages to communities both in the South and in the North about how change would, or could, occur. But even the most liberal journalists feared retaliation for overtly advocating for desegregation; ideologies of Southern liberals and conservatives only moved further to the Right when the issue of race was interjected into discussions of social and cultural mores (Kneebone, 1985).

NEWS AS MEANS TO PREVENT MIXING

America's worst fear of the past—and arguably of today—is the notion of inter-racial marriage (also known as *miscegenation* and *mongrelization*) and what that would mean for Southern culture—among other unpopular perceptions of racial and cultural outcomes (Hirsch, 2002; Kneebone, 1985). Mixing races was, perhaps, the lone issue that fueled such racial oppressions; indeed, Southern tradition dictates that white daughters are the representation of tradition, honor, valor, and civility—and that such purity should not be spoiled (Goodman, 1994).

In turn, Jim Crow laws maintained a distance between whites and blacks in large part to protect white women from black men who were deemed sexually aggressive and primitive, thought to be exotic and attractive to women, a mythical characterization that continues in news production today (Lule, 2001). The *Clarion-Ledger* and the *Daily News*—classified as Mississippi's two daily newspapers in its state capital—argued overtly against desegregation and racial mixing, and they did so aggressively (Davies, 2001; Roberts and Klibanoff, 2006). Editor Jimmy Ward and the *Daily News* once maintained a weeks-long crusade against Freedom Riders—those from the North who rode into the South to fight segregated busing—by claiming their investment in the South would undo racial order. In 1961, the newspaper "poked fun" at the riders, called federal involvement in Southern affairs a form of "invasion," and covered "black news" only when a black man was accused of violence (Davies, 2001).

Such efforts and actions maintained a conscious recognition of the dangerousness of mixing races and provided fodder for racial and violence reactions to a changing society (Davies, 2001). Therefore, when news appeared outside of any newspaper column that may have been titled "black news," even in the 1960s, stories about blacks were connected to issues of danger. This served two purposes: (1) to maintain a sense of fear about African Americans within communities in order to continue a sense of purpose for Jim Crow oppression and (2) to send a signal to blacks in the community to stay "out of trouble" and to "know their place."

News coverage of lynching, for instance, highlighted smiling faces of whites standing before a tree, a body hanging in a blur of black and white. These photographs became a message for blacks to keep themselves in line. Some 2,771 black people were hanged in the South between 1890 and 1930—well before Jim Crow, causing lynching to become a naturalized method for creating social order (Hirsch, 2002). Newspapers in Oklahoma, for example, tended to cover the lynching of a black man with detail and as news, including the cost of the rope that was sold after the deed was done, such as in a 1913 case in Anadarko, Oklahoma, in which news reporters detailed how the mob of whites nearly muted the screams of the black man as he burnt in coal oil and then hung. The message: this is how we deal with troublemakers.

Today, racialized discourse in the news tends to be less overt, yet it's expanded beyond that which we can recognize as being racial. Stories about city's "failing schools," for instance, ignore structural, cultural, and even pedagogical rationales for the state of education while supporting claims that the students just aren't learning, in part because of their behavior or home life. Voices of minority positions (racial and otherwise) are muted by journalists' dominant use of mainstream officials and dominant narratives. Stories that may otherwise appear to be news about community events, crime, and personalities are mired in tones of who deserves and doesn't deserve to have their stories covered at all.

As I discuss in Chapter 8, such layered and hidden discourse in terms of Iowa City's Southeast Side appeared predominantly in coverage of the city' schools. Therefore, below, I present a brief history of how the press has covered issues of race in American schools, a discussion that not only sets a historical foundation for understanding modern-day racialized segregation in our society and in education, but that helps to evaluate the institutionalization of practices and approaches to race that continue today in the news.

When Media Moved South: Media Mobility in Civil Rights Coverage

Schools were—and continue to be—social environments in which neighborhood and community issues are reflected within interactions between teachers, students, and peers (Noguera, 2008). It's in this space where a child's perceptions of her peers can be tested, and where a parent's fears are the greatest. U.S. Supreme Court cases *Brown* and *Brown II* intensified the demand for school desegregation, which led to mass protests, military intervention, and the threat that schools which did not integrate would be shuttered.

News Discourse About Desegregation

The year 1954 changed much for racial tensions within the U.S. as news coverage of what would become the Civil Rights Movement began surrounding school desegregation and the *Brown v. Board of Education* decision that ordered schools to integrate. While some schools did not "fully integrate" for at least ten years (Fairclough, 2008), the notion that the federal government would force local communities to send their white daughters to school with black boys seemed outrageous.

Many journalists at this time had recently returned from military service outside of the U.S. and had seen in those countries other cultures in which oppression between "races" and "skin tones" was not as accepted as it was in the States. Such perspectives of both Southern and Northern journalists influenced their interest in the racial tensions of the South and the protests, violence, and media events of school integration. On the other hand, for Southern school administrators and parents, the threat that schools would close and end the advancement of their own children worried them more than having their children interact with blacks.

Not all of the ideological work around desegregation occurred at the national level. Local newspapers, too, contributed, particularly to an anti–Northern position regarding military intervention in solving Southern racial conditions, such as in the Nashville *Banner* and the Memphis *Commercial Appeal* (Graham, 1967). Furthermore, the intervention of federal troops, legislation, and media powerhouses in the South (which would remain and grow in the following decade) enhanced charges from those in the South of Northern hypocrisy.

In Arkansas, specifically, a school desegregation movement in Little Rock brought about much attention in neighboring Tennessee. Indeed, in 1957, Little Rock became a site of confrontation of state and federal powers, a confrontation that Tennessee papers did not want to see in their state.

Covering Little Rock, Classrooms and Communists

The Little Rock controversy, once which included a large presence of federal paratroopers and National Guardsmen who stayed in the city for months, occurred along the geographic border of Arkansas' heavily black delta and hill country (Graham, 1967). The Little Rock case struck a chord with Tennessee newspapers, including the *Tennessean*, which was critical of the decisions to integrate schools through the presence of national troops that called attention to the region and issues of segregation.

The cultural themes at play in these news representations of race are rooted in the regional divide between North and South (state's rights and federal powers), and economic pressures that shift populations through Great Migrations (Wilkerson, 2010). The complexities of cultural pressures upon the coverage of Civil Rights, such as state rights and federal power, emerged during the coverage of desegregation—especially that of Little Rock schools— within the region. Newspapers in neighboring Tennessee watched the Little Rock instance closely, portraying the use of federal pressures to force integration at a state level as a possible foreshadow of integration in Tennessee (Graham, 1967).

Tennessee newspapers, in general, fought for integration (however slight or slow) not with the intention of developing equality among races, but to allow Southerners the ability to gain an education. Newspapers, including the *Journal*, the *Tennessean*, and the *Kingsport News*—all rooted in their individual political traditions—responded in part to the *Brown* decision and the use of federal pressures to integrate schools through political rhetoric and reporting, versus turning to overt discussions of race and the cultural meanings of school integration (Graham, 1967).

That the Northern press was willing to comment on the Southern tradition of racial oppression without discussing issues of segregation and discrimination occurring in many Northern cities revealed to some Southerners the complex and confusing purpose of Northern intervention. Indeed, intervention from the National Association for the Advancement of Colored People and other human rights organizations into trials and tensions within the South made way for Communist intervention as a means of supporting racial equality (Goodman, 1994).

Portrayals of Northern-as-Communist—in addition to the ideological

Communist threat itself—contributed to a lasting narrative of complete social and political upheaval throughout the South (Goodman, 1994). Communist publications emerged to fight for the rights of blacks—and future workers or Communist members. Teachers, blacks, and Northerners in the South were questioned about their political affiliations, a vetting designed to remove Communists from interjecting into the American—and the True American (the Southern)—way of life.

The complexities surrounding conflicts within schools and among other forms of integration and social change, now spreading to international fears of a Communist plaque, complicated the ideological work of newspapers. By choosing to all but ignore much of the school board decisions regarding desegregation, U.S. Supreme Court cases, and input of citizens about integration outside of editorial pages, Southern press tended to present the news as though racial tensions were not "as bad" as some had claimed, but that separate but equal was desired by both blacks and whites and that segregation was the only way for the two races to live in harmony to which the South was committed.

Niche publications, such as the *Southern School News*, did emerge to provide "objective" news on school-related issues. Acting as a news service once a month to provide other editors and reporters with details of what had been occurring within attempts to merge races (Roberts and Klibanoff, 2006), the publication tried to provide insights into issues that otherwise were not being discussed in the news.

Additionally, journalists' access and approach to covering the schools and the North-South divide changed when television took the stage as a growing form of news. Technological advancements in the news media and black diaspora to the North also influenced news coverage of racial tensions in the U.S. throughout the Civil Rights Movement.

A changing industrialization of Southern agriculture ended generations of sharecropping that many black families had performed. Northern machines put Southern men out of work. Meanwhile, Rust Belt industrialization occurring before and after World War II beckoned many black families to move out of the South for jobs—and, perhaps, for a sense of racial freedom. This shift of populations provided interesting cultural and sociological changes to both Northern and Southern communities in which races were slowly beginning to mix in cities and suburbs, providing their own conflicts, but also forcing some forms of segregation (Darden and Kamel, 2000; Krivo, Peterson and Kuhl, 2009).

The introduction of television news provided a select few within society the ability to observe the world from afar within the safety of their living rooms. As access to television expanded, television news overtook radio as an accessible and observed medium for information and cultural context of news events. It was at this point that the ways in which the public viewed segregation and the Civil Rights movement took on more of a human, personal tone.

Television news reports and documentaries on the racial divide of the South included the ABC News five-part series *Crucial Summer* about desegregation, which put the focus of the issues on the people involved. This connection with the viewer (both in the North and South, black and white) provided a new perspective on the everyday life of minorities and the institutionalized racism that mandated their lives (Roberts and Klibanoff, 2006). Television news programs also grew in length across the networks, providing more air time for deeper and more visual coverage of the people involved in the Civil Rights Movement.

By 1965, the press had come to adapt their practices to be available for breaking news, including violence and demonstrations surrounding racial tensions. This availability of the press—both print and television—also influenced the behavior of police and segregationists; police had to think twice about conducting violence, for example, lest it get captured by the camera and film. Coupled with another migration of Southern blacks to Northern states and workplaces, news media found themselves dealing with new audiences and new issues to cover in both geographies.

Advancements in television news and the introduction of Northern journalism powerhouses emerged throughout the South to cover violence (sometimes against journalists themselves) and the events of Red Summer—a violent season of bombings, mobs, and melees—and Freedom Summer—the Northern campaign to enter the South for peaceful protests, action, and education. Not until television began projecting images of protests and peaceful sit-ins into the homes, stores, and diners of Americans—both black and white—did the mass public begin to understand the humanity of the scenario playing out largely in the South (Graham, 1967).

The news media's ability to present the issues of racial oppression and violence in the South to Southerners allowed for social change to be seen as a real possibility: the words of the Rev. Martin Luther King, Jr. and other activists were able to appear in "real time"; and, television images of marches, demonstrations (peaceful and otherwise) and King's speech on the Mall in Washington, D.C., fed into a growing desire of the press to show images from breaking news and press conferences (Davies, 2001; Roberts and Klibanoff, 2006).

But when television cameras ventured deeper into the inner cities where many blacks had begun to settle in recent decades, news audiences began to see further into the black experience. Instead of expanding compassion for those struggling with and against oppression, U.S. audiences started to use scenes of violence and decline in the city to further marginalize and hate. Still, advocates for racial justice used this newfound press interest to their benefit.

BLACKS BACK IN THE NEWS: COVERING CITIES, SCHOOLS AND THE SOUTHEAST SIDE

The rise of the Black Panthers in the 1960s benefited from the use of press conferences, televised marches, and actions. By using the television to immediately respond to or propose political positions—and by viewing these images—the public began to believe social action was possible (English, 2011; Roberts and Klibanoff, 2006). Such methods would continue to be used in the Civil Rights Movement as they would in Vietnam to sway public opinion and perceptions about the ideological underpinnings of overt racial oppression.

And while the majority of the history I've presented above has focused on the coverage of race relations by white journalists of both the North and South, the black press of the mid–1900s did cover black communities and causes. However, movement North by many blacks in the Great Migration, the dismal economic conditions of the South, and the threat of violence and further oppression silenced many black newspapers. Used to empower and educate, these papers slowly began to stop publishing, while Northern black presses continued, especially in New York and Chicago. The *Pittsburgh Courier, Chicago Defender*, the *Baltimore Afro-American* (and later the *Black Panther*) emerged and were sustained in the North during the Civil Rights movement despite a decline in circulation in the South and the shuttering of many Southern-based black newspapers (Graham, 1967; Roberts and Klibanoff, 2006).

It's not until the rise of Black Power, though, that we see a revival of black press as a social tool in the 1960s and 1970s, as the *Black Panther* newspaper—attached to the social movement of the same name—emerged as a loud voice that furthered political action on behalf of urban blacks and fought brutal police responses to urban crime that targeted blacks (English, 2011). The *Panther*, a product of propaganda—but also a journalistic tool—came to represent generations of oppression and an act of agency to fight against hegemonic ideology that appears in racist reporting in mainstream press into the 1960s and 1970s. At that point, newsworkers by and large continued to ignore black issues and causes, diminished the importance of blacks, and presented government officials and police as the dominant and most trusted sources for what news was and what the newspaper's position on the news should be.

In the 1960s, newsworkers rarely covered black neighborhoods and black issues, they fought for further oppression in the name of social order, and they meekly attempted (perhaps to the best of their ability) to level charges against the "deviant, lazy, ignorant, and dangerous" black, the Vietnam War being a distraction from domestic issues at home. Yet desegregation was slowly advancing during the 1970s and the press had come to incorporate black issues into daily news coverage—at least in terms of the political nature of those fighting for their rights.

In comparison to the beginnings of the Civil Rights movement, black news in the 1970s and 1980s seemed to wallow and was soon replaced in the early 1990s by stories of drug dealing, rape and assault in American cities (English, 2011). At the rise of the "war on crime" in the mid–1990s, with images of Rodney King and O.J. Simpson in recent memory, notions of the inner city seemed especially on-edge (Bonilla-Silva, 2010; Stabile, 2006). Perhaps partly because of an increased presence of television media in America's cities, viewers saw past city skylines and into the city to images of violence portrayed by the press (Lule, 2001; Marable, 2011). This recent history of urban centers also associated images of decline and disorder with notions of America's "failing schools" in the early 2000s and, in the case of Iowa City's Southeast Side, served as a form of cultural mortar that the power elite used through the press to explain—and to try to expel—outsiders who had entered the community.

A Cultural Exploration of News: Textual Analysis

My reading of news-as-culture is the first of three methodologies used in this project. Mental mapping and interviews are discussed in Chapters 5 and 6. A tiered approach such as this helps form my thoughts of news place-making to better identify and articulate how news characterizes geography, especially through the dominant sociological and cultural expectations journalists have for themselves and the public.

Qualitative textual analysis explains how stories that are embedded in news, political messages—even fairytales—educate audiences about dominant social and cultural values (Bettelheim, 2010; Hall 1980; Meyers, 2004). While the specific approaches and methods one uses may vary, most textual analyses rely on a conceptual lens and rigorous and methodical reading (Carey, 2009; Lindlof and Taylor, 2010). More specifically, *narrative textual analysis*—the reading of texts for stories that invoke dominant ideological constructions—has been widely used in mass communications (Bird and Dardenne, 1997; Coman, 2005; Darnton, 1975; Ettema, 2005; Manoff, 1986) and is being applied here.

SELECTING AND READING NEWS TEXTS

Three local newspapers, *The Daily Iowan*, *The Iowa City Press-Citizen*, and *The* (Cedar Rapids) *Gazette* [*sic*], provided data for the next chapter's analysis of news events in 2009 and 2010. First, *The Daily Iowan*, a student-run newspaper at the University of Iowa, has a print circulation of 14,500 between August and May and 9,000 in June and July.[2] With its active website, the newspaper estimates its readership reaches some 50,000 readers. A student staff of about 100 and a paid advertising, design, and management staff of about 10 professionals work at the paper. Even though the college newspaper tends to focus its coverage on university news, *The Daily Iowan* does cover Iowa City government, police, and K–12 education.

Second, *The Iowa City Press-Citizen* is a Gannett-owned professional newspaper with a print circulation of about 15,000 and a staff of 50—about 10 of whom are reporters and editors. Since the early 2000s, this newspaper has focused on providing space for citizens to comment on local and national issues. More recently, writings by a dozen regular unpaid community participants in what the paper has called "The Writer's Group" has expanded from the newspaper's printed page to its website where writers run their own blogs and interact with commenters. People in this group are selected by newspaper editors and work closely with those editors in determining story topics and the language used in their articles.[3]

Lastly, *The Gazette* is a privately owned, professional daily newspaper based in Cedar Rapids, Iowa, about 40 minutes north of Iowa City. The paper has a print circulation of about 167,000 during the week and 200,800 on Sundays. While a majority of *The Gazette*'s coverage focuses on Cedar Rapids, an Iowa City reporting staff of about five reporters cover Iowa City government, breaking news, the University of Iowa, and Iowa City K–12 schools.

WHY NEWSPAPERS?

I selected newspapers for this study for two main reasons. First, while the Iowa City area is covered by newspapers, websites, and several radio and television stations, newspapers provide a rich source for discourse about the Southeast Side through letters to the editor, articles, editorials, columns, and photographs. Second, newspapers provided a convenient sample of discourse because each newspaper was available through online archives or microfilm and due to the fact that many of the print journalists, editors, and photographers who covered the events of 2009 and 2010 continued to work within local media or were otherwise accessible for interviews.

Such "convenience" allows a researcher to go deeper into her analysis by immersing herself in the community or data. In this case, I was able to spend more time with print reporters, because many of them lived and worked in Iowa City, close to rest of the case study participants, whereas almost all local television journalists were based and/or lived in Cedar Rapids and other cities, though they did cover some Iowa City news.

IDENTIFYING NEWS EVENTS

My analysis examines these three newspapers' coverage of six topics and events related to the Southeast Side during 2009 and 2010. By selecting specific instances and news events rather than conducting a census of all news coverage for two years, I was able to focus on a manageable volume of texts to explore how newsworkers constructed and characterized the Southeast Side. Fewer but more relevant texts allow a researcher to deeply explore cultural themes and meanings (Geertz, 1973; Lindlof and Taylor, 2010). Most of these events have been discussed already in this book, but the reader might benefit from a brief reminder of the events in 2009 and 2010 (Figures 3.1 and 3.2).

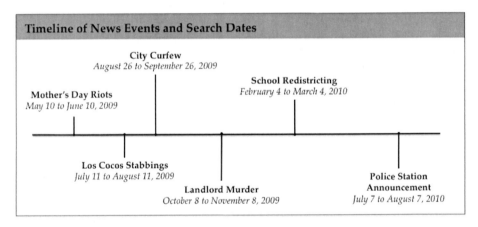

FIGURE 3.1. Analysis of news coverage surrounding six events over two years contributed to this project.

The first set of stories selected for this study surround "The Mother's Day Riots," a series of at least two neighborhood melees on Broadway Street in Iowa City's Southeast Side that began on Mother's Day (May 10), 2009. At least eight teenagers were arrested for their alleged participation in violence that involved as many as 60 people. The second set of news stories surround the closing of the Los Cocos Mexican Restaurant on the city's Southeast Side. During the summer of 2009, the restaurant had been a site of violence, including stabbings, fights, and shootings. The restaurant was closed in August 2009 after one woman was shot.

News Events, Topics and Search Dates			
News event or topic	Search start	Search end	n=
Mother's Day Riot	May 10, 2009	June 10, 2009	15
Restaurant closing	July 11, 2009	August 11, 2009	12
City curfew announcement	August 26, 2009	September 26, 2009	19
Landlord murder	October 8, 2009	November 8, 2009	15
School redistricting	February 4, 2010	March 4, 2010	13
Police Department opening	July 7, 2010	August 7, 2010	9
			83

FIGURE 3.2

A third set of news stories focuses on reports of violence on the Southeast Side in 2009, which led to a nightly citywide curfew for teens. The first discussion of the curfew appeared in late August of that year when the police chief asked the City Council to approve an ordinance ordering youth to stay inside at night. The fourth set of stories surround the murder of a white landlord at the Broadway Condominiums on the Southeast Side on October 8, 2009.

A fifth set of stories concern the redistricting of Iowa City Community School District elementary schools that was designed to lessen strain on the schools that service the Southeast Side. Redrawing lines that determine which schools students attend was supposed to ease overcrowding and spread the number of students struggling with educational and socioeconomic disadvantages more equally among schools. The sixth and final set of news stories surround initial reports of the Iowa City Police Department's intention to open a substation at the Pepperwood Plaza strip mall next to the Broadway Neighborhood Center on the Southeast Side in 2010.

ACCESSING ARTICLES

The Gazette and the *Press-Citizen* were read on microfilm, and *The Daily Iowan* was accessed through its online archive, which provides free access to PDF files. I conducted an initial reading of every issue of the three papers for each identified time span, selecting accounts, commentaries, photographs, and letters about the relevant topic or event and also items in those periods related to the Southeast Side in general. The resulting sample consisted of 187 news stories, editorials, columns, and letters to the editor.[4]

Once all news items from the first reading were collected, I created an electronic database to record my interpretations. To organize the news stories, each text's file name was coded based upon the newspaper in which it appeared, the respective publication, author name, page number, and headline.

IDENTIFYING THEMES IN NEWS TEXTS

My first reading of texts consisted of examining each issue of the newspaper within these time frames for stories related to the Southeast Side. I entered information about each of these stories into an electronic database. I used this database during a second reading from which I selected 83 stories that best reflected storytelling about place. In this second reading of the text—which consisted of exploring the news stories for their narrative qualities (Schudson, 2005)—I identified how the stories presented characters and sources from the Southeast Side or others who spoke about the Southeast Side. I was also interested in how the news stories applied language and literary devices, such as metaphor, to describe the Southeast Side and its problems, and how journalists overtly discussed elements of the Southeast Side's geography and explained the problems of the Southeast Side through larger social and cultural meanings. These findings were also coded and entered into the database to build a comprehensive map of the language, themes, and sources journalists used in their coverage.

I conducted a third reading to look deeper into the categories of storytelling with an intent to recognize the use of symbols and storylines that reflect larger meanings (Hall, 1980; Sillars, 1991).[5] In other words, I wanted to find how journalists connected the local stories to dominant narratives and explanations of everyday life. In this reading, I was interested in the news stories' sources and characters. When reading news as story, sources become characters that inform the story's plot and interact with the settings to "humanize" events (Bird and Dardenne, 1997, p. 343).

Interactions between characters, setting, and their experiences solving the story's problem reveal how the reader, too, can navigate through trials of life by turning to the social and cultural tools presented in the news story. Further, when evaluating who is—and who isn't—used as sources and characters, researchers are able to determine to whom the news story is written and for whom the news is produced (Bal, 2009; Sillars, 1991). To explore the category of sources and characters, I read the texts with the following questions in mind: Who are the sources for the story? Who is mentioned, and who is not? Are the sources providing perspective from inside or outside a particular place?

I also examined language and dialogue (or vocabulary) used to describe the Southeast Side. The vocabulary journalists use is important to examine what stories are "saying" about culture (Bal, 2009). For example, when the black boxer Mike Tyson was accused of rape in the 1990s, news stories referred to him as an "animal," a term that resembled a dominant stereotype of black men as primitive, savage, and sexually aggressive (Lule, 2001; Meyers, 2004).

With vocabulary in mind, I read stories about the Southeast Side while asking the following questions: How may specific phrases and language used in news texts depict people and place? Does language appear in quotes from sources or in journalists' own words? How might language be embedded with larger cultural and historical meanings?

During these readings, I was also interested in overt and explicit identifications and descriptions of setting and environment. In literature and story, place serves as a set upon which characters and themes can perform (Bal, 2009). To identify overt descriptions of place in news stories, I asked the following questions: How is a particular geography described? What is the journalist's proximity to specific places mentioned?

Finally, because the ways in which storytellers talk about geography—through place-making and place-naming that associate local places to larger social and cultural meaning—can influence audiences' connections to place and to the story's moral and social lessons (Hallin, 1986), I read news stories, asking: How may news texts refer to larger social and cultural constructions of place? How may journalists connect issues of geography to larger community/social themes?

I set out to approach news texts and interviews with journalists, officials, and Southeast Side residents guided by these questions and conceptual sets. However, to articulate the layered process of how news meanings about a neighborhood and its people were formed, I found the need to understand more about this community's dominant ideology. In this project, I consider even the most local of communities in the United States ones that not only benefit from power systems of national white ideologies that are embedded in public discourses, policies, and news practices, but that institute their own similar systems of oppression.

Conclusion

In this chapter, I have presented the final conceptual sets used in my analyses of how news media constructed Iowa City's Southeast Side. I presented a discussion about the power of whiteness via an evolving white supremacy in the U.S., the insertion of white ideologies into the country's social and cultural institutions—including the press, and a brief history of how the press have operated as a social institution in times of overt racialized tension that then naturalized particular narratives about race in news discourses that continue to appear today. This conceptualization was intended to frame the methods used to perform a critical textual analysis of news coverage about the Southeast Side, which appears in the next chapter.

FOUR

News of "The Inner City"

Racializing the Southeast Side

A black woman leans against the window inside Iowa City's homeless shelter. The evening shot from November 2011 shows her watching her children play in the building's warmth while darkness expands outside. The family waits for dinner as the woman's seven-year-old daughter looks outside where two figures—one who appears to be a black man in thick, winter clothes—lurk.

The page-one photograph on the cover of the *Press-Citizen* was a perfect image to reflect how the new shelter—about which the story and photograph were celebrating its first year in its new location—provides comfort, food, and safety for people in need.

But the photograph's cutline tells a different story, altogether.

"Originally from Chicago," it says, the woman "has been living at the Shelter House for nearly a year with her five children."

In just that single sentence, the photograph says it all: poor blacks (especially mothers) continue to come to Iowa City with their children (far too many for the women to care for) and take advantage of the city's good will and resources (by staying in the shelter for "nearly a year").

But the caption was wrong. The woman and her children had only been living in the city—and at the shelter—for a couple of months.

The homeless shelter doesn't even allow people to stay for a year.[1]

Inaccuracies like this happen for a number of reasons: poor notes, misunderstanding, bad typing—hell, even sources given bad information sometimes. But what was more interesting about this caption and photograph is how it matches with dominant discourse surrounding Iowa City's Southeast Side and the migration of folks from Chicago to Iowa City.

How people talk about new arrivals to Iowa City—especially black ones from Chicago—makes it sound reasonable that a mother of five children would want, let alone be allowed, to stay at the homeless shelter for that long.

Some of the believability that one could live in the shelter for so long and that the shelter would want someone to live there for so long comes from a dominant belief that a "welfare state" supports the indigent with housing, and money, and food and anything the homeless want, whenever they want it, and for however long they want it. These myths are even more believable when applied to mothers from urban areas who have multiple children (for review, see Omi and Winant, 1994).

Moreover, the photograph's setting contributes to these myths being applied in this case: outside lights in the pitch blackness, combined with a random man at the photograph's left side, resemble crime photos, with the night signaling deviousness and mystery; the light, surveillance; the random man once again, danger (Gutsche, 2011).

Even more troubling than what the photograph itself represents is that its cutline, before it provides any other information, identifies the mother as being from Chicago. As this chapter will show, in Iowa City, "Chicago" has come to mean more than just another city; it signals meanings of the ghetto, danger, blackness—and, most directly, of *not being from here*.

"This is the heartbreak," Shelter House's Executive Director, Crissy Canganelli told me when the photo appeared in the paper. The family, she said, had already felt unwelcome in Iowa City and by being identified first and foremost as being from somewhere other than the community to which they had moved, the cutline just made the family feel even more like they didn't belong. Indeed, soon after this photograph ran, the family moved back to Chicago, unable to find work, affordable housing, and the support that they needed to stay in Iowa City.

In this chapter, I identify several themes of news storytelling surrounding the Southeast-Side-as-place that help explain the coverage of those neighborhoods by not only describing what the coverage was but by surmising why journalists portrayed the Southeast Side as they did. These themes are presented below and serve as a starting point for interpreting interviews with journalists and their sources to reveal news place-making as an ideological process of the press in the following chapters.

Dramatic Storytelling from an Iowa Ghetto

Dramatic storytelling of "inner city culture" in the Southeast Side—such as violence and hip-hop music—in 2009 and 2010 quickly moved news stories away from describing events of Iowa City's southeastern neighborhoods to explaining—or interpreting—causes for social disorder there. For example, after violence forced a popular Southeast Side bar that featured hip-hop music to close, the news turned to urban stories to explain why. One *Gazette* story titled "Tough Crowd" opens with a setting of calm—"In the Southeast Side of Iowa City, in a quiet business district, sits the source of a lot of happiness and a lot of grief" (Shurson, 2009).

Deeper in the story, police officials counter accusations that race motivated arrests at Los Cocos, citing that officers had been called to the bar "almost 210" times and had made about 90 arrests, which "consumed more than 200 officer hours." One police official explicitly rejected notions of racial profiling: "The bar's clientele is predominantly black," he said, "[but] race isn't the issue; it's people who want to be thugs" (Shurson, 2009). The news story then quickly turns to a complicated discussion about racism, with the bar's owner blaming violence on a constant police presence at the bar, which was frequented primarily by racial and ethnic minorities. "If you treat a person like an animal," she said about the police's intervention at her bar, "they are going to act like an animal."

Perhaps Los Cocos was a dangerous place that required police attention, and maybe news told that part of the story accurately; however, my analysis is not to argue whether or not crimes happened or if the press covered the "facts" of these events "accurately." Instead, I am interested in how storytelling in news of the Southeast Side—such as Los Cocos closing—was told through narratives of "The Inner City" (Burgess, 1985), relying on notions of urban culture, crime, and welfare that "explained" causes for social conditions in the Southeast Side.

In the case of Los Cocos coverage, for example, news stories focus on explanations of how hip-hop music—and the kinds of people it attracts (i.e., "thugs")—closed a Southeast Side bar, though even the bar's owner suggests the closing was more complicated than the music she played. News from *The Gazette*, *Press-Citizen*, and *Daily Iowan* focused on similar characteristic of Los Cocos patrons and their problems, often explaining that hip-hop music attracts "thugs" who then start fights.

Indeed, a *Press-Citizen* story claims that the club's closure was not surprising: "hip-hop clubs have not been successful in the past in Iowa City ... [even though] police have worked hard to try to make Los Cocos the exception" (O'Leary, 2009). In another news story about a shooting at Los Cocos that calls the bar a "troubled Iowa City nightspot," several black suspects are identified (O'Leary, 2009a). Yet another story tells about a "two hour barrage of reports" about crimes at and around Los Cocos (Hermiston, 2009a).

Through dramatic descriptions of hip-hop's influence on Los Cocos violence, news coverage tapped into notions of the dangerous, black inner city to explain the bar's problems. Perceptions of hip-hop's connection with urban geography, deviance, and culture (Katz, 2012) provided a recognizable answer for disorder among blacks on Iowa City's Southeast Side. Since its early days when hip-hop radio stations shared "shout outs" about urban neighborhoods, housing projects, and streets, hip-hop has been portrayed in popular culture as a black or "ghetto thing" (Forman, 2002). Hip-hop is also increasingly confused with rap music and images of black men wearing chains ("bling") and brandishing handguns (Forman and Neal, 2004).

The Gazette's story about "Tough Crowds," then, may be the most explicit story about how Los Cocos—and its hip-hop—attracted the city's blacks and connected black and "inner city culture" to the Southeast Side as a whole. A photograph accompanying the "Tough Crowd" story, for example, shows dark-skinned patrons being "checked" by security outside Los Cocos at night. Other news photographs during this time period also cast Southeast Side spaces— such as apartment buildings and crime scenes—in dramatic shadows, suggesting that Iowa City blacks live in desolate, devious, and dangerous places (Gutsche, 2011). News stories portrayed the people living there, too, as being dangerous.

One *Press-Citizen* story about an older resident's interactions with young men in the Southeast Side describe young suspects—"a dark-skinned black man with a goatee and a black man wearing a black shirt and shorts"—threatening people in their cars by "taking off their shirts, jumping up and down and yelling obscenities" (Hermiston, 2009b). Perhaps this tale of young black men "jumping up and down and yelling"—or something like it—did happen in the Southeast Side. But, what makes the story even more believable in terms of how it constructed a "ghetto scene" is how well its description resembles decades of descriptions of young black men elsewhere in local press, specifically dramatic stories of young men "jumping up and down and yelling," that presented them as though they were primates living in an "urban jungle."

Indeed, the *Press-Citizen's* use of the word "thug" in reference to violent, urban blacks, such as in Los Cocos coverage, has been associated with violent blacks in mass media (Chiricos and Eschholz, 2002), and the term's inclusion in this news story—and descriptions of young black men as animals—seem more than coincidental. History on the use of such of subtle racism appearing in news is just as strong as the press' past use of overt racist descriptions. For example, Ewen and Ewen (2008) suggest that *The New York Times'* enthusiastic report about a 1906 museum exhibit featuring a caged African headlined "BUSHMAN SHARES A CAGE WITH BRONX PARK APES" represents dominant ideologies of the audience at the time:

[the Bushman] was an immediate sensation. For an Anglo-American population fearful of the masses of influx of immigrants that was underway, and struggling to control a large free black population, the spectacle of a man living in the same cage with an orangutan offered tangible reassurance that the world was, in fact, inhabited by people of unequal worth [p. 136, capitalization in the original].

Not much has changed in news coverage of blacks since the 1900s, however, and despite the scholarly work on how blacks are depicted to be violent more than whites in news coverage (Entman and Rojecki, 2000; Stabile, 2006), news has adopted notions of subtle racism in which a perpetrator's race need not be mentioned for audiences to assume the violent characters are most likely male and black. Parisi (1998) calls such subtle coverage an "ambiguous melding of mythico-aesthetic grandeur with contemporary phrasing and personified framing [that represents] only a sophisticated new form of the denigrating discourse of race in the press" (p. 247).

Local coverage of violence in the Southeast Side used specific words that marked the people in the Southeast Side as people living in an urban jungle, a space that endorses and breeds violent blacks. One story, for example, details the Southeast Side as a place full of "youth roaming the sidewalks late into the night, causing trouble, making noise and being disrespectful" (Heldt, 2009). Similar language appears throughout newspapers. A *Press-Citizen* editorial (*Press-Citizen,* 2009) argues that a youth curfew would stop youth in the Southeast Side from "congregating, loafing and loitering" and would be a fair response to what the newspaper claims are community concerns about "youth roaming at all hours, small children out alone without supervision, loitering in large groups, throwing rocks, blocking traffic on streets and chronic truancy."

Terms such as "roaming," "animals," "youth," "loafing," and "congregating" in Southeast Side coverage sound like actions of zombies or animals (attributes that have also been assigned to urban blacks) thereby serving as euphemisms for black, inner-city living (Meyers, 2004; Wilson, 1997; 2009). Meanwhile, notions of "small children out alone without supervision" smacks of descriptions often used to describe and chastise urban black families—and mothers in particular—who ignore their children's needs (Katz, 2012).

Ultimately, these subtle, dramatic scenes and language used in news to describe the people and activities of the Southeast Side were reminiscent of settings and terms used to describe the Southeast Side as yet another inner city ghetto that then was connected to its leading archetypes, which are discussed below.

The Chicago Story: Gangstas and the Ghetto

News stories about Iowa City's Southeast Side tended to racialize and urbanize descriptions of social disorder there through storytelling by sources outside of the Southeast Side and language that reinforced urban tales of deviance (Lule, 2001; Parisi, 1998; Stabile, 2006). In the end, multiple storylines that connected the neighborhoods, its people, and problems with people and problems from outside Iowa—particularly of Chicago—strengthened storytelling of the Southeast Side as "The Inner City."

Stories about "those people from Chicago" tapped into a long-time local legend of a Chicago-to-Iowa City migration. The story of black Chicagoans moving to Iowa City for social welfare has been a local narrative for nearly 30 years. How many people—particularly black people—have moved to Iowa City from Chicago or other places *specifically for social welfare* in recent years is not quite clear, though a 2010 ethnography (Keene, Padilla and Geronimus, 2010) of those who moved from Chicago to Iowa City following the collapse of Chicago's public housing program provides some data:

> The Iowa City Housing Authority (ICHA), which serves all of Johnson County, reported in 2007 that 14 percent (184) of the families that it assists through vouchers and public housing were from Illinois, and according to housing authority staff, virtually all of these families are from the Chicago area.... Additionally, the ICHA estimates that about one-third of the approximately 1,500 families on its rental-assistance waiting list are Chicago area families [p. 277].

The study of black families who moved to Iowa City from Chicago by Keene, Padilla, and Geronimus also focuses on the newcomer's sense of "rootlessness." After feeling forced out of Chicago by gentrification and then trying to live in Iowa City, participants said that they felt like they did not have a "home" since leaving Chicago and felt pressured to return by some in Iowa City, a mostly-white community. The study's authors write that participants'

> quests for opportunity in Iowa bring them to a whiter community, where they confront head-on the systems of racial exclusion that have produced the profoundly unequal geographic distribution of resources and opportunity that they seek to escape. Many participants describe how this geography itself serves as a marker of difference and how "Chicago" has become a code word for deeply rooted stereotypes of an urban "underclass" used by white neighbors to marginalize them [p. 282].

Participants told researchers that they came to Iowa City for steady employment, safe neighborhoods, and good schools for their children; however, portrayals of blacks who moved to Iowa City from Chicago fit closer with archetypes often applied to those from "The Inner City," and especially with that of the "Welfare Queen"—women who steal welfare—which constructed a divide between those living in the Southeast Side and the rest of the city.

When Iowa City officials announced the opening of a police substation to address crime at Los Cocos and other places in the Southeast Side in 2010, for instance, newspaper coverage avoided a complicated cultural or social explanation for violence in lieu of stories about urban violence and illicit drug use. More specifically, news stories told tales of blacks who moved to Iowa City from Chicago to cheat the welfare system and to participate in gang violence, creating a "you-me and us-them" structure (Katz, 2012, p. 83) between the Southeast Side and the rest of Iowa City that then applied specific characteristics, values, and experiences to particular places—despite the experiences of people who lived in the neighborhood that were rarely reported.

Even though people of the Southeast Side—both blacks from Chicago and longtime white residents—were seldom mentioned by name and interviewed as individuals in news stories to explain the Southeast Side's social conditions, they were often grouped together as a collective via rhetoric, separated from the rest of the city in ways that suggested the Southeast Side operated as its own entity.

In fact, sources and journalists alike often referred to Southeast Side residents as "those people" and "these kids" (Hermiston, 2009c) as though the entire neighborhood was of one people. Indeed, in a 2010 *Press-Citizen* (Hermiston, 2010) story about a black, 17-year-old man charged with murdering Versypt, the white landlord, Iowa City Police Chief Sam Hargadine described the Southeast Side as a "'tight-knit community' of people who 'don't rat each other out.'"

In an ultimate "us/them" construction (Katz, 2012; Said, 1979), Southeast Side Iowa City crime in 2009 and 2010 was attributed not to people from Iowa City or even people living in Iowa City, but to people who had moved to Iowa City from Chicago searching for welfare. Newspapers published opinion pieces and news stories that told of Chicago residents coming to Iowa City strictly for easy access to affordable housing, despite public data that shows two-thirds of low-income households registered with the city's Housing Authority assists were elderly and disabled, not poor, black, and from Chicago (Spence, Lawson and Visser, 2010) or, as the newspapers described them—hoodlums, gangstas, and welfare mothers from the Chicago ghetto.

A *Press-Citizen* news article following Versypt's murder used more veiled language, describing people living in the Southeast Side as migrants "taking advantage of subsidized housing and other need-based services here ... [who] come from inner city neighborhoods with radically different cultures" (Elliott, 2009). The article, written by a community member who was part of the newspaper's Writers Group (and selected by editors to be published under the auspices of *The Press-Citizen's* Writer's Group), also argues for an orientation program for people coming to Iowa City to help them assimilate in order to live well alongside long-term Iowa Citians.

The Welfare Haven: Rise of the Welfare Queen

When Southeast Siders who came to Iowa "from Chicago" were overtly used as sources in news coverage, they were not only identified as being *from Chicago*, but often were suggested as negatively influencing everyday life in Iowa City. A page-one *Press-Citizen* story about the increase of homelessness in and around Iowa City is a good example of this. The article was published with a photograph of the story's main character, Shamika Miller, who appears to be black, and who is sitting with three children on the front porch of the homeless shelter. The story, however, appears to be more about her character and the drama surrounding her homelessness than about homelessness as an increasing concern in Iowa City. The story starts:

> Shamika Miller has been homeless for about three weeks now.
> Coming to Iowa City a year and a half ago, she stayed at the Domestic Violence Intervention Project shelter after leaving her boyfriend behind on Chicago's Southside. She had a job at a packaging plant until she was laid off four months ago, and she and her four children had an apartment on Benton Street until they were evicted three weeks ago, landing them at Shelter House.
> "I was one month behind (on my rent)," Miller said. "(The landlord) took me to court and she didn't want my money. (But) I've been cool since I've been here" [Daniel, 2009, parentheses in original].

And while the story continues by discussing increasing numbers of homeless school children in Iowa City and how much the city spent to build a new community homeless shelter in 2009, how Miller became homeless is not overtly described, but is assumed as the story discusses illicit drug use and violence that caused both her and a Chicago man to become homeless and in Iowa City:

> One current resident of the Shelter House, Kenneth Porter, said laws and attitudes toward the homeless and those with criminal backgrounds need to change in order to alleviate the homeless problem. Born and raised on the south side of Chicago, Porter said he came to Iowa City via Madison, Wis., in January, planning to be near his daughter, Marie, who lives in Marion. He said it took him until May to find a part-time job as a janitor despite his experience in driving a forklift and in the food service industry.
> Much of his problem, he said, comes from his conviction in 2005 for dealing

drugs in Illinois, a part of his past that continues to haunt him in housing and employment applications.

"Most of the people are homeless because of employment and housing," Porter said. "Because of your background ... people don't want to rent to you. If you haven't been in trouble for three years, what's the problem? They make me feel like once a criminal, always a criminal."

By focusing only on homeless in Iowa City who had moved from Chicago—and, particularly on a young black mother and a violent male drug user—this story serves as what Manoff (1986) calls a *shadow text*—a story in which cultural meanings and messages are embedded in what appears to be representations of reality and objective truths. More specifically, this particular story puts a face on "those people from Chicago" who fit notions of the Southeast Side as being a ghetto and Iowa City, generally, as a place that attracts poor and deviant blacks.

More specifically, Miller's "shadow text" in the story above affirmed the archetype of the "Welfare Queen"—usually used to portray low-income, inner-city black women (whether or not they use social welfare) as "using" and "cheating the welfare system"—that was often associated with "people from Chicago" in local press. The story does not specifically mention whether Miller received a welfare check—though she is using another form of social welfare via the homeless shelter, is black, and is shown to have multiple children in the page-one photograph, a perfect example of the Queen archetype.

Stories of the "Welfare Queen" describe a woman who has more children in order to increase her welfare payments. She then spends the extra money on drugs, material goods, and supporting her lazy boyfriends (Blank-Libra, 2004; Gilliam, 1999). While the "Welfare Queen" is a gendered archetype, both black women *and men* were accused of abusing social welfare in coverage of Iowa City's Southeast Side in ways that fit with the "Welfare Queen's" devious nature.

For example, a guest opinion written by a former Iowa City police officer selected to run in the *Press-Citizen* blamed "tax-supported programs" such as affordable housing for having "introduced a culture of violence" to Iowa City (Roth, 2009). The author also writes that welfare programs, such as affordable housing, attracted people to Iowa City who bring with them an urban culture that has "endangered our children," has "ruined some of Iowa City's schools," and has "destroyed some property values and businesses."

Miller's connection to the "Welfare Queen" archetype is further reinforced when the news article discusses how homeless people moving to Iowa City have increased the number of those receiving money from the "county's general financial assistance fund." Yet, most troubling in this news story on homelessness was how the "problems" were not at all influenced by local politics, values, economies and social conditions. Instead, problems were cast as extensions of Chicago's inner city and black "culture." Indeed, coverage focused on distancing the people who arrived in Iowa City from somewhere else as the most undesirable outsiders, and examples of this are numerous.

Take for instance a story adjacent to Miller's story on homelessness that was headlined in bold letters "Refugees' pasts can haunt them in U.S." (Hermiston, 2009d). Focused on the police shooting of a John Deng, a homeless Sudanese national but who was living in Iowa City that same year, the story's use of the term "refugee" when discussing homeless blacks or Africans strengthens the narrative of dark-skinned people embodying inner-city deviance and hunger for welfare handouts moving to Iowa City. Indeed, the term "refugee" carried such connotations used by news media to describe thousands of poor black residents who had evacuated New Orleans following Hurricane Katrina (Shah, 2009).

News scholarship reveals a recent history of using the term "refugee" to stereotype poor blacks. Masquelier (2006) writes that "[b]y referring to stranded residents as 'refugees,' … journalists effectively misidentified them: Many so-called refugees felt they were being singled out on the basis of an invalid criterion" (p. 736). Therefore, coupled with the story on local homeless and stories on "refugees," this storytelling strengthened a divide between Iowa City and those who live in the Southeast Side, casting that part of the city as though it was from another part of the country—or the world.

Southeast Side as Gangsta Land

But the Southeast Side was never meant to be compared to anywhere but nice Iowa. That changed in 2009 and 2010. Following an announcement that the city would open a police substation on Iowa City's Southeast Side in 2010, a guest opinion in *The Daily Iowan* described dominant perceptions of Southeast Siders as Chicago transplants: "a black teenage boy, fresh off the bus from Chicago with a few ounces of crack. He has an unmarried mother, probably just as strung-out, and for fun he likes to rob some nice white native Iowans" (O'Reilly, 2010).

Most other news coverage of the Southeast Side, however, was less explicit in describing "Welfare Queens" and "Gangstas" moving to Iowa City. For example, a *Press-Citizen* story about a black Chicago man suspected of robbery ended with a promise from police that the man would be returned to Iowa City under extradition "should he surface in Chicago" (Conzemius, 2009). That the man might "surface in Chicago" seems to suggest he has entered some kind of Chicago underworld, a haven for those who commit crime in Iowa City and escape.

Notions of gang violence on Iowa City's Southeast Side that were influenced by Chicago's inner city culture further distanced the people and the problems of southeastern neighborhoods from the rest of Iowa City. A 2009 *Press-Citizen* story about potential gang violence in Iowa City, for example, used dramatic storytelling that set Iowa City on par with gang-infested urban centers. The story—which appeared as city officials announced a new police station in the Southeast Side—begins:

> Picture a place where gang members outnumber police four to one.
> A place where those gangs have carved out a piece of turf they use to brazenly peddle drugs on street corners and enforce their territory and rules with assaults, stabbings and drive-by shootings.
> You might be envisioning the streets of Chicago, Detroit or Los Angeles, but this was the scene in Iowa City in 1998 [Hermiston, 2010a].

The article continues by celebrating local police officers who took over policing of gang violence in Iowa City and quickly begins to read more like the plot of a crime drama than a news story about gang prevention:

> What was meant to be a temporary unit has become a fixture in the department.
> Gonzalez and the five-man SCAT [gang-prevention] team was out-numbered, so it had had [*sic*] to use strategy to pick off members one or two at a time, they said. The result, Batcheller said, was like taking a "sledgehammer to a pile of mashed potatoes."
> However, Gonzalez said that although police got smarter in their approach to the gangs, the gangs got smarter, too.

The story ends with a fear appeal that connects past gang violence with more contemporary times, saying that gangs from the 1990s "remain" in Iowa City, and, in one police officer's words, "It's never stopped.... It seems like almost every year it comes out."

By connecting the efforts of police from the past with a perceived gang problem of today through official sources and tales of danger, journalists relied on nostalgia and news narratives about ghetto life to frame the gang problems of today as being just as threatening or that they ever existed to begin with. In this case, journalists also suggested the same solutions to similar problems—increased policing.

More interesting, however, is how these most recent news reports further located the Southeast Side as an "urban" place instead of describing the causes and consequences of gang violence. Such news reports about gangs and violent crime would make it appear that crime was a big problem in Iowa City in 2009 and 2010. In 2009, 23 percent of police calls were from Iowa City's southeastern neighborhoods (Hennigan, 2010); Iowa City had seen a 24 percent increase in violent crime generally and a 27 percent increase in property crime in 2008 (Hennigan, 2009). Still, the majority of the violent crime was in a concentrated area other than the Southeast Side—the city's downtown bar district that's frequented by university students.

Supporting College Violence and Criminalizing the Southeast Side

A 2010 report by graduate students at the University of Iowa about Iowa City's southeastern neighborhoods showed that the city's downtown tended to have more crime in the mid–2000s than anywhere else in Iowa City (Bailey, Law, Mason and Phillips, 2011). Such ideological work is further developed by local news coverage of fights and disorder among mainly white college students in Iowa City's downtown, the space where police reported the most violence in 2009 and 2010.

Whereas Southeast Side violence was cast as extraordinary through the use of racialized verbs, suspect descriptions, and comparisons to urban and black culture, downtown violence was presented as common and somehow safer. An April 2009 *Daily Iowan* article, one of three stories published in a series on downtown violence, said that "in the chaos of downtown, passersby tend to see an assault as a normal occurrence, at times even considering it 'entertainment'" (Zilbermints, 2009).

While *The Daily Iowan* series did not mention the race of victims or suspected assailants—as coverage of the Southeast Side did—a page-one photograph shows a white male with blood on his face, providing a visual signal of the race, gender, and age of those involved in downtown violence. Under the headline "IC's Mean Streets," the photograph's caption labeled groups of drunken and violent men in Iowa City's downtown as "roving packs" out to hurt each other. From around the same time period, a *Gazette* story described the downtown college violence as an "exuberance of youth" (Belz, 2009) and explained the group violence this way:

> They are in college. They will never again be this free. And they are drinking $2 beer at sweaty nightclubs, smoking cigarettes under streetlamps, falling down, getting arrested, getting angry, getting to know each other, fighting, kissing, hugging, yelling and laughing.

Just as news coverage explained downtown violence as a natural college experience, news coverage normalized Southeast Side violence as being the effect of urban black culture. News stories indicated that drunken "packs" of college students were isolated to the downtown, whereas Southeast Side violence was described as infiltrating the city's schools, social services, and public safety.

With the news articles' characters identified as violent, young men— many of them black—through language and scenes, news articles create a vivid description of those who went to Los Cocos or who participated in activities throughout the Southeast Side. For example, a *Press-Citizen* story turned to police officials—and police verbiage—to provide authority to otherwise baseless claims of increasing danger and violence in the Southeast Side. The article stated that "Police learned a group of 25 to 30 teenagers, some as young as 12" were contributing to a "high volume of foot and vehicular traffic," though the story still lacked authoritative statistics and context (Hermiston, 2009b).

Other news stories used generalizations and anecdotes to bolster reports of the unruly Southeast Side. One *Gazette* story (Petrus, 2009) said that "juvenile crime is taking over (Southeast Side residents') community." A quote from one resident added drama to news coverage that was otherwise matter-of-fact: "You drive down your street to get to your house and you can't get through," the resident said, "because the street is blocked by kids and they won't move." Another story, this one also from *The Gazette*, focused on similar dramatic descriptions of setting, action, and characters that added emotional ties to dominant narratives:

> The neighborhood has seen three riots this week—widely reported street fights involving dozens of people using baseball bats, boards, knives, chains and fists.
>
> It's quite a change from what one long-term resident remembers of the area.
>
> "The most we've had is speeders up and down the street," a woman, who asked to remain unnamed, told *The Gazette* on Wednesday. The residents, she said, now keep their "eyes and ears peeled and one hand on the phone."
>
> The woman, "grandmother-aged," has lived on Hollywood Boulevard for 25 years. She said she watched nervously from her kitchen window Sunday as a mob-like group stood across the street, yelling and taunting neighbors to come out and fight.
>
> "The street was covered with people," she said [Keppler, 2009].

These stories of the Southeast Side as a place of constant activity, including increasing street and gang violence, loud youth taunting the elderly, and general disorder, mirrored another image of "The Inner City." For example, a *Gazette* story about "a recent rise in violence in the southeastern side of Iowa City" (Petrus, 2009) presented an extreme version of neighborhood concerns without providing specific data of how much violence—and what kind of violence—was occurring there.

Neighborhood Nicknames:
Renaming the Southeast Side

On multiple occasions, notions of the Southeast Side as an especially violent place allowed newsworkers to rename the Southeast Side in ways that highlighted its perceived deviance. For example, the headline "Fight Central" topped a *Daily Iowan* story about the aftermath of street violence in the Southeast Side (Zilbermints, 2009a). Harried details from residents and police officials contributed to a tale of danger that began with one woman's personal story:

> One Iowa City woman has pulled her children from school and said she is leaving the city following a series of riots outside her home.
>
> Iowa City police responded to a fight Wednesday at City High, 1900 Morningside Drive, which they say is related to a slew of massive fights in the area. Two juveniles were arrested at the scene, authorities say.
>
> The incident was the fourth related confrontation since Sunday involving a series of events police say are unprecedented.
>
> "It's spiraling out of control," said Iowa City police Sgt. Troy Kelsay. "We haven't dealt with this on this scale. This has blown up very quickly."

The story continues by revisiting police descriptions of the fight, and the mother from the story's lead reappears on the page-three jump:

> "This has got to stop—if my kids can't be safe at home, where are they safe?" said Necey Patterson [*sic*], the owner of the Hollywood Boulevard residence, a one-story, green house with walls adorned with her children's academic awards and sports medals.
>
> Patterson said her kids—a 16-year-old son and 15-year-old daughter who were both injured in the confrontations—would not return to City High.
>
> "I can replace my stuff," she said about the damage done to her home. "But I can't replace my kids."

The story ends with warnings of future violence, suggesting that stories such as this from the Southeast Side may continue indefinitely:

> Police expect more related incidents in the coming days and more charges to come, [Sgt. Kelsay] said.
>
> "The whole thing is just so foreign to me," he said. "A group of 50. Kids and parents. It's ridiculous."

News coverage that both overtly and covertly characterized groups of people as deviant blacks from Chicago who settle in the Southeast Side became so established in news coverage that journalists were able to assign the Southeast Side a secondary place-name. Place-names such as "Fight Central," and "Tough Crowd" carried warnings to readers that they should avoid the Southeast Side. Indeed, placing the Southeast Side as a "tough" place at the "center" of Iowa City's criminal underworld similar to the "seedy" cities of New York, Los Angeles, and Chicago. Place-naming in these instances showed the strength of normalized notions of the Southeast Side as a deviant place in that journalists were able to apply to that location a secondary place-name without much explanation of exactly the place which they were describing.

Another story, this one from *The Daily Iowan*, labeled the Southeast Side a "No Go Zone" (Valentine, 2009) after a pizza company announced that recent robberies of delivery workers in the Southeast Side forced the company to halt future deliveries. (Indeed, even in 2013, a friend of mine who lives near the Southeast Side told me that she had to get a manager's override to have a pizza delivered to her home.)

In an explanation for the crime, the newspaper connected the new place-name to other recent stories of Southeast Side crime: "The robberies are similar to crimes committed by members of the Broadway Goons, a locally brewed gang mostly made up of individuals age 17 and under...."

Perhaps the most blatant example of Chicago storytelling that also used secondary place-names appeared in 2010 at the top of the *Press-Citizen* opinion page. Headlined "Perpetrators of urban decay," the story names the Southeast Side "Little Chicago," a smaller version of an inner city that is infested with gang violence, welfare mothers, and children in public housing:

> When will Iowa City have done enough to serve as a sanctuary city for those whose Chicago projects have been torn down and not rebuilt? How much "Little Chicago" can Iowa City afford to absorb and hopefully, some day, supposedly assimilate?
>
> After all, few signs point in the direction of assimilation. We're left wondering, just who is changing whom?
>
> It doesn't matter if we have the best intentions in the world. Looking at the matter pragmatically, how many inner-city refugees can a city the size of Iowa City absorb without:
> - More police officers?
> - Higher taxes?
> - More money for schools to assist special-needs, developmentally delayed children who have little stability or emotional support in their lives?
>
> As a former social worker, I used to fill out housing applications at the Hawkeye Area Community Action Program. I asked applicants why they came here.
>
> "For a better life for myself and my children," each parent would say. "Fewer deadbolts and locks on my doors."
>
> But then who do they bring with them?
> - Boyfriends not on the lease and possibly wanted in Chicago.
> - Relatives and friends who need a place to stay.
>
> These lodgers—invisible to the public housing bureaucrats—bring their bad

habits with them, and soon Iowa City residents have more dead bolts and locks on their doors.

Just who is changing whom? [Conzemius, 2010].

While this piece was not written by a newspaper staff writer, it was selected by an editor and commissioned by the opinion page editor; in fact, after this story appeared in 2010, I spoke with both the author and the editor about what I considered its incendiary language (i.e., "inner-city refugees"), broad characterizations (i.e., "perpetrators of urban decay"), and how this particular story contributed to overall coverage of the Southeast Side. Both the article's author and the editor said that the language was provocative, but said that, in fact, that is what they wanted. Indeed, Conzemius told me that her opinion page editor encouraged her to "stir up" the opinion page and blogs through her writing.

These secondary place-names solidify ideological constructions of a place considered once safe and homogenous but that has since been influenced by "juvenile crime." Such discourse revealed a belief that a utopian community, Iowa City—a traditional, wholesome, and safe place—had become corrupted, influenced by urban and black culture from a neighboring city. These news stories relied on narratives of places outside of Iowa City to describe a less-desirable portion of the hometown that exists as its own entity, thereby releasing the wider community of responsibility to positively influence those neighborhoods.

Conclusion

In the end, there appeared to be little change over the course of the coverage of the Southeast Side in 2009 and 2010. While local news media may have begun referring to Southeastern neighborhoods as the Southeast Side in the mid 2000s (Spence, Lawson and Visser, 2010), the term took on specific meanings in the news in 2009 that was maintained and strengthened throughout 2010. The Southeast Side became not just a place or a particular geography but a mythological setting that houses and breeds racialized social disorder. In this way, the "Southeast Side" became an *ideograph*, a recognizable, rhetorical symbol of cultural values and ideology (McGee, 1980) that journalists then assigned to a cluster of neighborhoods as a means to express community disdain for its existence.

By turning to an ideograph such as the Southeast Side, journalists embedded a deep history of urban narratives and stereotypes of black city dwellers to explain social conditions among newly arrived blacks to a small, Midwestern city. Indeed, as future chapters will show, comments by journalists, officials, and residents confirmed that the term Southeast Side was code for "black people from Chicago," "the bad side of town," or "the ghetto," and consistent storytelling in the news that not only described but *interpreted* social conditions in Southeastern neighborhoods affirmed this racialized archetype.

Crime stories from the Southeast Side—and especially dramatic stories—became the mainstay of describing and discussing the Southeast Side, and crime stories that focused on urban gang violence that tapped into riveting narratives of ethnic gangs plaguing U.S. cities from news and popular entertainment. More specifically, officials described the Southeast Side in terms of its disorder—violent youth, crime reports, loitering, and fear. Little news reporting provided more complex explanations and descriptions that may have revealed influences in the Southeast Side that came from outside the space, such as economic or racial inequalities. Journalists consistently cited police sources who charged hip-hop as an element of urban culture and deviance, and news reports told stories that fit with other dominant perceptions of urban settings—young men "congregating, loafing and loitering," "chronic truancy," and black youth "roaming" the streets.

Stories about the Southeast Side not only mentioned a suspect's race—a common practice in crime reporting—but also included descriptions of suspects' clothes and other identifiable features, which ultimately gave the audience characters and imagery to be applied to the Southeast Side and furthered a narrative of blacks-as-gangbangers. Such visuals, combined with particular language such as "thugs," "animal," and descriptions of young black men "jumping" and "yelling," as described above, act as rhetorical tools used to connect behavior in the Southeast Side to narratives of primitive and dangerous blacks (Stabile, 2006) and urban environments (English, 2011; Massey and Denton, 1993; Wilson, 1997).

Characterizations of the Southeast Side as "The Inner City" or as "ghetto" were reinforced, however subtly, in several ways. First, coverage of crime among black youth on the Southeast Side was compared to crime in big cities. News stories referred to homeless people—both from Iowa City and Chicago—as "refugees" and as "The Other." Such subtle and lasting tales worked in conjunction with other covert forms of characterization, including the secondary place-names "No Go Zone" and "Fight Central" used to re-label the Southeast Side, and by turning to official sources rather than Southeast Side residents to define and describe the neighborhood.

News coverage about the Southeast Side seemed to be just as much about creating a geographic difference between Southeastern neighborhoods and the rest of Iowa City as it was about informing the public about social conditions there. Throughout these two years of coverage, the "Southeast Side" became a geographic place that represented dominant beliefs about an urban, black ghetto as a way to define and separate some Iowa City neighborhoods from each other.

Such a divide is especially clear in coverage of violence among youth downtown versus in the Southeast Side. Whereas both groups of youth were referred to as "packs" and roaming or crowding streets, explanations for the college students focused on the joys of college life and described ruckus and violence from college students as being ordinary and expected. On the other hand, the term "pack" became racialized when viewed in context with other storytelling about animalistic, urban behavior among young black men in the Southeast Side.

Starting with the next chapter, I use this textual analysis to support an analysis of interviews with journalists, officials, and residents of the Southeast Side that focuses on how each group characterized spaces of Iowa City—and the Southeast Side in particular.

FIVE

What's the Southeast Side?

Using Mental Mapping to Construct Place

Michael moved to Iowa City in 2007, right before the "Floods of 2008" that decimated much of Iowa's lowlands.[1] Waters pushed some six feet higher than shorelines, thousands were displaced from their homes, and pressure from water altered both natural and built environments for years to come (Mutel, 2010). Because the Cedar and Iowa Rivers carve the state into distinct regions, and their estuaries curve throughout hills and valleys and weave through neighborhoods and farmland, when rain poured and saturated at levels not seen in hundreds of years, the water had nowhere to go except to spill into people's lives.

As a journalist in his mid–30s at the time, Michael had already covered disaster. He was ready for it. What he wasn't prepared for, though, was how flood waters that spread across acres and acres of Iowa City and the region—shutting down highways and interstates, closing bridges, hiding landmarks and city features that people relied on to give directions and carry out their lives—made it especially difficult to become familiar with the city's landscape.

"When the flood started, I still wasn't really familiar with the area," Michael says. "And I still have this geographic inability to figure out what's east and west," because the Iowa River swelled so much and many of the city's physical features and main arteries were hidden under flood waters or morphed by the surge.

Even before the flood, Michael welcomed information about the city. What are the different neighborhoods? Where are specific streets, buildings, parks, places where he needed to do his reporting? There were some places Michael learned about faster than others.

"It didn't take long after I moved here to hear about the Southeast Side [as being] a poor, black—I hate to use the term, but—ghetto part of Iowa City," Michael says. "Coming here from outside, people taught me the stereotypes to know what they were talking about, shorthand, whether they were true or not."

Michael also says that he would listen to a morning show on the local KCJJ radio station that played Elvis Presley's "In the Ghetto" when it aired police reports about Southeast Side crime.

Michael wondered: "What's the 'common knowledge' that would make this joke funny? How is the Southeast Side a 'ghetto'?" "Hell," he even wondered, "Where is the Southeast Side?"

He asked his friends. His family. (New to the city, would they even know?)

Michael ultimately found his answers from other journalists, city officials, long-time residents, and from his own experience when he covered the violence of 2009 in the Southeastern neighborhoods. He said these few experiences in the Southeast Side ultimately shaped his personal knowledge of and beliefs about that neighborhood.

"There's a perception that there's a large amount of crime there," Michael says. "Large might be an exaggeration; however, my personal experience is that I've been there. I was there after that landlord got shot, covering the police action there, and one time I was doing a ride-along with the police and just by coincidence there was a report of shots fired."

But how did Michael's experiences, the stories he was told, and the reasons why he ever even went into the Southeast Side shape how he would cover the neighborhood for the newspaper?

In December 2011, I interviewed three sets of people in Iowa City—journalists, public officials/community organizers, and residents of the Southeast Side, which provided a deeper understanding about how news comes to characterize place.

As seen with Michael's story, unpacking his ultimate understandings of the Southeast Side shows they were constructed by a complex set of events and key players.[2] As Shoemaker and Vos (2009) write, news media research should incorporate the study of social institutions, news processes, audience reception, and inquiry that focuses on news texts and creation.

With this approach in mind, all interviews focused on interviewees' perceptions of news coverage, Iowa City environments, and activities of the various spaces and places throughout Iowa City. More specifically, participants were asked to discuss their perceptions of geography—neighborhoods, spaces, and places—throughout the city.[3]

Michael's story, for example, contributes to understanding the complexities of experiencing and learning about place, especially in terms of how he learned about the Southeast Side as both a new arrival and as a journalist. His example also highlights the degree to which these storytellers relate to each other, their sources, and the narratives they are told about neighborhoods that then appear in their coverage.

As a journalist, Michael was exposed to local city and community leaders as part of his daily job. He was exposed to media—media beyond that which he created and that came from his own newspaper. Michael also had an expectation of being familiar with the community enough to represent it in some authoritative, mediated manner via his journalism, which required him to be mobile, to enter and exit city spaces, and to find an "objective" narrative to tell about people and places.

In this chapter, I present an analysis of how journalists and their sources—particularly city officials—operated within a shared interpretive community in that they applied similar ideological explanations of geography, local culture, and social conditions that ultimately shaped mediated characterizations of the Southeast Side. I begin this chapter with a discussion about how I selected participants and conducted interviews.

Most interesting in this initial description of my methodology is a discussion of how journalists and their sources, independent of each other, provided nearly identical (and complicated) demarcations and characterizations of the Southeast Side. Equally important—and directly connected to my formation of *news place-making*—is the following explication of this concept as a process. Below, I discuss the qualitative method of mental mapping through which participants draw and explain maps of their environment as a means to cull meanings participants assign to particular locations.

Selecting Journalists as Storytellers

I gathered names of journalists and photographers that appeared in bylines of news stories used in my textual analysis to build a list of 15 potential participants; 11 participated (Figure 5.1).[4] Journalists ranged in age from 20 to 37. All had lived in the Iowa City area for at least three years. Ten of the journalists identified as white; one identified as Hispanic. Three were female. Seven had been working at the same media outlet since 2009 or 2010. One journalist had moved into a new position at another Iowa City news outlet, one had left the Iowa City area, but remained in media, and two had left the field entirely.[5]

Journalists' Demographics				
Name	Age	Newspaper	Race	Gender
Annika	20	Daily Iowan	White	Female
Ashley	20	Daily Iowan	White	Female
Barb	36	Gazette	White	Female
David	33	Press-Citizen	White	Male
Duncan	21	Daily Iowan	White	Male
Gary	33	Press-Citizen	White	Male
Jeff	41	Press-Citizen	White	Male
Len	29	Gazette	White	Male
Max	28	Press-Citizen	White	Male
Roger	35	Press-Citizen	Hispanic	Male
Ulrich	37	Press-Citizen	White	Male

FIGURE 5.1

Identifying Public Officials as Sources

I also compiled a list of 13 names or positions of public officials and community leaders cited in the stories used in the textual analysis (Figure 5.2). This list included those from particular public institutions, including schools, the police department, and city public service agencies, such as the housing authority. Community organizations that operated in the Southeast Side, such as neighborhood associations and neighborhood centers, were also included. Six public officials and community leaders (fewer than half of those I contacted) agreed to participate by responding to my initial email.[6]

As with all participants, I began the interviews by answering participants' questions about the project and asking for their demographic information, including age, race, and their length of time living and working in Iowa City. I also asked participants to clarify their jobs and involvement in the community.[7] All of the officials and community members identified as white; one was female. Participants ranged in age from 31 to 54. Five participants considered

Public Officials' Demographics

Name	Age	Affiliation	Race	Gender
Allen	49	Police officer	White	Male
Bill	54	City official	White	Male
Fred	45	School official	White	Male
James	31	Neighborhood association	White	Male
Paul	32	Police officer	White	Male
Susie	40	Neighborhood center	White	Female

FIGURE 5.2

themselves long-term Iowa City area residents. One (the school official) had lived in southwestern Iowa City for about two years.

Searching for Southeast Side Residents

Another purpose of the interviews with journalists and officials was to have participants explain what they thought of the Southeast Side and where they thought the Southeast Side was located. Finding the exact boundaries of the Southeast Side isn't easy. City officials don't offer a specific description of the space and the space's contested nature makes its borders ambiguous at best.[8] Thus, near the end of their interviews, I gave journalists and public officials an aerial photograph of a Southeastern portion of Iowa City and asked them to locate the city's Southeast Side (Figure 5.3).

This assisted me in the subsequent step of selecting Southeast Side residents by identifying where participants' spatial definitions intersected in order to find specific sets of residents that represented the Southeast Side as characterized in the news. These residents were not long-time, white Iowans who were seen as being "invested" in the city; rather, news stories tended to discuss poor, black, transient, and deviant people as "infesting" the neighborhood. Those, then, were the people I wanted to talk to, and I wondered: "Where were these people? Who did journalists and officials think they were talking about?"

By using a highlighter, journalists and officials drew borders for the Southeast Side on the photograph. The majority of these participants located three versions of the Southeast Side. Each version of the three Southeast Sides carried its own meanings (Figure 5.3). The first included Court Street at the north, South Gilbert Street at the west, and the city borders on the south and east ends. Shown with a black border around the edges of the map below (and labeled 1), participants said that this Southeast Side contained more businesses and economically and racially pluralistic residential neighborhoods.

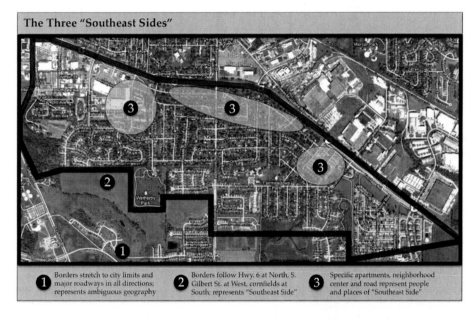

FIGURE 5.3. Journalists and officials alike independently described the city's Southeast Side in three ways.

A second Southeast Side focused on neighborhoods bordered at the north by Highway 6, at the west by South Gilbert Street, and by cornfields and city parks at the south. The eastern edge for this version of the Southeast Side seemed to appear near a trailer park and elderly care facility. This version of the Southeast Side (marked on the map by a dark boundary labeled 2) was considered to include more low-income housing and more pockets of racial and ethnic minorities.

The third Southeast Side was comprised of three separate locations within the inner dark boundary marked on the map by numbered circles (labeled 3). Locations within this third Southeast Side included the Dolphin Lake Point Enclave apartments (formerly the Lakeside Apartments) near Lakeside Drive[9] at the far right edge of Highway 6; a stretch of Hollywood Boulevard between the Dolphin Lake Point Enclave and the Broadway Condominiums on Broadway Street; and, the Broadway Street Neighborhood Center (BSNC) near Cross Park Avenue at the map's far left, which provides residents with preschool and afterschool programming, parenting classes, tutoring, clothes, and food. Participants said that this version of the Southeast Side is "what the public means by the Southeast Side" in terms of it representing the "black ghetto."

IDENTIFYING RESIDENTS

I selected the Broadway Street Neighborhood Center (BSNC) as a site to conduct interviews with residents from Iowa City's Southeast Side, because the center appeared as a common location used to describe and explain the Southeast Side and who lived there. Also, for practical reasons, the BSNC provided shelter from the weather, had space to meet and talk without interruption, and had tables that participants could use to comfortably draw their mental maps of the city. The neighborhood center was a place where I could meet residents without intruding into their homes or personal spaces. The neighborhood center is also a place where people choose to enter, where they

BROADWAY STREET. The Broadway Street Neighborhood Center in Iowa City's Southeast Side serves as a resource for local residents. Photograph by Alicia Kramme.

have built relationships with other residents and, in many cases, with center staff.

Admittedly, making the center my base restricted the sample of those living in the Southeast Side in that those who use the BSNC are a subset of neighborhood residents in terms of race and socio-economic status. Furthermore, limiting this study to what researchers call a "convenience sample" limits perspectives of this study's findings to that particular group and may lead to an oversimplification of insider/outsider perspectives of the Southeast Side.

However, this selected group of participants does help me address this project's larger focus—that of understanding the power (or lack thereof) of residents to shape media characterizations of their neighborhood. Indeed, journalists and public officials identified BSNC clients as representing the "Southeast Side," describing that they carry negative stigmas associated with Southeast Side neighborhoods and the BSNC, itself: according to the center's director, roughly 69 percent of the 1,800 BSNC clients are under the age of 18; 47 percent are male; and 49 percent are black. These residents, then, provide perspectives from within the neighborhoods, among those who themselves carry a stigma associated with young, black men who cause riots and general disorder.

I spent at least four hours a day for five business days over two weeks in December 2011 at the BSNC to meet with clients. BSNC staff allowed me to use a large table near the back of the main lobby and an office space, as available. During my visits, I approached clients in the center to measure their interest in participating in my study. Once I met those who wished to participate in the study, a BSNC director served as a facilitator to guide us to a table or room that was available where I spoke with participants.[10] Five people declined to participate; 17 others agreed to participate at our first meeting (Figure 5.4).[11] All 17 participants from the BSNC identified as black and ranged in age from 20 to 57. Ten of the participants were women.

At the time of the interview, 16 residents either lived in the Southeast Side at one time or had recently moved from the Southeast Side to another part of the city. Participants were asked how long they had lived in Iowa City, their employment status, and about their other social connections in Iowa City. The remainder of the session was devoted to the creation and discussion of mental maps, which is described below.

Community Storytelling: Exploring Place Through Interviews

Each group of participants likely held differing stakes in their community storytelling that should be understood before we go further. The following

Residents' Demographics

Name	Age	Race	Gender
Alicia	27	Black	Female
Amanda	23	Black	Female
Angel	23	Black	Female
Beth	35	Black	Female
Cordell	53	Black	Male
Jacque	29	Black	Male
Johnny	20	Black	Male
Lisa	23	Black	Female
Maria	33	Black	Female
Michelle	34	Black	Female
Nene	44	Black	Female
Nevaeh	57	Black	Female
Sandra	51	Black	Female
Slimmy	47	Black	Male
Ted	49	Black	Male
Tom	22	Black	Male
Tony	21	Black	Male

FIGURE 5.4

discussion, therefore, is not to present concrete findings about these participants, but to deepen an understanding of the participants themselves and their roles in the community and in this study. First, public officials and journalists tended to be long-term residents who had—or were planning to—raise a family and spend much of their careers in the Iowa City area.

Having spent a significant amount of time in their respective social roles in the community, these participants have the ability to create a lasting story about the city and are particularly invested in forming and maintaining dominant stories of the city. These two groups also served functions in the city that influence their perspectives on the purpose and value of storytelling about the community.

Officials, for example, have become involved in city governance and planning; their interest in city storytelling is likely related to building positive perceptions of what they consider their home territory. Journalists also likely have an investment in sustaining a positive perception of the dominant community's which they cover in conjunction with local political and social institutions, a process called *boosterism*, the act of journalism as a means to advance and maintain positive perceptions of their geographic community, often through business news and *fluff* (Burd, 1977; Kaniss, 1997).

Second, student journalists, a subset of the group mentioned above, operate as journalists in the community, but as college students they are transient residents. In most cases, student journalists live and work in the community while school is in session. They can come and go during the academic year and can vacate the community during summer months. While previous research suggests student journalists prefer to identify with their journalistic selves before their student selves (Gutsche, 2011a; Gutsche and Salkin, 2011), students tend to maintain a close proximity to the university campus and operate within highly structured experiences related to coursework and social interactions determined through their role as a college student.

Their stake in storytelling about the city beyond the university campus may be slightly different than professional journalists and public officials in that students are more likely to leave Iowa City after graduation and, therefore, may not share the same sense of community as journalists and officials who plan to stay in the city for the foreseeable future. Student journalists lack the same risks of professional journalists and officials in their storytelling; if they see the community as a temporary home, they may have less at stake in how it is portrayed in their work.[12]

Finally, Southeast Side residents I spoke with are a mixture of long-time residents and transients who have been in Iowa City for a short time and may return to their homes in Chicago. But even those who lived in Iowa for 10 years and consider Iowa their home travel back and forth between Iowa City and Chicago to visit friends and family members. These residents share a sense of being outsiders in Iowa City. Like those residents who moved to Iowa City to find work and escape what they considered dangerous neighborhoods in Chicago, they continue to balance the possibility of returning to their homes and families there. Constructing a sense of community and "home" for this group then, is a complex assignment of meaning between two cities, rather than a single, favored, and permanent place.

Maps as Storytelling

While journalists and officials were interviewed in advance of Southeast Side residents in order to determine how these dominant storytellers defined the Southeast Side, interviews with all participants followed the same pattern after they shared with me their basic demographic information. I asked each of my interviewees to draw a mental map of Iowa City to widen my understanding of how participants experience and interpret the city as a whole, before focusing our discussion on their perceptions of the Southeast Side. *Mental mapping* allows participants to draw maps that identify and explain natural or manmade boundaries in geography from their own vantage points (Wood, 2010).

Lynch (1980) writes that such maps are "speaking landscapes" of words, images, colors, and one's personal experiences with geography. By asking participants to draw their neighborhoods and the city as a mental map—and by asking them to describe their maps as they drew them—together, we were able to identify evidence of different concepts of both place and story which extended to authority, power, and social and cultural barriers in Iowa City.[13]

I encouraged participants to see these maps as drawings that told people where they went in the community and what they knew about different parts of the city. I told them to feel free to think of these more like drawings than absolute representations of space with scale and proportion (Johnson, 2007). While I asked participants to identify where they lived, I did not encourage them to place any other specific items or locations on their maps.

For up to 10 minutes, I would read or check e-mail while people drew, so as to not distract or intimidate them by watching. I then asked them to describe their maps, to tell me what types of people they thought lived in different neighborhoods, who enters and exits the space, and what they think happens in that space (Entrikin, 1991; Soja, 2010). My questions included: What do you know about this part of town? What do you think of people who live in that part of town? Who lives in this neighborhood? What kind of news comes from this part of town?

Wood (2010) writes that a person's map as story can be understood by turning to Barthean semiotics. All maps begin as empty, blank spaces that are either filled or left void, the reasons for which explain how one interacts with a specific environment. These decisions can be revealed through a critical analysis (King, 1996). Barthes has been credited for providing a means by which to recognize and "read" signs embedded in messages through multiple and deep readings. Cloke, et al. (2004) employ a Geertzean (1973) approach of "thick description" to reading maps that "emphasizes the complex layers of meaning that can attach to what are often apparently simple social behaviors" (p. 308). More specifically, Cloke, et al. (2004) suggest cartographers and geographers become "insiders" (p. 309) to study culture. Therefore, to interpret mental maps and the process of place-making, I turned to information and perspectives gathered from exploring the Southeast Side phenomenon for three years and from interviews with residents, journalists, and officials to identify categories or aspects of maps related to how participants constructed place. When I came to read the maps, I looked at three particular characteristics of the drawings.

First, I was interested in the selection and promotion of items on mental maps. Monmonier (1996) writes that mapmakers select, suppress, and emphasize elements of maps to tell stories. A traveler's roadmap, for example, likely shows the most accessible means of travel, emphasizing interstates in lieu of back roads. However, an atlas or plat map—used for detailed representations of terrain, property lines, and natural resources—would likely include back roads and alternate paths. Both types of maps tell different stories for different purposes. Therefore, evaluating the map's purpose—or multiple purposes— is an essential first step to understanding what is shown, what is not, and how.

Second, I was interested in how geographic boundaries demarcate real and perceived social and cultural territory (de Certeau, 1984; Johnson, 2007). More specifically, I was interested in the boundaries that mapmakers drew, which buildings and streets were shown, and which routes were described (Cloke, et al., 2004). Ladd (1967) also used mental maps to explain the experiences of youth in Boston's Mission Hill neighborhood. Children's drawings, then, allowed Ladd to identify the emotional, mental, and physical barriers that youth experienced in that environment. His work is especially important to my study in that it shows how people can connect to their physical places through memory and emotion.

How people describe their interactions with space leads to my third category—the use of symbols and words to express story (Blaeser, 1997; Johnson, 2007). Whereas the previous categories dealt with what participants chose to include in their maps, this category is interested in *how* those items were included. In this discussion, symbols, lines, streets, and words come to represent not only geography, but also stories that are shaped and coded by the mapmaker's ideology (Cloke, et al., 2004; Monmonier, 1996).

Conclusion

In the next chapter, I delve into an analysis of how journalists, public officials, and other "outsiders" regarded the Southeast Side as a place based on their work and personal experiences in the community. I found that journalists and officials typically turned to familiar sources and narratives—such as official reports and anecdotes from longtime residents—to guide their interpretations of the area, interpretations guided by a complex set of ideological steps.

SIX

Whose Southeast Side?

Mapping Place

Slimmy got his name for being tall and skinny. So tall and so skinny that at 47, he still looks like he could kick your ass at basketball—or any other sport—but with a heart kind enough that you wouldn't mind losing.

For the past 20 years, Slimmy, a black man who moved to Iowa City from St. Louis, lived in and around the Southeast Side. By the time we talked in 2011, though, he had been living on Iowa City's East Side for six months, in a white neighborhood, where he and his family didn't know anyone and no one would talk to them. He carried the stigma of the Southeast Side with him when he moved and told his neighbors where he had come from, he said.

Such news didn't go over well.

"It seems that black people are allowed to live in only certain parts of the city," Slimmy says.

There can be a price to staying in the Southeast Side, too, though. Slimmy has seen the drugs there. He's seen the gangs. He's been around long enough to see both the highs, the lows, the playin,' the distraction.

In fact, *these are the stories* that people want to hear about the Southeast Side: Slimmy's often asked to speak to groups about drugs, violence, and living amongst other blacks in an enclave of sorts smack dab in the middle of white Iowa.

But are these the only stories that should be told from the Southeast Side?

What happens in a city when the larger community wants to hear only a portion of someone's story? Specifically to Slimmy, how do these particular stories about living in Iowa City and the Southeast Side—the ones of *most interest* to those outside of his neighborhood—contribute to forming dominant understandings of the Southeast Side and those people in it?

In this chapter, I turn to the methodology of mental mapping to complicate characteristics of Iowa City's Southeast Side as a ghetto. In exploring the maps and discussions that were presented to me by journalists, officials, and Southeast Side residents, I am mainly interested in the wayfinding associated with people's explanations of city spaces. Therefore, I present participants' stories of experiencing the city via themes of place-making as a comparison between residents and dominant storytellers in the media—journalists and their official sources.

I begin the analysis with place-making among journalists and officials before presenting a comparison of place-making among all participants, including residents. (Not all mental maps are presented in this chapter, but can be found at www.robertgutschejr.com/transplantedchicago.) I then conclude with an initial analysis of the cultural meanings inherent in comparing participants' place-making. A discussion of how this study contributes to understanding the ideological power in news place-making and implications for journalism and journalism research appears in Chapter 7.

Talking About Neighborhoods from the Outside

By and large, journalists and officials relied upon personal and work experiences with particular Iowa City geographies to describe the city. These places, participants said, were most preferable for working and were where they felt most comfortable. In turn, participants also said that their perceptions of place influenced their perceptions of the people who lived or frequented particular Iowa City neighborhoods.

Safe Places

Journalists said that their perceptions and knowledge of Iowa City places, particularly the university, the downtown, and some residential neighborhoods influenced what they covered as news. Ashley—a white, 20-year-old college journalist at *The Daily Iowan*—described Iowa City based upon the news that occurs on and around the college campus (Map 6.1). Such news includes geographies of the University of Iowa, Iowa City's downtown business and bar district, city government, and police department.[1]

In addition to seeing the city through the perspective of a journalist, Ashley located "Hickory Hill Park" at the top right of her map and wrote her feelings about the spaces ("safe/homes"; "neighborhoods"). In her map's top left,

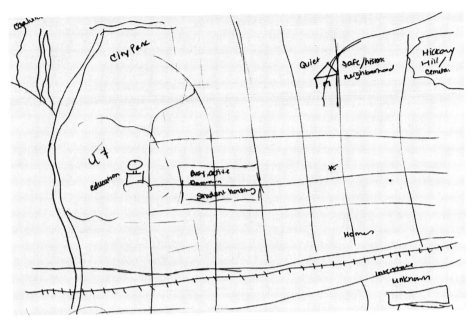

MAP 6.1. ASHLEY'S MAP. Ashley, a journalist, drew a "bubble" around the downtown and university to show her connection to people and places in those environments.

Ashley shows the city of Coralville, home to a shopping mall that she frequents. The grid that dominates much of her map represents streets that she considers "residential neighborhoods" and that are also "safe" and "nice."

THE DAILY "BUBBLE"

Journalists and officials alike showed a preference for institutions and geographies that were closely related to their daily lives, places that they could easily visit, and where they felt safe. Ashley's map, for example, is especially telling in how it reveals her connection to local institutions, particularly in how she demarcates the University of Iowa's physical boundaries. Instead of drawing landmarks such as buildings or streets to show the university's borders, for example, Ashley draws the university in what she called a "bubble." This "bubble," she said, shows the university as "an entity" that heavily influences local culture, politics, and economy. The university's political power "ebbs and flows" beyond any specific geographic boundary. "Some things can't happen in the community without university approval or their support," she said.

Ashley's descriptions of the university, for instance, revealed the school's institutional power and place within that geography, particularly in terms of its proximity to institutional and ideological spaces. As further evidence of this, Ashley's identification and description of other spaces in Iowa City, including the Southeast Side, were also shaped by her perceptions of the university and other institutions, such as police, city government, and businesses—all located in the city's downtown. These institutions and geographies, it seems, receive a unique amount of attention as journalists construct the news. Again, Ashley drew boundaries as boxes or "bubbles" around important places: the downtown is labeled "busy" and "active"; another space is labeled "student housing."

THE EAST/WEST DIVIDE

Barb, a white, 36-year-old *Gazette* reporter, said that her map shows how she moves around town as a reporter and as a mother (Map 6.2). Inside Iowa City, Barb draws her downtown office, the Old Capitol on the university campus, and the public library. She also locates her favorite grocery store and her children's daycare. On the map's left side, Barb drew a large circle that she labeled "University Hospitaland" to represent the university's medical campus west of the Iowa River. "University Hospitaland," Barb said, is where she "gets

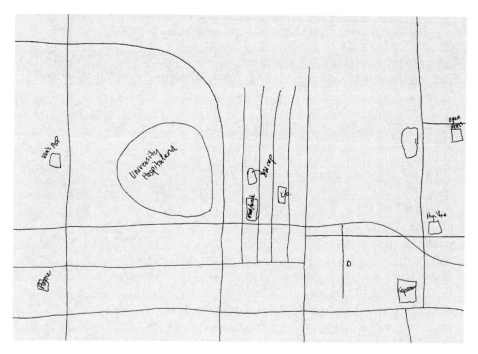

MAP 6.2. BARB'S MAP. Barb's map represents how journalists focused on "official" parts of the city to find their news, such as government offices and the hospital.

a lot of [her] news," specifically from press releases about medical research and the hospital's finances and employees.

As Barb shows, and other participants explained, news is partially influenced by the geographic location of institutions, such as the hospital, police department, and business districts. In this case, Iowa City is small enough that these places are all close to the journalists' offices, homes, and institutions they rely upon for news are close to each other. Barb said that she focuses more on what she perceives as an east-west divide in Iowa City geography because she has children in the school district and just purchased a home on the West Side. "This really is the divide, I think, that defines Iowa City," she said. Riverside Drive—the curved line between "University Hospitaland" and downtown—represents both the Iowa River and a physical entry point to either the East or the West Side.

As Barb explained this divide—the city's West Side, for instance, "is full of rich people" and "the more wealthy"; whereas, the East Side is home to "history" and "culture"—it sounds as though she is describing two different cities. Barb said that the meaning she assigns to different geographies helps her determine the news audience and the importance of what might be covered in different parts of the city.

UNKNOWN PLACES

All journalists said that they did not know much about several areas of the city, including the Southeast Side, and that their understandings of these spaces were shaped by information from city agencies, including the police, the school district, and the City Council. Stories from longtime Iowa City residents are also valuable sources of information, participants said.

Ashley, for example, said that she knew about the people and places in and around the university and downtown, because she spends most of her time in these areas, but that she did not know much about who and what exists outside these spaces. While the Southeast Side appears on her mental map, bordered by railroad tracks and confined to a small rectangle that she labeled "unknown," Ashley said she included those neighborhoods because she knew my study dealt with that space. However, she said, "That really is what I think about it." She added:

> I really don't know what is there.... There is not a lot of focus (on the Southeast Side) compared to the downtown and university. And, I am largely affected by what the public says. Because I can't say from personal experience, I have to go off what the public says, as a person who is part of the media. I don't have a car and I am not able to go down into this area, so I have to rely on what people report about it.

Mapping Mobility

Other participants said that even though they are able to move around the city (illustrated by the various roads included on their maps), they must rely on multiple sources of information to understand some of Iowa City's city spaces that they have never visited and that appear as blank spots on their mental maps. For instance, Barb's drawings of crisscrossing streets take her to the city's edges and run off of the map's edges, leading to neighboring communities of Cedar Rapids, North Liberty, Hills, and West Branch.

While her sketch shows her ability to move throughout the Iowa City area, including to the Southeast Side, where she has done some reporting and exercises at a neighborhood gym, Barb said that she relies on the work of other reporters to inform her about those neighborhoods. Similarly, Annika—a white 20-year-old reporter at *The Daily Iowan*—said that she drew spaces where she spends most of her time, particularly downtown and at a shopping mall in Coralville. Annika said that because she does not have a vehicle, she struggles to get around the rest of Iowa City, which has stopped her from experiencing more city neighborhoods and meeting more people.

However, Annika said that even though she has never been to the Southeast Side and left that space empty on her map, she still "know[s] about it" from conversations with police officials, other reporters, and city leaders. She explained:

> I think community members, and I think readers, have negative connotations of over there. I think you have this whole thing where community members think all these people are coming from Chicago, they're causing gang activity and all of these problems, and we need more police over there with all of this gang violence, and it's not safe, no one knows what happens over there.... I probably don't spend enough time over there to say.
>
> I feel that whenever there is coverage, people in the Southeast Side are more grouped together than maybe in other neighborhoods. Sometimes I feel like it's another chip in the pile of what's happening in the Southeast Side. If the same events happened in some other neighborhood that happened in the Southeast Side, would they be covered differently? I don't know.

Maps of "Other People's Stories"

Some participants were very clear about how local storytelling—particularly stories embedded in anecdotes from longtime residents—informed their perceptions of city spaces. Michael, the *Press-Citizen* reporter discussed in the previous chapter, said his ideas about some blank spaces on his map come from stories of social disorder that had "been told to me by people" (Map 6.3). Such reliance on anecdotal information about the Southeast Side that often

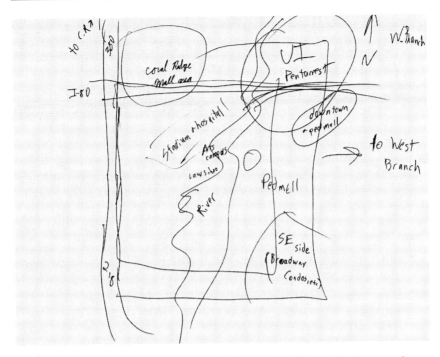

MAP 6.3. MICHAEL'S MAP. Michael identifies the Iowa City landmarks he uses to locate where he lives and works in the community.

excluded residents—and specifically the residents news stories were focused on—is representative of how journalists and public officials discussed how they learned about city spaces and constructed their personal beliefs about Iowa City.

Indeed, two police officers who frequently contributed to news reporting about the Southeast Side discussed how they formed their perceptions of place from a combination of personal opinions and experiences from responding to crime in the Southeast Side. The officers also said that they relied heavily on police department data and news reports about black violence to shape their characterizations of the city, generally, and the Southeast Side in particular. The men's experiences as police officers, interactions with the same department, other officers, residents, and journalists led to similar interpretations of space, evidenced by their almost identical mental maps.

WORK(PLACES)

Allen, a white 49-year-old officer, drew his map with the Iowa River, a box around the university, another box around the downtown, and numbers that identify police patrol areas. Fellow officer, Paul, who is white and 32, also drew roads, the Iowa River, and other landmarks, such as a highway, the downtown police station, and the Southeast Side police station.

Even though Paul did not place numbers on his map to identify patrol areas as Allen did, Paul did talk about Iowa City geography in terms of the types of calls police respond to in particular city spaces. Indeed, Paul said that while "I consider Iowa City a community," his map excludes landmarks and other points of interest because they were "insignificant" to his work. Though both officers said that they spend personal time in Iowa City beyond their work hours, they viewed city spaces according to what areas attract the most "business." Interestingly, these officers' maps match the police department's patrol, or beat, areas (Map 6.4).

Just as police officers subscribed to their department's interpretation of space and place, Gary—a white reporter in his mid–30s who lives near the outer edge of the Southeast Side—shows how institutionalized notions of place enter into the journalistic community as reporters and sources work together. On his map, Gary drew circles that reflect his perceptions of news that comes from geographic areas. His circles are based on perceptions of who lives there and who would be interested in reading news from those spaces.

Gary's first circle encompasses Iowa City's downtown and the university campus, which has "bars," "retail," "education," and other "development." News from this area, he said, relates to business owners, city officials, the university community, and police. Gary's second circle includes residential neighborhoods, a "housing mix" of students and professionals. Gary said that crime in this area mostly involves college drinking and property damage. News from this area relates to college students, city officials, and long-time residents.

News from outside of these two circles focuses either on schools, gov-

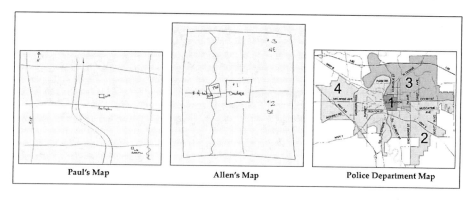

| Paul's Map | Allen's Map | Police Department Map |

MAP 6.4. PAUL AND ALLEN'S MAPS. Police officers Paul and Allen draw the city in ways similar to each other and to an official department "beat" or "patrol" map.

ernment, or business, Gary said. News from the Southeast Side, however, (which is in its own circle) is a complicated collection of "a housing mix" and racial and ethnic changes that are difficult to report. News from this area relates to the neighborhoods' racial and ethnic changes and crime. Even though such coverage tends to focus on "negative news," Gary explained:

> I don't think there is any intentional.... And there is that accusation that's out there that people are intentionally trying to make the Southeast Side look bad or writing one story and ignoring another. And I could not disagree more with that. I think people who are in the news business are in it for altruistic reasons. It's not like you make a lot of money. You know you want to make your community a better place, so I could not disagree more that anybody that I know of is doing it intentionally. You follow the news, right?

THE SOUTHEAST SIDE

Gary said that politically progressive Iowa Citians have contacted the newspaper to complain about journalists' use of the term "Southeast Side" (representing the ideograph of the "Southeast Side" discussed in previous chapters) and how the newspaper covers those neighborhoods. However, he said, the Southeast Side term is used by officials, residents across the city, and other journalists. The newspaper, Gary said, does not make changes in how it covers the Southeast Side—or in their terminology—because making changes because of reader input may undermine the newspaper's objectivity. He explained:

> The "Southeast Side" means more than a geographical reference to the community... There was definitely pressure from groups like the neighborhood's center who said the press makes the Southeast Side look bad. I don't think that's the case at all, but there is pressure to do stories that focus in the Southeast Side, because people are saying, you only do crime stories.

Gary's explanation of how local news characterized the Southeast Side is representative of how journalists as a group show a reliance upon public officials to explain and perpetuate social conditions with an authority that further legitimizes the news.

Explaining Place with Stories of Authority

Journalists and public officials revealed a need for stories about place that held traditional notions of authority, such as statistics, police reports, and personal experiences. Interviewees said that stories of dramatic violence among blacks in the Southeast Side as told by police and other official sources (such as with the "Mother's Day Riot") fit their perceptions of urban-like places—even though most of them said that they had never been to the Southeast Side.

For instance, Len, a 29-year-old white reporter who worked at *The Gazette* in 2009 said that "people in Iowa are soft" when it comes to living in diverse neighborhoods (Map 6.5). Compared to residents near a racially diverse boarding school he attended in Georgia before moving to Iowa, Len said whites in Iowa want to live only by other whites. "They want to live out in Waukee (a Des Moines suburb) so that they are safe, but (black neighborhoods in Iowa are) not really that unsafe. I don't even feel it at Broadway (in the Southeast Side)."

Indeed, Len's map of Iowa City's includes more features of the Southeast Side than most of the other journalists, possibly showing his feelings of greater comfort there. His map includes an apartment building, streets, a shopping mall, and a park in the Southeast Side. Len, who has since moved away from the Iowa City area, explained why other white people might not be comfortable in black communities:

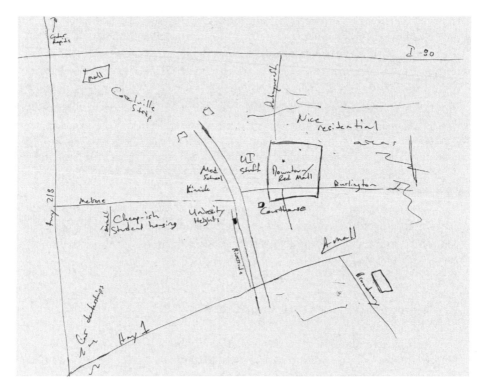

MAP 6.5. LEN'S MAP. Len's map shows a sense of comfort with the Southeast Side, but still shows a lack of familiarity.

You walk through the street and you see more black people.... I think there is a lot of racism still, you know. That's no secret. Like, you grow up in a town of 500 or 5,000 in Iowa like most people around us did and you never saw black people except for on TV. You will want to live out in Waukee where you are as far away of them as possible.

In addition to individuals' personal experiences and values that shaped their interpretations of place, dominant cultural narratives of urban black neighborhoods, as discussed previously, held such cultural authority that notions of race and welfare from other parts of the country emerged as some participants explained their mental maps. Bill—a 54-year-old, white official in Iowa City's affordable housing department—said that he constantly reads local newspapers, while looking at a map of Iowa City that shows public housing scattered across the city. Bill said that he reads newspapers for police news that may show residents who receive housing assistance as violating their agreement with the city to stay out of trouble.

"Official" Places

Bill said that he is so familiar with the map—and its meanings—that when I met him in his office and asked him to draw his mental map of Iowa City, he turned to his housing map, unrolled it across a conference table, and asked, "Can't I just use this? This is what my map will look like anyway." Indeed, when Bill finished drawing, portions of his mental map did resemble his "official" map: the Iowa River snakes through Iowa City, several major streets stretch across the city, and the municipal airport appears below Riverside Drive on the map's left side.

As Bill explained his map, he turned to his past experiences overseeing affordable housing programs when describing the Southeast Side. He openly discussed the controversies about neighborhoods with dense numbers of racial minorities. Bill described a city that seems to relate race to poverty and welfare, such as affordable housing and neighborhood disorder to urban crime. He also said that explanations of black and urban culture and disorder from other cities help explain social conditions in the Southeast Side:

What's happened is this is really sort of where the issues started—the Broadway area. The city put public housing in down here. The [Housing Fellowship nonprofit] has added to rentals down here, Habitat has built some owner-occupied homes down here. I think what has happened is this is where it started, but then you have African American families down here, you have assisted housing ... and therefore the people are making connections that you had crime over here, and assisted housing—that assisted housing equals crime.

While he talked, Bill pointed to his mental map, reminding me that it resembles his "official" city map and that because the map reflects facts from statistics and information from the city, it is an especially accurate tool for discussing what types of people live in different neighborhoods. As shown with Bill and the police officers, Paul and Allen, public officials generally preferred to describe Iowa City based on "official" and "authoritative" maps. So too, journalists tended to reinforce that their own maps were "not to scale" and often corrected where streets "actually are" as a way to make their maps more "realistic," in an attempt to bolster their maps' authority.

Journalists and city officials, including police officers, made their maps in other, comparable ways, as well. For example, striking similarities appear when comparing the map-making of a school official and an education reporter. Fred—a white 45-year-old who works for the school district—drew his map in terms of how it relates to his job. He explained that his map largely resembles an official placement of schools in his district.

SCHOOLS AS PLACE-MARKERS

After drawing major roadways and the Iowa River, Fred placed elementary, middle, and high schools (Map 6.6). Almost immediately, he started talking about Iowa City as a school district, a subset of the larger community. Even items that may seem out of the ordinary were mentioned on his mental map: Fred identified the county landfill, the National Guard Armory, and the Johnson County Emergency Center. Each location is marked because of how they relate to the schools he oversees: Fred identifies the landfill because local officials were looking into smells that were impacting a nearby elementary school; he located the armory and emergency center because he had been asked to speak about leadership at both locations.

Fred also used schools on his map to talk about the people of Iowa City. For example, on the city's West Side, he said, students who attend Kirkwood Elementary and Coralville Central Elementary had:

a higher proportion of students that are in lower socio-economic strata. And then if you look at Lincoln Elementary School, Horn Elementary School, Weber Elementary School—both high socioeconomic status. Roosevelt, closer to the river, lower socioeconomic status. So you've got a bit of a mix in there, and then you move out here (Southern Iowa City), you get more rural and there's a lot of poverty out there. I know a lot about the demographics for ya.

Just as Fred's place-making relied on perceptions of how place affected his work, so did Roger's, a 35-year-old Hispanic reporter for the *Press-Citizen* who covered K–12 education. Though his map includes his church, his home, and several neighborhoods, Roger's focus is primarily on schools and the types

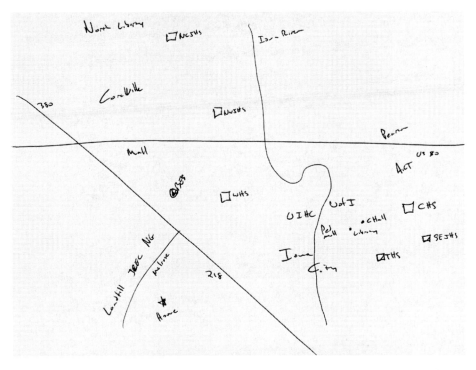

MAP 6.6. FRED'S MAP. Fred's map represents how officials described and explained city spaces based upon their professional experiences.

of students that they serve (Map 6.7). He said that his reporting on the socioeconomic status of elementary schools during redistricting influenced his perceptions of who lives in Iowa City neighborhoods.

"You should have seen [how parents discussed their desire to keep children apart] in redistricting," Roger said, especially "[w]hen parents were saying, 'I don't want my child going to *that school*,'" meaning, he explained, that the pairing of students from diverse economic and racial backgrounds was not appealing to some parents.

ASSIGNING PLACE NICKNAMES

As journalists and public officials described their maps—and the Southeast Side, in particular—they said that the "Southeast Side" label, though not an official term, has become accepted and widely understood. They also said that they were aware that news reports might further negative stereotypes of those neighborhoods; however, participants said that the term helped express complicated social conditions in a quick way.

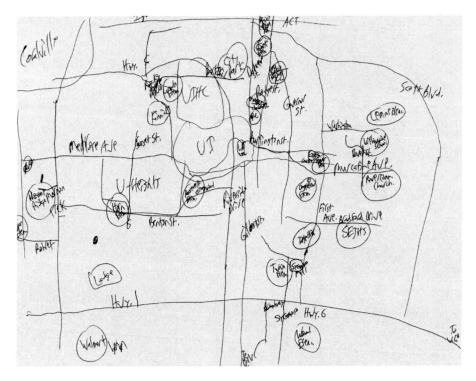

MAP 6.7. ROGER'S MAP. Roger's map shows how journalists tended to relate to city spaces in similar ways to officials—based upon their professional experiences.

As Len said, "it just takes time and effort to get to the level of [neighborhood or street] specificity that is respectful for the story and still helpful for the reader." And Barb, who was mentioned above, said that such place-names are "like a shorthand" and that while "it is unfortunate that you could pigeonhole a bunch of people who live in one area," she often uses the term "Southeast Side" in her coverage of those neighborhoods.

Like Barb, David, a white 33-year-old *Press-Citizen* reporter, said that place-names help report the news (Map 6.8):

> What a lot of people really care about is what's going on in their neighborhood and what's going on with their kids. So they care about the schools, prep sports, and crime. And so when we're saying that police have arrested somebody for stabbing someone—something that's going to draw your attention—I think the first thing people want to know is "Where did that happen in relation to where I live? Am I in danger? Did something dangerous happen near me?"
>
> So a quick and easy way to establish, generally speaking, where that is is to say Southeast Side, Iowa City. So three fourths of the community can say, "OK, that's not my back yard."

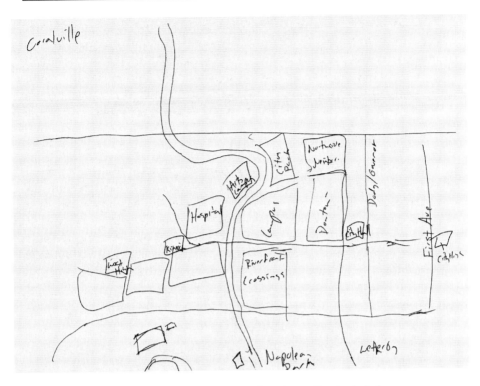

MAP 6.8. DAVID'S MAP. David's map represents how journalists included government buildings and businesses to explain city spaces.

Positioning the Southeast Side—or any geography, perhaps—in relationship to the readers' location solidifies the journalist's authority by relating the place that's at the center of the story to the reader herself, personalizing the story, in fact, and strengthening the ideological relationship between the journalist and reader.

(DE)VALUING ALTERNATE AUTHORITIES

Journalists and officials alike adopted the Southeast Side label as a geographic and ideological shorthand that, because journalists had built themselves as authorities on explaining the social conditions there, became acceptable to them as a collective and likely "readable" by the audience. Susie—a white, 40-year-old woman who works at the Broadway Street Neighborhood Center and who is often quoted in news about the Southeast Side—said that "sensationalized" media coverage has contributed to public perceptions of the Southeast Side as a neighborhood of "poor black people doing bad."

Susie said that the news ignores that "there are poor black people all over the city," and that the Southeast Side label has become synonymous with notions of a black ghetto. "I find it interesting that this is the only neighborhood that is identified as a neighborhood, routinely," she said. "If you ask people where the Southeast Side is, they may all have a difference in the starting and ending of streets, but they have a pretty good idea of where it is."

THE "OTHER" OFFICIALS

James, a white 31-year-old neighborhood association member in the Southeast Side, had similar thoughts on news coverage of the neighborhoods he represents.[2] James also said that media focused on "negative" news from the Southeast Side. He said, "I think that when out-of-season [farmer's] markets happen at the elementary school... that gets covered, but that local media are "writing from press releases" when news from police and city leaders emerge that simplify and explain Southeast Side news.

Relying on these releases and the "official" explanation for events without confirming or complicating the story by talking with residents, James said, shows him how journalists "are playing up some of [the] tension" of the story rather than "covering" it. He explained:

> It is a neighborhood that has changed a lot in the last decade and has moved away from being older, working class families ... and is younger and is more diverse. And I think that ... the people that complain are the ones that can tend to drive news coverage.
>
> There is the old white lady who lives right behind us and who is big on the neighborhood watch thing. I wouldn't say she is racist, but certainly sees young black kids who [pause] when you're driving around and there are groups of young black kids riding their bikes or walking down the middle of the street, it is a little intimidating.
>
> But because it is groups of kids walking in the middle of the street [pause] and I don't know if it's a cultural thing or a kid's thing or what it is, but I think some people see that kind of thing and feel like it is, "Well, there goes the neighborhood."

On the surface, mental maps by Susie and James look similar to those by other officials; however, they explained city spaces quite differently than other public officials. On her map, Susie placed major streets, the Manville Heights neighborhood, Hickory Hill Park near her home, the University of Iowa, and the "Southeast Side." Susie also included two schools (Mark Twain and Grant Wood) near the Southeast Side and marked the space as "low-income housing" as a way to distinguish the space from other neighborhoods. Susie also drew the Iowa River as a major divide in the city that demarcates East from West in a similar way to other participants, such as Barb.

However, Susie's explanation about the divide is much more focused on the cultural interactions between people. "In the (school) boundary discussion," Susie said (see Chapter 8), "there is a feeling of 'We want to stay put, and don't you dare move us across the river.'" However, Susie is quick to explain that the city's "primary divide is the Highway 6 divide," which borders the Northern edge of the Southeast Side. She added:

> North of the Highway 6 you would consider—although you have various types of neighborhoods—this to be the tracks. If you were to say there is the "wrong side of the tracks" in Iowa City ... there is this barrier of a simple four-lane highway, even though the schools that some of these students go to are on the other side of the tracks.
>
> If I were to describe Iowa City to someone, I would say we have placed the low-income here (South of Highway 6) and this [divide] appears as though we can't cross it.

James also described neighborhood boundaries on his map. First, he drew a square around two neighborhoods and labeled them ("Northside" and "Goosetown"). James included the Iowa River, Interstate 80, his home (starred in the lower right corner), and several streets that he uses to enter and leave the city. Yet, his interpretations of meanings behind the boundary lines, for instance, deal with issues of social power, a perspective lacking in many interpretations by journalists and officials.

For example, James drew the University of Iowa in a circle similar to Ashley's "bubble," and does so because it is "disconnected" from the rest of the community. Whereas Ashley discussed how the university's power "ebbs and flows" throughout the community as a kind of connection, James said:

> (The university) doesn't pay taxes, so it doesn't support the city in that respect.... It doesn't use municipal services. It is self-contained. Like, it worries about its own power. It worries about its own water. The university, essentially, could lop-off Iowa City and be OK. Like, if the zombie apocalypse comes, you could barricade yourself in the university and have access to a lot of stuff.
>
> I don't get a sense that the university does anything for "the community," the wider Iowa City community. It does things for the "university community" and obviously that entails a lot of people in Iowa City, but I don't think that entails my neighborhood.

Interestingly, both James and Susie drew maps of Iowa City that resemble an official, city neighborhood map, yet they expressed different concerns about the Southeast Side and how it is portrayed in the news.

James and Susie may be outliers among public officials and journalists in how they described place, perhaps because they work so closely with people in the Southeast Side, are protective of its reputation, or feel they have a greater understanding of the neighborhoods' complexities. Regardless, the narratives presented by James and Susie were not as strongly represented in news texts discussed in the previous chapter and were set aside in lieu of information and explanations that seem to better resonate among police, city officials, the school district, and journalists.

Countering Dominant Stories: Neighborhood Mapping

Lisa—a 23-year-old black woman—moved to Iowa City from Chicago a year before we met, looking for a "change" in her life (Map 6.9). During her time in Iowa City, Lisa's been able to enroll at the Kirkwood Community College, where she wants to study psychology, and placed her children in the neighborhood schools. Lisa said the neighborhood is "safe" and the schools are "good."

These details—missing in even the home neighborhoods of journalists and officials—showed local place as contested and more complicated than news stories would lead one to believe.

MAPPING THE UNKNOWN

On her map, Lisa shows how close her home is to schools, parks, and shopping. She drew a shortcut through her neighborhood to her child's elementary school that cuts through a grove of trees that she found one day when she got lost while walking her children to school. The route became a shortcut, she said, that she enjoys taking each morning. Lisa also included her routes to the playground at the Broadway Street Neighborhood Center (BSNC), Kmart, and to her brother's house. She said that these paths—details of a neighborhood that were absent in maps by officials and journalists—remind her of how quiet Iowa City is compared to Chicago. "I like walking down the block and not feeling like you're going to die," she said.

But Lisa's knowledge of Iowa City, she said, is limited to what she can see and visit via the city buses. "I don't know (the city)," she said, "but I want to." And though Lisa is aware of negative stigmas about the Southeast Side (still, she said, it's better than where she came from), she described her neighborhood as "nice or quiet or boring." Her labels such as "home" and a smiley face near the BSNC show elements of her everyday life living in Iowa City's Southeast Side and is representative of how Southeast Side residents showed a preference for the Southeast Side and expressed feeling unwelcome in other places of the city. For Lisa, she said, the downtown and the university, the same places where officials and journalists said they spent most of their time and felt the most comfortable, were "unwelcoming" and "unsafe."

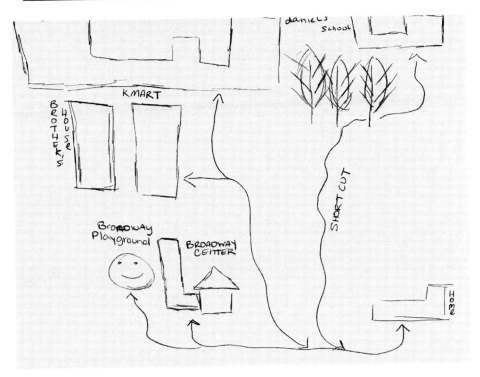

MAP 6.9. LISA'S MAP. Lisa used her mental map to show her feelings of safety and happiness as a resident in the Southeast Side.

MAPPING PROXIMITY

By and large, all residents used their maps to represent a distance from the downtown and much of Iowa City while revealing a closer connection to the Southeast Side. Residents tended to highlight particular roads, businesses, social services, and spaces they spend their time in and around the southeastern neighborhoods. Michelle, a 34-year-old black woman who has lived in Iowa City since 2001, drew Kmart, the Pepperwood strip mall, and her apartment on Taylor Drive—all of which branch-off from Highway 6 in the Southeast Side (Map 6.10). Michelle said that the Southeast Side is safer and quieter than Chicago and was the main reason she moved to Iowa City nine years earlier. "When black people are over here, they kind of portray you in a certain way," she said. "This place is better than what they portray it to be—a ghetto, worse side of town." In Iowa City, though, children "can be active" and it is where she can find work and attend college, Michelle said.

While looking at her map, Michelle said that residents outside of her neighborhood "know what type of people live in the Southeast Side and what

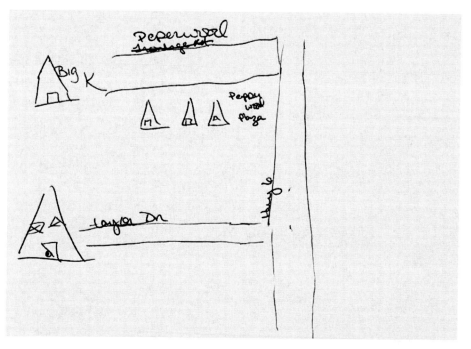

MAP 6.10. MICHELLE'S MAP. Michelle's map is similar to other residents in that she uses it to compare the Southeast Side to her former Chicago neighborhood.

the Southeast Side is supposed to be about." Despite assigning positive attributes to Iowa City—which all residents mentioned—participants often focused on concerns about their safety or lack of involvement elsewhere in the city. Michelle, for instance, said that her map—which includes only her home and neighborhood stores—shows how she stays close to home, in part, because she feels that the larger Iowa City community "seem(s) to be afraid" of blacks who have moved into the city and that she is not welcome elsewhere. In particular, she said, her map's roads—Taylor Drive in the Southeast Side, the Kmart parking lot, and Highway 6—were the best way to show where she lives and how she moves around the city.

And, as with most participants—journalists, officials, and residents, alike—roads became a description to articulate not only their geographic proximity to places in the city, but that also came to represent racial inequality.

MAPPING RACE

While journalists and officials drew broad sketches of roadway and streets that led to neighboring cities, residents focused much more on the roads themselves, drawing them wide and crowded with traffic. Consider, for instance, Jeff—a 41-year-old white man and reporter who has lived in Iowa City for 13 years—who drew his routes out of Iowa City to visit in-laws, a music school, and other cities. By and large, journalists and officials drew their routes through the city as thin, interwoven lines, while residents—such as Tom, a 22-year-old black man who moved to Iowa City from Chicago six years ago—drew streets that took up most of their maps, complete with vehicles and hash-marks, signs of how much time they spend on the streets (Map 6.11).

Additionally, residents drew narrow lines that represented bus routes that showed how they navigated the city. Tony—a 27-year-old black man who had been in Iowa City for nine years, performs service at the Broadway Neighborhood Center and has friends in the Southeast Side—drew only the places he goes, including where he lives in Coralville ("CV"), his uncle's house ("U"), the neighborhood center ("NC"), and the warehouse where he works ("W"). Tony said he tries to "stay at home" and "stay out of their (long-term, white Iowa City residents) way" to avoid a "run-in" with police, who he fear will

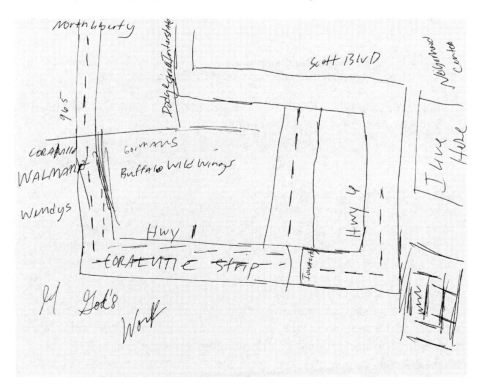

MAP 6.11. TOM'S MAP. Tom's map represents how many residents drew roads and bus lines that circumnavigate the city's downtown.

MAP 6.12. TONY'S MAP. Tony's map represents how residents used mental maps to show a lack of integration into the community and feelings of isolation.

target him because he is black. His map, barren of city landmarks and physical features, then, seems to reflect a feeling of isolation (Map 6.12).

MAPPING TO DISSECT "DIVERSITY" AND MEDIA

It was more common for residents, without prodding or priming, to discuss Iowa City's spaces in terms of race relations, particularly how white residents treat blacks and portray the Southeast Side as a black ghetto. Tom, whose map is shown above, said that those who live outside of the Southeast Side rely on what they "think" happens in the Southeast Side, not on what they "know" from personal experience. "They should live down here and see nothing [bad] goes on," he said.

Tom's map is representative of those by other Southeast Side residents in that it presents an image of Iowa City that is quite different than those of journalists and officials. Whereas journalists and officials showed how they move throughout the city, including to the downtown, Tom's map shows how he avoids the downtown, because, he said, "It's not a place for me."

Through their maps and descriptions of Iowa City, Southeast Side residents explicitly questioned the authority of those outside of the Southeast

Side who would call the neighborhoods a "ghetto." Tony, from above, for instance, said that the Southeast Side "ain't the ghetto. I been in the ghetto [in Chicago], and this ain't it."

And though residents acknowledged that crime does occur in the Southeast Side—while noting that more crime happens downtown among college students—they say the extent of crime is not close to what they experienced somewhere else and that local media and police overreact to crime in the Southeast Side. Amanda—a 23-year-old black woman who moved to Iowa from Chicago when she was a child—said that she spends about "60 percent" of her time in the Southeast Side, most of it at her mother's house, the Crisis Center, and the Outlet, where she gets cigarettes. She echoes other residents when she says that her neighborhood is often misrepresented in the news.

"In the media," Amanda said, "they portray more than three people standing together as a gang.... That's what you hear sometimes on the news, but people should not say it if they don't know." Instead, residents, including Amanda, focused on other disorders in the city, such as a lack of mass transit and overt racism, nodding to these as causes for social conditions in the Southeast Side. For instance, she said, people in the Southeast Side feel abandoned and confined, and that the neighborhood is quickly becoming gentrified for people who don't need to use the buses and who are valued more by the rest of the city.

"They are trying to make it available to college kids and higher," Amanda said, forcing many residents out of the neighborhood to Coralville or Cedar Rapids, a city that's some 30 minutes away by car. For the most part, she added, the news media will continue to report on "this area as a bad neighborhood" until black residents have moved out.

DRAWING DEEPER MEANINGS OF PLACE

Residents recognized a difference in how the Southeast Side was portrayed in the news compared to other city geographies, particularly in terms of how reporters focus on stories of black crime that do not go "deeper" to explain causes other than culture. Such criticism seems to highlight notions of Skogan's (1990) *social disorganization* or *broken windows* explanations for urban conditions, in which neighborhood disorder is brewed by the deviousness within and is shown and encouraged by physical signs of disorder.

Overall, residents said their own stories and experiences never appear in the news and that journalists just report what the police tell them about the neighborhood. Beth (Map 6.13), a 35-year-old black woman who lives in the Southeast Side, for instance, said that local reporters discuss race and "black culture" through veiled language, such as by calling the Southeast Side "a

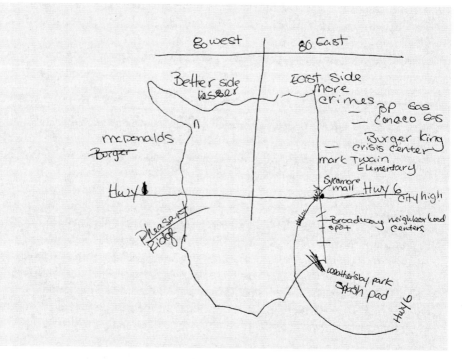

MAP 6.13. BETH'S MAP. Beth's map represents how residents focused on their personal experiences and feelings to explain city spaces.

poverty area," which she described as being people on Section 8 housing, with "lots of kids." Part of the problem, she said, is that reporters do not spend time in the Southeast Side, rely on what police "have to report," and "say nothing about West Side bank robberies" and other crime. Beth says that this kind of reporting is "unfair." "They say what they want to say about the Southeast Side," she said.

Beth's description of news coverage about the Southeast Side reveals how people "inside" and "outside" of the neighborhood seemed to rely on different aspects of evidence and how they assigned authority to different types of data about the space. Such a distinction appears in a comparison between Beth's map and one by David, a 33-year-old white reporter.

David's map (Map 6.8) includes the jail and sheriff's office, businesses along Highway 1, and the university hospital. He said that he constructs his ideas about the city in terms of journalistic beats—specifically that of city government. David's map focuses on the courthouse, the roads he takes to get to places where he reports, city hall, the university, schools, and residential areas. These are places where police, city government, and businesses offer news events and topics for journalists to cover, he said. Beth, however, focused much more on a detailed and complex environment south of Highway 6. Beth, who moved to Iowa City from Chicago 10 years ago, said that the Southeast Side is home to support systems, a splash pad waterpark for children, large parks, schools, and businesses.

Comparing maps and explanations of place by Beth (the city is about her own experiences) and David (the city is about where news happens) reveal how these two sets of people—residents and journalists—relied on very different sources for explaining place: While journalists described geography based upon the role of social institutions and experiences of authorities within particular spaces and how those institutions described the city, residents turned to personal experiences with their environments and focused their thoughts more on how Iowa City residents treat racial minorities and people in the Southeast Side.

Through their maps and descriptions of Iowa City, Southeast Side residents challenged the authority of those who speak publically about the Southeast Side as a "ghetto," articulating specific challenges to dominant explanations of social conditions. Journalists and officials tended to speak in broad terms about the entire city when drawing their maps, focusing on wide geographies, while residents—partly, they said, because they felt confined to the Southeast Side—provided a deeper explication of their neighborhood characteristics and charged "outsiders" (i.e., reporters) with misrepresenting their home.

The wide and generalized descriptions of the city by journalists revealed a sense that their authority to characterize geography in the news spanned miles of space. Max—a 28-year-old white reporter at the *Press-Citizen*—was particular about including numerous landmarks on his map, branching west from the Iowa River to the university football stadium to new neighborhoods at the east. He also included cemeteries, parks, grocery stores, and several other locations, such as his newspaper office and police station. Max said he included these in his map as he was concerned about being "accurate" and "to scale."

Residents, on the other hand, tended to go much deeper in their map-making, telling stories of people's homes, events, and discussing their emotional connections to their environment. Angel—a 23-year-old black woman who had lived in Iowa City for two years, after moving from Chicago—drew the Southeast Side with trees and places she frequents. Her illustration includes the homeless shelter where she and her family stay near the Southeast Side, Kmart, Stuff Etc. (a discount store), her former apartment off of Broadway Street, and her favorite Mexican restaurant (Map 6.14). Angel said she didn't know much more about the city, but considered herself to be, at this point, "from" Iowa City. "They don't know this side of town," she said about residents and journalists who call the Southeast Side a ghetto.

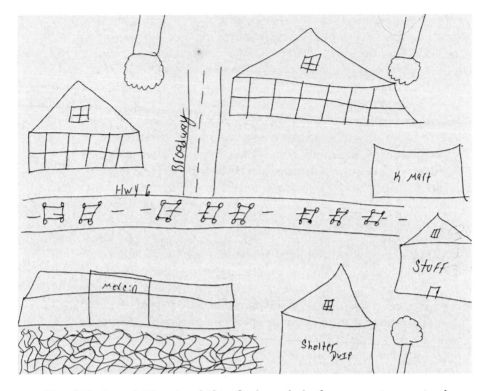

MAP 6.14. ANGEL'S MAP. Angel identifies how a lack of transportation restricts her ability to explore much of Iowa City.

And even though Angel said that she has positive feelings about her neighborhood, her stories about the Southeast Side reveal the trouble she has had integrating with the rest of Iowa City. Angel said that she "came [to Iowa City] for help," but that the city is "depressing" in that "you get set up for failure down here." Angel said that community members "set (the Southeast Side) up to be what it is" by placing clusters of low-income blacks in one space and then telling stories about their perceived deviant and dangerous behavior and culture. Many residents described both positive and negative experiences living and working in Iowa City and discussed at length what seemed to be interest in knowing more about the city, but wanting—and needing—to stay to themselves and in their own neighborhoods.

Conclusion

Through their maps, residents unpacked the ideograph of the "Southeast Side" as being an urban ghetto, ideologically separated from notions of a "safe" and "good," white Midwestern city. These maps, however, also challenge dominant characterizations made about their neighborhoods by journalists and officials. Residents resisted narratives of urban spaces that were applied to the Southeast Side.

Several interesting outcomes that highlight this resistance deserve further explication. First, comparisons between maps by residents and those by journalists and officials are quite telling in what some participants included and others did not. For example, 16 of the 17 journalists and public officials drew the Iowa River—most of those at the center of the map—and said that the river was a major feature of the city. Of the 17 residents, only one did; most said that they did not know about the Iowa River or where it was, and that it was not an important part of their lives.

Residents Beth and Amanda are prime examples of how residents said that they did not know about or see the river as an important part of their daily lives. Conversely, journalists, such as David and Max, said the river was crucial to the city's identity. Tight circles on residents' mental maps show how they experienced the city from the bus or in transit to and from work. Blank spaces in the center and on the edges of these circles reveal the spaces and places where residents say they do not go—most notably, downtown, the university campus, and most of the city's neighborhoods, parks, and landmarks.

Such striking comparisons reveal how drastically residents, journalists, and officials experience and define the city. By sharing details of everyday life in terms of what was "important" and how they got around, residents provide alternative meanings of place. They referred to the Southeast Side as their "home" and demarcated other city spaces as places that they feel unwelcome, focusing on inadequate public transportation, overt racism from white Iowa Citians, and personal experiences in city spaces that influenced decisions to spend most of their time in the Southeast Side.

These personal stories about moving about the city, residents said, directed their feelings as a whole based upon their interactions—or lack thereof—with the rest of the community. Nevaeh (a name she created by spelling "Heaven" backwards), for instance, a 57-year-old black woman who moved to Iowa City from Chicago, wondered how much the stereotypes of the Southeast Side and its people influence public policy, in part because of perceptions about people from her neighborhood and the lack of integration. "We are a target over here," she said, "put all together over here, [not] allowed to get out at this point." And though Nevaeh recently had moved to Coralville and then to North Liberty to find affordable housing, she said a lack of public transportation to and from the Southeast Side made her feel "confined to one place" and that such an experience still makes her feel unwelcome anywhere else in the city. Indeed, these participants questioned the validity of Southeast Side stereotypes by comparing the neighborhood to their past experiences in other geographies, such as black neighborhoods in Chicago.

Perhaps the most striking insight from interviews with journalists and officials that became even more apparent in discussions with residents, is how officials and journalists applied their place-making to their mental maps. In particular, officials and journalists drew and explained mental maps in ways that closely resembled each other and that seemed to mirror "official" maps that they used in their work.

Bill, a city housing official, for instance, drew his map to match a departmental map that showed placements of affordable housing clients; police officers Paul and Allen drew nearly identical maps to each other that resembled the police department's "patrol map"; and *Press-Citizen* K–12 reporter, Roger, drew elementary schools to describe neighborhoods in an identical process to that of Fred, a school official. This reliance on what they considered objective, official, and authoritative descriptions of place showed the close connection between sources and journalists that shaped place-making and explanations, seeming to relinquish journalists from exploring the spaces deeper from those living there.

A second interesting comparison between the explanations of the Southeast Side by residents, journalists, and officials is in how each group legitimized their own interpretations of space. By describing their mental maps—and their own neighborhoods, specifically—residents expressed frustration that news media demarcated and characterized the Southeast Side as a ghetto without expressing the residents' alternative views and the challenges inherent in being black in a white town. In effect, residents questioned the legitimacy and authority of journalists to make claims about the Southeast Side and its people, because their voices were silent in the coverage of their neighborhoods.

Such "muted voices" allowed for racialized and stereotyped news narratives of urban people, places, and "problems" in the Southeast Side to form an ideological boundary between those in and outside the neighborhood. Such a place-making process also created a category of people who could construct dominant characterizations of city geography and its values, subjugating the Southeast Side's cultural diversity and its people, presenting them as being counter to Midwestern values and a threat to notions of a safe, white and historically homogeneous community.

Part of maintaining the city's traditional values meant keeping residents outside of this expanded interpretive community and restricting them from contributing to the dominant, mediated definition of the neighborhood. These people, after all, represented culture and characters tasked with demolishing the city's history and bright future. For example, journalists and officials relied on "official" reports and statistics to define the Southeast Side as a "ghetto," "urban," or an undesirable place to live.

Residents, on the other hand, often compared the Southeast Side to what they described as safer and quieter spaces than their Chicago neighborhoods. Journalists and officials said that their impressions of particular spaces, such as the Southeast Side, were influenced by stories from long-time Iowa City residents and by how urban environments were portrayed in popular culture and news. Simply, the two sides to the story didn't match.

In the next chapter, I discuss the ideological function of news place-making with a deeper analysis of how power and narrative operated in the dominant characterizations of the Southeast Side.

SEVEN

The Subtle Power of the Press

Place and Its Ideological Function

Comparisons of interviews and mental maps among journalists, officials, and residents of Iowa City's Southeast Side presented in the previous chapter reveal interesting patterns about how dominant storytellers there explain how they experience the city. Some examples:

- Fred, a school official, drew and explained Iowa City based upon the schools he oversees and visits both professionally and personally. Similarly, Roger, who had reported on schools for the local newspaper, also focused on schools as prominent tools for place-making in his professional and personal life.
- Police officers Allen and Paul drew their maps to resemble an official police department map of police patrol areas, and both men said that city spaces—even in their daily lives—mattered only in terms of the territories they were familiar with based upon their jobs. Gary, a local journalist, also drew the city based upon the places from which he reported the news.
- Bill, a housing official, drew and explained Iowa City based on an official city map that he used at his job and said that even though he visited a wide range of spaces in the city in his personal life, his job focused how he described city spaces—and their social conditions. These descriptions and explanations mirrored those by several journalists, including Annika, Barb, and Michael.

And, by and large, Southeast Side residents—despite their individual differences—seemed to say the same things in their interviews and mental maps:

- Iowa City's spaces are defined by perceptions of who lives in what neighborhoods, and public and news discourses use these perceptions to racialize events and issues in the Southeast Side that are more complicated than blaming problems on "bad people" from Chicago.
- A lack of access to public transportation and built environment restricts many newly arrived black residents who moved to the Southeast Side from urban centers to their neighborhood. And, if and when residents do move beyond their neighborhood, they feel unsafe and unwelcome.
- Police, city leaders, and journalists operate to stigmatize the people of the Southeast Side, furthering a sense of hostility among many long-term whites in the community toward black residents—particularly the youth.

In this chapter, I surmise as to the cultural explanations behind the similarities and differences among and between these participants' mental maps as a means to express their lived experiences of Iowa City and the Southeast Side. First, I discuss the meanings associated with the ideological power of the press in its news place-making and the power behind their ability to shape dominant characterizations of geography, especially in terms of how the dominant, mediatized characterizations of the neighborhood differ so greatly from people living there.

Next, as a means to better position these interpretations of participants' mental maps and explanations for neighborhood disorder that appeared in local news, I further apply news place-making to a brief example of how the Southeast Side was characterized in local and regional media through subtle explanations of disorder elsewhere in the community based, in part, on racializing place and its people. I conclude the chapter with a discussion on using place identifiers as race identifiers that will assist an analysis in Chapter 8 of how "official" data appeared as discourse about race and place as a prominent vein of news coverage about the Southeast Side.

Identifying Power in News Place-Making

Analysis thus far in the book suggests that the creation of Iowa City's Southeast Side was just as much about creating an "Inner City" (Burgess, 1985) as it was about constructing notions of Iowa City itself, in part because the press presented the neighborhood as an ambiguous space that couldn't be identified. While news articles may have mentioned streets or specific addresses for where events occurred in the Southeast Side, stories did not provide readers with maps or consistent indications of where the Southeast Side was—and wasn't. Journalists did not overtly identify physical boundaries for the Southeast Side; they allowed the audiences' perceptions of boundaries and the place's meanings to be left undefined and debated.

And it was the subtleness of this place-making that released journalists and their sources as a shared interpretive community from being accused of racism by relying on "official" explanations of the place and its social conditions. Indeed, this project suggests that journalists and officials operated together as an interpretive community, which perhaps could be viewed as a second sphere of the journalistic interpretive community—one that extends the power of media to a select group of like-minded sources and that, in turn, allows journalists to share in the ideological authority and legitimacy of their sources, at least among dominant society.

This reliance on "official" and "authoritative" explanations of space and place resulted in participants (no matter if they were authorities in their own neighborhoods) being marginalized, ignored, or overruled on defining the Southeast Side. Furthermore, such a reliance on "official" descriptions and explanations show the degree to which journalists and officials rely upon each other to define and explain social conditions and their causes.

Beyond sharing dominant place-making processes that deepen an understanding of how the two groups reinforce each other's explanations of city geography—such as in the cases noted above and in previous chapters—journalists also showed great power in their choice to name particular neighborhoods as the "Southeast Side" while also recognizing that the term may stigmatize and stereotype. The term, journalists said, served as short-hand for identifying physical space, though some journalists suggested the name may be problematic. Barb, with *The Gazette*, for example, said: "It is unfortunate that you could pigeonhole a bunch of people who live in one area." Other journalists seemed to recognize similar dangers of using the "Southeast Side" place-name, but did so more cryptically, often in phrases of "I know about *that place*," and then describing the Southeast Side either as "mostly black," "crime-ridden," or "poor." The construction of the Southeast Side as a term— an ideograph (see Chapter 4)—to quickly identify a particular place and people, then, constructed a place-name that came to hold a particular ideological power that took on authority and resonance to condition audiences to recognize or adopt its racialized meanings.

Therefore, this analysis suggests that physical and philosophical connections between journalists and officials assign a form of authority to interpretations and explanations of everyday life. Journalists operated at a cultural level, embedding historically dominant racialized narratives of black communities and geographies in local news, and diverging from their normative operations. In other words, journalists believed "official" descriptions of the

Southeast Side and its residents, in part because "official" explanations fit other dominant narratives rooted in a history of racial injustice and oppression that is maintained in popular culture and mass media.

Journalists followed narratives that suggested the Southeast Side was built around urban, black, and deviant culture, which gained further legitimacy through similar tales told by local police and government officials and long-time Iowa City residents. These ways helped journalists *describe* place, but not to prove the veracity of their descriptions. Such ideological work is evidenced by Annika, a journalist who said that even though she has never been to the Southeast Side, police officials, city leaders, and other journalists told her about the place to the point where she said she "know[s] about it."

Michael, also a journalist, said that people he considered authorities on Iowa City spaces quickly—and consistently—talked to him about the Southeast Side as a ghetto from the moment he arrived in the city, which formed his foundational understanding of the city space. By not providing specific details about where the Southeast Side started and stopped, they created an ideological construct of the place that could be formed and altered based on the needs of a particular story.

In turn, the narratives used by journalists to cast the Southeast Side as a ghetto, reiterated by officials, carried such authority that journalists did not need to enter the Southeast Side to report about the neighborhoods. In effect, journalists extended their interpretive community to include officials as full-fledged participants, challenging the notion of journalism as an independent watchdog institution rooted in objective and citizen-based reporting.

News place-making in this case, then, was just as much about the power of the language as about the descriptive nature of journalism, because the notions of place relied on the rhetoric and the ideological notions of urban cities and the power differential of the people who told stories and those who didn't. Furthermore, these findings suggest that the institutional role of local journalism perpetuates dominant ideologies on race, class, and place in the U.S. by representing local place and people in comparison with popular narratives of deviant, urban geographies.

And, the mental mapping that's at the center of this study helped articulate how ideology related to urban narratives was applied to the spaces of Iowa City—to the degree that even the spaces in which participants didn't draw roads, streets, and landmarks held meaning related to place-making. Indeed, city spaces that participants said they did not know about were left empty on their maps. These blank spaces—often including in the map's southeastern portion—were described as unsafe, stigmatized, and "ghetto." Empty spaces on mental maps of journalists and public officials reveals an important aspect of place-making in that ideological frameworks rely on empty spaces to be filled with dominant perceptions of culture (McGee, 1980).

This lack of boundaries allows the audience to apply mythical constructions of place and people to further develop the ideograph of the Southeast Side as a particular type of place. Indeed, these places of the "unknown" are filled with *local legends* that are used to "explain ambiguity—something does not quite seem to belong or stands out from its surroundings" (Bird, 2002, p. 525). That journalists drew vast geographies in and around Iowa City further reveals journalists' abilities to move in and out of social settings and geographies—a level of power not revealed by residents. Ideological constructions of the Southeast Side as a black, dangerous, and deviant place branded not only that space, but people of a particular skin color that would follow them throughout the city (Figure 7.1).

Characteristics of Place-Making via Mental Mapping

	Describing the City	Experiencing Local Geography	Conceptualizing Neighborhoods	Describing Place-Making via Mental Mapping	Explaining Place-Making via Mental Mapping
Journalists	Thin roads reach wide geographies; show social/physical mobility; use personal experiences to select spaces	Inform "official" narratives; show how limited geographic experiences maintain dominant tales	Turn to "objective," dominant narratives and professional experiences to explain blank spaces on maps	Journalists and officials showed a certain degree of geographic similarity and access;	Maps identified subtly and ideological power of place-making in local news;
Officials	Thin roads reach wide geographies; show professional activities; use narratives to select spaces	Show narratives similar to journalists; show how limited geographic experiences maintain dominant tales	Use "objective" news reports, "official" data, and professional experiences to explain blank spaces on maps	Journalists and officials revealed personal and professional limits of exposure to particular city spaces;	Maps reinforced dominant place and race news narratives used to blame residents for social conditions;
Residents	Wide roads, caricatures/drawings express emotion; tight/small maps show limited exposure to space	Focus on neighborhood stories/mobility within space; show narratives that challenge news of neighborhoods and spaces	Identify distance and hostility to explain outside interpretations of neighborhood; turn to dominant narratives of spaces avoided	Southeast Side residents illustrated poor integration of neighborhoods because of limited access and mobility	Maps stigmatized residents of Southeast Side, preventing them from being valid sources for characterizing place

FIGURE 7.1. Mental mapping helped shape several outcomes and understandings related to exploring place-making among all participants.

More specifically, journalists and officials—many lacking personal experiences in these particular neighborhoods—relied on neighborhood demographics, housing and school district statistics to describe who lived there and what the environment was like. These "official" reports that were rooted in statistical data, often coming from city agencies and local police, held a kind of objective authority for participants, and this perceived objectivity of "facts" seemed to bolster the participants' perceptions of their own objectivity in assigning meanings to geography.

By focusing upon cultural elements of urban and black poor in the Southeast Side as a means to explain data, such as school demographics, Census data, and housing and other city statistics, newsmakers ignored structural ele ments of the environment that residents discussed, such as the role of low-income housing, lack of transportation, and inequality in education (see Chapter 8) upon the conditions and perceptions of that part of the city. Beyond providing information about community issues and social conditions from southeastern neighborhoods, then, the very term "Southeast Side" performed a singular ideological purpose: to identify and maintain dominant community values throughout the rest of Iowa City.

Placial Politics: Using Trailer Trash to Ghettoize the Southeast Side

In 2010, at the height of the Southeast Side coverage, a juxtaposition of news coverage about the Iowa City neighborhood and a mobile home court outside of the city revealed the complexities in assigning meanings of those who "earned," or who were unfortunate to experience poverty through coverage of place and people. That summer, *The Des Moines Register* published an investigation into the condition of homes within the Regency Mobile Home Park that's just south of Iowa City (Rood, 2010; 2010a; 2010b; 2010c).

The newspaper's investigation revealed dozens of people living within deplorable conditions in the trailer park with unclean drinking water and in dilapidated and unsafe homes. Because the *Register* is owned by the Gannett company, which also owns the *Iowa City Press-Citizen*, news articles about the park appeared in both papers. Additionally, because of the *Register's* reporting, other news outlets reported on the newspaper's work, which then made coverage about the trailer park a local news story, even if the dominant newspaper covering it was located on the other side of the state.

More than roughly 20 stories positioned one area of disorder to another through attribution of blame (Iyengar, 1991) in which those in the trailer park were described as being of the *deserving poor* (see Introduction) while those in the Southeast Side were cast as causing their poverty. Attribution of blame and responsibility as a theory has come to explain how audiences use information to make judgments to find blame for social conditions and issues, such as welfare (Sotirovic, 2003) and crime (Iyengar, 1991). Individuals have been shown to place a majority of blame within either institutions and structural influences (external factors), or within individuals themselves (individual factors).

Stories that focus on the individual through personal stories and anecdotes tend to lead readers to blame the individuals themselves for their problems, which has especially been the case in discussing poverty, racial conflicts, and reasons for social welfare programs. On the other hand, readers tend to blame structural influences for social conditions when news stories focus on those structural factors, such as governmental or institutional influences upon social issues (Iyengar, 1991; Sotirovic, 2003). Further, research also suggests that the more "negative" the news story about a person or social issue, the more likely one will see a causal attribution (Bohner, Bless, Scharz, and Strack, 1988), in part because more negative stories are viewed as more relevant and persuasive (Rozin and Royzman, 2001).

Attribution of responsibility has been used in conjunction with research on framing to explore the use of personal stories within news coverage of social issues (episodic framing) in which readers tend to blame the individual for his or her problems, while news reports that focus more on larger facts and themes (thematic framing) tend to result in readers blaming structural factors (Iyengar, 1991). While one's personal beliefs and experiences have been suggested to be a major influence upon where one places blame, responsibility for social conditions described in the news tends to be more of an influence upon these decisions.

In addition, attribution of responsibility has revealed that the race of individuals involved in the news stories may also influence a person's perceptions of blame, which is central to this study. Blacks as a group, for instance, have been shown to be more likely blamed for their own social conditions among white Americans, as are those who accept social welfare (Ben-Porath and Shaker, 2010; Gandy and Baron, 1998; Iyengar, 1991). Such blame was extended for reasons beyond welfare and personal experiences of those described in the news, but specifically by relating them to the dominant characterizations of places from which they had arrived.

The subtleness of the ideological work of place in the news as explanation and description of social conditions and cultural differences that's most interesting in this study is how perceptions of one place (Chicago) were used to describe and explain Iowa City's Southeast Side, while the people of the trailer park were from white, Midwestern America. Yet, the process of characterizing the Southeast Side in terms of its relationship to the rest of the Iowa City community also used areas within the city to differentiate and divide.

Here, I present a brief analysis of how journalists attributed responsibility and blame for social conditions in each of the neighborhoods based on three main elements—the characterization of people as a characterization of place, environmental descriptions to explain the culture of neighborhood residents, and the grouping of people within a geography to explain social conditions in that place.

Casting the Crew: People as Cause for Place-Meanings

While U.S. Census data do not specify the number, race, and socioeconomic levels of residents within the mobile home park, initial newspaper reports said many of the park's 600 residents were "unemployed, disabled, elderly and immigrant," though none of the newspapers' coverage overtly indicated the racial or ethnic makeup of the "immigrants."[1] News reports that appeared in the *Register*, the *Iowa City Press-Citizen*, and *The Gazette* out of Cedar Rapids portrayed those in the Regency Mobile Home Park as *trailer park trash*—a concept "synonymous with being a Southern 'redneck'" and with other characteristics of a "Southern kind of poverty" (Harry, 2004, p. 218) but that is also rooted in traditional Southern and American values. The Southeast Side, on the other hand, was compared to "The Inner City" (Burgess, 1985).

Despite obvious differences between the two neighborhoods—such as the racial makeups—the settings for these stories of social strife and poor living conditions were very similar: both neighborhoods suffered from substandard housing; people in both neighborhoods experienced environmentally caused illness; both neighborhoods struggled with poverty. Yet, in attempting to explain the complexities of the social conditions within the neighborhoods, journalists at three newspapers turned to very different resonant news narratives to place blame for the civil unrest and deplorable living conditions.

Stories about park residents focused on their inability to care for themselves, pitting them against the landlords and the corporation that owned the park, which was ultimately charged with creating such poor living conditions. One article in the *Press-Citizen* told the story of one couple who was threatened with eviction because of a mix of financial mismanagement at the park and high rents (Schettler, 2010). In addition to describing living conditions within the park, the story also explained some of the residents' inabilities to pay rent. The residents "both work full-time," the paper said, "but" the residents are "not sure how they will afford the rent." The paper then quotes one of the residents as saying, "We're not slum people."

News stories from the city's Southeast Side also told of a vulnerable population, new to Iowa City after escaping the dangerous Chicago ghettos. However, few articles focused on the detailed experiences and needs of individuals, their finances, or their work that would have complicated dominant stories about these people's experiences. Instead, stories focused on fears of violence, a space that was out of control, and some residents (mostly youth) who were preying on each other.

A pathological breakdown of family structure (Heldt, 2009; Keppler,

2009) that caused a reliance on welfare and affordable housing (Rhatigan, 2009) also fueled conversation about who lives in the Southeast Side. For instance, one resident was quoted as saying that youth will ignore the evening city curfew created to keep young adults off of the streets because their behavior is already violent; they already break laws, such as using illegal firearms. "If they don't care about that, why are they going to care about a curfew?" the woman asked (O'Leary, 2009b).

The people of the place, then, became just as strong of an explanation for social disorder as anything else, casting them as either victims or as being responsible for their environment's social conditions.

Building the Set: Environment as Cultural Message

News stories about the Southeast Side and the mobile home park set the scenes for interpreting and explaining social disorder in both of those places through environmental descriptors. Stories about the mobile home park focused more on details of dilapidated mobile homes with mold, unclean water, and abandoned structures (Rood, 2010). The park was described as ripe with litter, unmowed grass, and garbage in driveways. Abandoned trailers have "ripped-out doors and broken windows and smell of urine. Strewn inside ... are beer cans, blankets, old computers and broken TVs" (Rood, 2010). A source in one story called the Regency Mobile Home Park "the Appalachia of our area," words that also scrawled as a sub-headline in the paper (Rood, 2010), a nod to America's "white trash" that despite their culture of poverty still try to uphold traditional American values. But white trash is still a valued community who, for the most part, keep their problems to themselves while those of the inner-city present problems for society as a whole.

The mobile home park was also described as a place that could be considered home. One trailer has a "lawn trimmed short and flowers [that] brighten up the outside," one article states, while another trailer has "parakeets [that] chirp in a cage outside of the home while the children watch a movie" (Hermiston, 2010b). The space is deemed, despite its issues, as being a place full of life. When the state's attorney general appeared at the park for an inspection, he said, "We saw three little kids running around at one of the trailers down there. My heart goes out to those little kids. They deserve a good place to live" (Schettler, 2010a).

The environment of the Southeast Side, however, was cast in a very different way. Descriptions focused more on the activities of people who live in the space and less on the details inside homes. Instead, news stories focused on the perceptions of the space: gunshots at night, streets filled with youth, and gang activity (Hennigan, 2009a). One Southeast Side resident told a newspaper that she felt "like the neighborhood is out of control" after reports of four or five gunshots and word that a youth had been shot (Gallegos, 2009), though police found no evidence of shots fired or an injured youth. These descriptions about fear of gang and youth violence resembled stories about urban cities in the 1990s that have spread into America's suburbs (Garland, 2009) and have come to represent one of the worst elements of the inner city—and its effect on neighboring spaces.

In its initial reports about the Regency Mobile Home Park, the *Register* told many personal stories of park residents that included financial and personal reasons that kept them in the park. Indeed, the series of stories in the *Register* was titled "Trapped." Stories included phrases such as "...the 57-year-old who was broke and fighting prostate cancer..." (Rood, 2010a), and "Williams, who is divorced..." (Rood, 2010b) to explain why they would live in such circumstances. More blatant explanations included one couple, that said "[l]eaving the park is not an option. [The resident] is unemployed, and the couple live on [the spouse's] disability check" (Rood, 2010c).

These explanations, though focused on the individuals in the case of the trailer park, painted the residents as more vulnerable to the external causes of their poverty—corporations motivated by profit—who suffered from the forces that damaged their homes. Those in the Southeast Side, on the other hand, seemed to be charged in the press with destroying their neighborhoods, altering them from being homes to being the 'hood. The 'hood's environment, then, becomes representative of its people's disorder.

Printing the Playbill: Grouping as Cultural Meaning-Making

News reports about the mobile home park focused on city and county ordinances that were not enforced by state and local agencies (for example, see Hennigan, 2010b), and press descriptions of the park's problems showed the residents as being an entire group of victims. Poor drinking water, dilapidated housing, and alleged financial mismanagement of the park's owners were explained as caused by greed and a lack of oversight (Schettler, 2010b; 2010c). News reports detailed the work and responses of county and state officials that would ensure "everyone's protected" while attempting not "to trample on anyone's rights," an assistant county attorney told the newspaper (Schettler, 2010c).

Because the *Register* provided the initial reports on the mobile home conditions, news reports from that publication moved from telling individual stories about those living in the mobile home park to the state and local laws that were either not enforced or were allegedly broken. Stories also began mixing personal tales of safety problems, responses from state and local official sources (Rood, 2010), and stories of law enforcement charged with investigating the park conditions. Such a movement to state and local laws provided attention to structural influences upon the environment and the residents, who as a group deserved the same kind of public concern.

News coverage of the Southeast Side, however, contained stories that seemed to place blame upon all of those living within the neighborhood, turning to parents, gang activity, and poor behavior of neighborhood youth as causes. Early in the coverage of the Southeast Side in 2009, police officials indicated that the initial melee on Mother's Day included parents and children (Keppler, 2009), suggesting that both adults and children were "lacking maturity and good decision-making ... these adults are lacking them as well, and kids are modeling after that," a police spokesman said (Keppler, 2009).

Issues of juvenile crime continued into coverage that fall (Gallegos, 2009) that placed the blame for the Southeast Side on all of the people there—not on issues of poor transportation, racial discrimination in schools, housing, employment, economic and other social inequalities, and stigmatization that limited integration of Southeast Side residents to the rest of the city.

When more shots were reported in the "Southeast Side" in August— after a summer of community tension and discussions over race and violence— one news account said the recent flare of violence occurred because some youth did it "just for fun" (Hermiston, 2009b). In turn, very little news coverage of the Southeast Side dealt with issues of structural factors, though one story did mention that the city police department was working with "public housing staff" to remedy the violence among a group of neighbors who construct their dangerous neighborhood (Rhatigan, 2009).

Race was also a strong undertone in many other stories that grouped people of the Southeast Side, appearing in comments from city residents and officials who indicated that much of the public conversation about the Southeast Side revolved around "those people from Chicago" or "black residents and people from Chicago or other metropolitan areas" (Hermiston, 2009c) who then contribute to crime in Iowa City through gang activity (Shurson, 2009a).

Other comments in news coverage about violence, gangs, and the evolution of the Southeast Side into a space perceived to be unsafe tended to be summed up as being too large of an issue in which to find blame, sometimes referred to simply as "this challenge" (O'Leary, 2009c). However, journalists were much clearer about providing causes for disorder at the Regency Mobile Home Park. By and large, local press blamed structural influences, such as poor management by the mobile home owners, lack of governmental oversight, lack of access to legal assistance among the mobile home residents, and a string of lawsuits involving the management company regarding several of its properties in Iowa and across the country.

Instead of discussing what led to the poor living conditions in both spaces—a combination of failing city and country housing ordinances and larger social and economic pressures—newsworkers turned to the powerful (and possibly believable) myths available: violent blacks became denigrated and degraded through the blame placed on them for a summer of violence, whereas structural, political, and legal factors were the cause for the troubles of the mostly white trailer park. By focusing upon cultural elements of urban and black poor in the Southeast Side, newsmakers ignored structural elements of the environment, such as the role of low-income housing, lack of transportation, and inequality in education upon the conditions and perceptions of that part of the city.

Conclusion

Because I acknowledge my interest in critical approaches to race, news, and geography, my characterization of news place-making can't be separated from lines of scholarship that include notions of power as the purpose and process of an ideological project that is the press. What I have produced thus far, then, relies, to a degree, on a type of feminist ethnography and critical, cultural studies in the sense that news place-making attempts to reveal the positions of the oppressed and marginalized to explore how mediatized geography appears in the press.

Interactions between powerful messages about place and the devices and explanations of geography in coverage of the Southeast Side bolstered dominant cultural explanations for everyday life in a changing Iowa City while simultaneously suppressing alternative explanations from subjugated audiences. Therefore, residents' counter-narratives to mediated definitions of the Southeast Side presented in this project reveal several implications for the traditional role of journalism as a tool for democratic representation and self-governing.

A seminal voice in the democratic value of the press, Meiklejohn (1965) writes that government should not be ruled by the elite, businesses, or politicians, but that citizens are—and must be—deeply involved in governing, which includes an involvement with the press. Additionally, Kovach and Rosenstiel (2007) argue that journalists have an obligation to engage with the citizenry in producing and disseminating information and building public involvement in democratic efforts.

Indeed, they write, journalism's "first loyalty [is] to citizens" (p. 5). However, this study addresses questions of whether journalism really is about serving the public or maintaining the status quo. In terms of the trailer park coverage, for instance, the press showed an interest in revealing wrongdoing by private business and in determining the responsibility of local governments to protect its citizens. Coverage of the Southeast Side, however, showed itself as a tool for and an extension of the police (and the state) as an apparatus by which to maintain dominant ideologies of who is considered an acceptable citizen and to oppress those who operate outside of that ideology through the coverage of people's places.

In the end, this study reveals place-making as a fundamental role of the journalistic community and identifies another ideological function of the press in that they assign power and meanings by describing news where it happens. It also deepens understandings of ritualized patterns of journalism and institutional power in that while grassroots interpretations of the news and neighborhoods are accessible to journalists, ideological connections between journalists and other institutions hold an authoritative power and exclusivity that is virtually unshakable.

In the next chapter, I explicate a specific element of coverage about the Southeast Side through the lens of Iowa City's schools to further understand the subtle ideological work of news place-making, specifically in how it contributes to acts of social control.

EIGHT

School News

Press Constructions of
Schools-as-Place

Nell's problems with Iowa City started in her children's school.

Having moved with her five children from the Calliope projects of New Orleans in 2001—a predominantly black and rough part of the city, the kind of place Master P raps about—Nell planned on her kids walking each other to school. Even though Iowa had safe neighborhoods, Nell found, there are few places in the world where elementary students should walk to school alone.

Even Iowa isn't that nice.

All went well for Nell's first year in Iowa City. She found work and she started studying for her associate's degree at the city's Kirkwood Community College. But it was only a matter of time before her black kids would stand out in their mostly white North Side school.

The voices of Nell's children seemed to come out a bit faster and carry a bit more than others. It's not unfair to say that communication in Iowa is a bit slower, quieter, and follows the rules of Standard English. At some point, her children's being "not from here" caught up with them: one of Nell's three sons got suspended. At the same time, one of her elementary-aged daughters found herself in detention, leaving one of the girls to walk home by herself.

Nell says she had told the elementary school staff that her daughters were supposed to walk together—no matter what. But for some reason, she says, school staff sent one daughter out alone, and she was "jumped" by other students.

Balancing work and family is hard, Nell says, and when this shit happens, it's neither good for the individual child nor for the family as a whole. It throws everything off.

More than that, Nell was furious that her orders for her daughters to walk together were overruled, and she went to the school to complain.

Bad move.

Apparently, the principal wasn't ready for Nell's concerns, and Nell certainly wasn't ready for the principal's explanation.

"Well," Nell was told, "if you got off your behind and walked them, then maybe this wouldn't happen." Nell lost it. Who was this woman to suggest she didn't work and didn't care for her kids? she thought. What did that principal know about her, anyway?

"So I went off on her," Nell says, "and called her a few names."

Maybe that wasn't right, she says now, but she didn't think the argument justified calling the cops. The principal, however, did.

In the end, Nell was banned from the school, charged with "verbal assault," and fined $250.

"I'd never heard of that (charge)," Nell says, "and I was so confused. So [the principal] can say whatever she wants because she's the principal of the school and I'm a nobody and just wasting my time?"

In New Orleans, Nell says, had the principal made such a comment, "I had every right to tag her behind."

But in Iowa City, Nell said, she was expected to take the insult silently.

More than anything that happened that day, Nell got hurt.

"It made me feel really low," she says. "She only looked at the outside of me—that I've got five kids and I'm black, sitting at home."

Since then, Nell's finished her associate's degree and has been working in daycares and for community resource centers. She's been on and off of Section 8 affordable housing, often finding ways to pay the bills without the help. But one of her sons has since moved to live with his father in Georgia, and the other two moved back to New Orleans.

"They couldn't take Iowa anymore," Nell says.

Her family still struggles with cultural clashes in the schools. When we talked in March 2013, one of her daughters had been suspended from school and was wearing a GPS bracelet on her ankle during her home detention.

Nell says it's easy for someone to blame her and her children for these problems, but this isn't about black kids acting badly. Instead, it's about an unfair set of rules being applied to kids that look like Nell's and attributed to notions of "black culture."

"We don't need to explain our behavior to anyone or to ourselves," Nell says. "So why are we asking why *black* kids are fighting? Why do we even need to ask?"

Instead, she asks, Why don't people ask about why kids feel the need to fight, generally? And, Why don't people ask more questions about how some kids are treated differently than others?

Indeed, Nell's got enough stories to start the conversation: the next-door white college students who had a party and Nell got kicked out for making a little noise of her own; the time a white parent chaperone slapped Nell's kid on a school trip and apologized with a letter and four coupons for ice cream (not even enough for all of Nell's kids); and the time when one of her children was told by a white schoolmate, "Ya'll need to get back on a bus and go back to Africa."

When stories such as these come up from new blacks in Iowa City, they are always asked why they stay. Why not just "go home?" these arrivals are asked, and Why can't you just follow the rules and become part of the community?

Why should she leave? Nell asks, and Why can't people see that part of the problems people like her experience come from within the community just as much as out of it?

"I came here to better educate myself as well as my children," Nell says. "I am working and my kids are in school. And even though they want to put us out or call the police, when they are teaching the class they have to teach that little white child, they have to teach my child, 'cause they have to get to that little white child."

And here's my favorite part of what Nell's saying, the part that shows the real agency of new arrivals, the determination and persistence to talk back to members of the community who don't want to share their schools: "As long as they keep my kids in the room," she says, "they can't stop teaching the class, 'cause they want to teach their kids."

Nell's experiences with Iowa City tend to resemble many interactions with institutions that were described to me by residents I've spoken to for this book. Nell's in particular, in that hers are related to conflict in the schools, reveal deeper influences upon the constructions of Iowa City neighborhoods and how new residents have been treated poorly by local governments and officials—even those such as schools, police, and the press that are said to be there to help the community.

Just as the previous chapter examined the press as a racialized institution that relays cultural and social norms of oppression as a means to maintain the status quo, so do schools. Building this argument and connecting it to Iowa City is crucial for recognizing how "refugees" from Chicago have failed to be integrated into city spaces outside of the Southeast Side. Below, then, I present how concepts of the *undeserving poor* and *banishment*, which were discussed previously in the book, were applied to press coverage of schools. My main argument is that such banishment occurred in how these residents were ignored in public discussions and debates about their schools that appeared in the press.

This discussion, therefore, requires an understanding of progressive scholarship about the role of schools in embedding dominant ideologies and in, at the very least, maintaining the social order through racialized power dynamics in the classroom and through policing. Following that introduction, I present a brief analysis of how local press covered two major issues related to Iowa City schools in 2009 and 2010—coverage that I used in this project's previous analysis of how journalists characterized the Southeast Side. Discourse surrounding the closing of Roosevelt Elementary School and the redrawing of school boundaries to equally disperse poor and minority students throughout the district served as a form of ideological social control that shaped juxtaposing newswork about the Southeast Side with subtle coverage of public policy said to be rooted in notions of "equality."

In the end, this chapter builds a foundation upon which I base the conclusion: place (in this case, characterized through narratives of neighborhoods and school environments) serves as a rhetorical construction of racial identity.

Schools, the Press and Racialized Rhetoric

News media tell us about our communities through schools (Collins, 2009). The press cover local sporting events, governance, and neighborhoods by presenting classrooms as extensions of neighborhoods, the children as a community's future. Indeed, because America's public schools are paid for, in part, by local property taxes—whether or not property owners have children in the schools—the schools are presented as a means by which to contribute to the future of a larger community. News about schools, then, is presented under the auspices of the "public's right to know" and as a valuable source for tracking American educational progress and local events and personalities.

Despite all that communities invest in schools, the strength of national rhetoric about the importance of public education, and the amount of energy local news media put into covering schools, the press continue to undervalue deeper, cultural implications of public policy and rhetoric that fuel the influence of oppression, inequality, and racism that comes from our classrooms and curricula. At a time when urban schools continue to be attacked for overspending on students and neighborhoods deemed too dangerous or too-far gone to save and rural schools are ignored by national press and politicians (as many rural issues tend to be), news media tend to focus only on the larger economic and political elements of the education debate (Delpit, 2006).

Media coverage about Iowa City's changing classrooms continues to emerge in 2013 and 2014, in part, because of an influx of low-income blacks from Chicago turned to speculation about gang violence, those seeking easy access to affordable housing, and "black culture" in the Southeast Side. Stories about neighborhood schools, then, became more about the neighborhoods than about the schools. In this section I discuss the dominant narratives about education in the U.S., focusing solely on how mainstream media discuss the role of neighborhood schools and the cultural role schools play in society.

WHAT WE SAY SCHOOLS DO

By and large, schools as an environment and institution have been labeled the space to become "the great equalizer" (Downey, von Hippel and Broh, 2004), in which learning environments and curricula erase education gaps along socio-economic and racial lines. Yet, public discourses about communities, schools, and education are built on a background of this nation's racist history, intertwined with narratives about geography, class, economics, and whether children are to achieve and advance through intellectual study or through vocational training (Anderson, 1988; Kozol, 2005; Payne, 2008). How well schools meet the end of equalizing education and the chances for success has become, possibly, the biggest debate among those interested in public education.

The evidence of how schools don't work for some is widespread. In *The Trouble with Black Boys,* for instance, Noguera (2008) writes that by 2006, black men accounted for 50 percent of adult men in prison, though black men make up just a fraction of the country's population. At the same time, he writes, dominant stories about the disproportionate incarceration of blacks (many who are jailed for non-violent offenses) trumps deeper discussions about what this over-incarceration means to society. Among Noguera's concerns is the social and cultural effects of removing members of families and larger communities in terms of how these people can provide financial support for schools, improve students' home lives and environments, and contribute to a stronger sense of community that could surround strong schools.

Moreover, such a discussion amputates the public's ability to focus on what resources these schools may need to assist students both in and out of school. Instead, policymakers and the press continue to discuss incarceration and the "deterioration" of inner-city families, neighborhoods, and schools with notions of "black culture" and what I call the *ghettoization effect.*

This ghettoization effect consists not just of the real influences of ghettoization upon an individual's psyche, but also the broader effect of characterizing a neighborhood as a ghetto upon the local, regional, and national understandings of place. Public characterizations of a neighborhood as a ghetto not only serves a rhetorical function of "othering" those residents and removing them from the mainstream, but allows governments, businesses, and individuals to enforce predatory institutions and policies in these spaces. This "effect" is even more dynamic in that it ascribes these notions of ghetto onto the people of that place so that they carry with them the fluidity of place elsewhere into their worlds. Such perceptions are revealed in fairly popular phrasings similar to, "You can take the man out of the ghetto, but you can't take the ghetto out of the man."

Such a "ghettoization" has also created a pathology of its own in the concept of "black culture" that then fuels the "normalization of failure on the part of Black males" in all facets of public life—including schools (Noguera, 2008, p. xix). In turn, this "normalization of failure" has built a divide between which children schools are meant to serve, especially if ghettoized black youth and their "pathologies" will ruin the education of non-blacks.

In an attempt to equalize any divides among rural/urban/suburban schools and across racial lines in the U.S., the federal government initiated the infamous No Child Left Behind legislation in the early 2000s. This approach focused on using standardized assessments of student knowledge and teacher performance to measure student learning, teacher effectiveness, and proper use of school funding.

Despite strong opposition by classroom teachers and education scholars who argue against the validity of standardized testing, the legislation continues to shape dominant educational practices. Teachers are increasingly held to assessments based on standardized tests, as are their students, and are labeled as "failing" based on test results (Payne, 2008).

Lost in these education practices that are often implemented and maintained at the local level and surrounded by discourse about how "education is the key" for individual and mass advancement, however, is the recognition that, in the end, schools aren't designed to equalize, but to normalize dominant explanations for everyday life and to oppress those who fail to adhere to the mainstream (Alexander, 2010; Bourdieu and Passeron, 2000). If dominant understandings of what role education plays in society and dominant culture are to increase an individual's intellect and agency and to create an engaged citizenry, that citizenry would likely be charged with and supported in questioning the status quo.

To limit the ability of education to inspire mass challenges to dominant culture and social norms, schools operate with standardized stories of history, literature, and science set by private textbook publishers, local cultural leaders, and federal educational guidelines that insert dominant ideological meanings into curriculum and instructional material in an attempt to pacify learners.

Assessment and other policies that standardize what and how students learn and experience social control in schools solidifies dominant ideological functions of education.

And, to keep the lid on the pot, news media report only on the schools' sports teams, teacher retirements, and on the results and outcomes from school districts and state tests. Rarely do the press report on the larger cultural and social implications of education practices. Specifically, news media are more likely to report on school disorder—minor school violence (small fights and disruptions)—rather than how and why the complexities of pedagogy, teacher/student interactions, zero tolerance policies, and disproportionate suspensions contribute to perceptions of out-of-control students.

Such reporting veils cultural elements of education and naturalizes the approaches and practices of educators—even when educators choose to criminalize school children.

SCHOOLS AS PIPELINES-TO-PRISONS

Under the guise of being an objective watchdog for the "public good," news media attempt to serve as an accessible forum through which the public can engage in a hearty debate about its social institutions, including education (Gans, 2004; Kovach and Rosenstiel, 2007). However, it's the alternative media and scholars that seem to provide the dominant arena for discussion about how schools and their communities respond to learning, behavior, and cultural conflicts in the classroom. Increasingly, this effort is accomplished through studying policing. Several scholars have come to call the over-policing and militarization of schools, the implementation of zero-tolerance policies, and out-of-school suspensions—all efforts that are targeted at minority students—a *school-to-prison pipeline* (Kim, Losen and Hewitt, 2010).

The school-to-prison pipeline captures the ways in which the educational system in the U.S., from federal policies to local decisions, operate a police state within the established legal system that's been injected into America's schools to deal with the most minute disruption. To be clear, the pipeline is not addressing massive scenes or threats of disorder in schools, such as mass shootings that placed names like Columbine and Sandy Hook into the American consciousness, but is instituted to subjugate those who think outside the mainstream, who express themselves differently than the mainstream, and whose personal experiences, histories, and futures are different than the mainstream and that cause a frustration that is often exposed within the structure of school.

Under zero tolerance policies that many school districts have implemented, for instance, the loudest voice in the classroom, essays and papers with explicit violent or sexual scenes, debates between teachers and students that are perceived as disrespectful or threatening, and aggressive physical play lead to intervention by armed police.

Instead of inspecting schools and the educational system for inequalities that may contribute to tensions between teachers and students or housing and policing inequalities that effect some students' home lives and not others, the pipeline paints schools as an environment of constant surveillance where a single misstep leads to a police record and sets students up for an early—and usually a difficult—introduction to police and control. In their book *The School-to-Prison Pipeline*, Kim, Losen, and Hewitt (2010) note startling statistics that represent the disproportionate effects of the pipeline along racial lines:

- Between 1973 and 2006, black students who were enrolled in public schools and suspended within a given school year increased from 6 to 15 percent [p. 34].
- Black and Native American students are overrepresented in being identified with and evaluated for intellectual deficiencies, based, in part, on classroom behavior and that, once in these programs, they receive "vastly unequal support and services, especially compared to their white counterparts" [p. 54].
- Zero tolerance programs, which allow school officials to suspend or expel children "from school for everything from weapons to drugs to smoking to fights" circumnavigate due process for youth and immediately place these children—including grade school children—in contact with law enforcement and interactions with the legal system that have generally been saved for adults [p. 79].

Many schools are already "underprepared" with few resources to meet diverse needs of students. Poorly trained teachers, little money for innovative and advanced pedagogies, and substandard curricula with which educators struggle to prepare students for college and intellectual thinking heighten in-class tensions between students and teachers. The burden of achievement and development is rested upon the youth themselves. America's children operate within a testing atmosphere that pushes students out of school. In turn, students aren't exposed to the arts, to advanced placement courses, or to environments that build upon students' natural gifts and interests.

Discipline, becoming increasingly harsher as years progress, combines with over-testing and boring teaching material and delivery so that when grades are measured through culturally insensitive standardized tests—and nothing more—students are held back in both their grade level and in their ability to grow emotionally and cognitively. Behavior that's normal and acceptable for some students, such as arguing about what is taught and what isn't (a freedom awarded many gifted and talented students, for instance) is viewed as aggressive or disruptive and usually results in punishment in most classrooms. In the end, too many students are "pushed out" and leave school because they feel that they are not cared for, and, for the most part, they are right.

"These push-outs," write Kim, Losen and Hewitt (2010, p. 9), "range from nondisciplinary measures, such as disenrolling truant youth from high school or counselors encouraging struggling students to enroll in GED programs, to harsher forms of exclusion, including frequent suspensions, exclusions, and school-based arrests." Furthermore, news reporting about these schools include only those events that are deemed by police and school leaders as violent, or are simple readings of student demographics and testing data skew public perceptions about what's going on in schools.

Indeed, several recent changes in urban school districts have led to national discussions focused more on political and philosophical approaches to publically funded education than on the complex social *and cultural* explanations for the state of urban schools. In 2013, school districts in Chicago (Yaccino, 2013) and in Washington, D.C. (Khalek, 2013) closed dozens of schools in heavily black neighborhoods. Since at least 2008, an exodus of citizens and economic downturns in cities such as Milwaukee, Detroit, Atlanta, and Kansas City have complicated race relations in suburban school hallways (Holland, 2012; Ispa-Landa, 2013) and have left urban schools abandoned and deeply segregated (Saulny, 2010). In 2010, black boys in Nashville were found to be roughly four times more likely than any other student in the K–12 system there to receive out-of-school suspensions because of perceived behavioral problems (NPR, 2010). While discussions about these topics in the press have been presented with criticism against school officials, little of the discussion questions how normalized and naturalized such outcomes have become and how widespread the cultural implications for such measures are.

Indeed, the destruction of public education as a means to equalize and engage the nation's citizenry tends to be discussed in the press as though the decisions were normal and acceptable, as though closing dozens of schools and disproportionate suspensions are acceptable and unsurprisingly commonplace. Noguera, in his book about black boys, writes against judgments made by teachers of students mainly that young, black males aren't interested in learning without understanding the social and cultural influences that shape students' perceptions of school as a key for success.

"When teachers and administrators remain unfamiliar with the places and the ways in which their students live and their lives outside the school walls," Noguera writes, "they often fill the knowledge void with stereotypes based on what they read or see in the media, or what they pick up indirectly from stories told to them by children" (p. 105). Not only does Noguera's logic fit with similar ideological work journalists and officials make about "blank spaces" in their understanding of city spaces—as I've discussed earlier in this book—but also in how news media, generally, articulates complex issues of schools.

Because journalists are insulated from alternative explanations for social conditions they are limited in presenting to the public complex understandings of the everyday. Instead, reporters choose to dissect issues related to schools through the sanitized, non-human lens of statistics and "official" explanations. They report on what they are told through means that present notions of objectivity—reports made by officials about schools from the perspective of serving the "public good" and, particularly, the children. In this way, the news is color-blind; data represent "reality" and remove complexities. But alone, data are absent of explanation.

Below, I show how such color-blind and "objective" interpretations in local news coverage about school issues in Iowa City operated as a discourse separate from that about the Southeast Side but served as a supplementary discussion about the changing city. More directly, news reports about the city's diverse students and families—specifically the influence of low-income students on classroom learning behavior—reveals an intentionality of talking about the challenges of integrating new arrivals to the city without implicating the local community for failing to adapt to change.

Iowa City press, then, became a subtle but direct influence on covert, local place-making by relying on rhetoric about neighborhood and school culture and disorder as being one, subtly introducing the idea of increasing social control of neighborhoods through schools.

Forming the Southeast Side Through Schools

The 2009–2010 academic year in the Iowa City Community School District was one of controversy surrounding how fears about a crime wave in Iowa City's Southeast Side would influence classrooms of students throughout the community. Letters to the editor, columns, and news stories in local press carried comments about the local violence and its connection to an influx of blacks from Chicago, as well as a preponderance of low-income, Section 8 housing recipients living in the Southeast Side (Gutsche, 2011).

Here, I discuss two news events that provided the arena for a veiled debate about the Southeast Side—the closing of Roosevelt Elementary and proposed boundary changes, a process called *redistricting*, to distribute poor and minority students throughout elementary schools in the city. While Roosevelt didn't serve students from the Southeast Side, the closing called for the construction of a new elementary school and a possibility that significant policy changes would alter the city's commitment to neighborhood schools.

Redistricting furthered concerns that the district would lead to fewer neighborhood schools and would allow for students from the Southeast Side to attend other city schools, reducing those schools' quality of education. In the end, debates about changing city schools were rooted in dominant ideological explanations for urban culture and the affect spreading the urban culture across the city would have on a traditional, white Midwestern city. Schools, then, became a way for the community to subtly construct deeper impressions about the people and place of the Southeast Side and its relationship to the rest of Iowa City.

The Roosevelt Story: Schools as Neighborhoods

Early in 2009, the Iowa City community learned that its school board planned to close the city's oldest elementary school, Roosevelt Elementary, on the city's West Side. The school served a neighborhood from the top of Benton Hill, a wooded lot that in the 1930s was on the "outskirts of town." An architect's review of Roosevelt, which was built in 1931, showed the structure needed $5.1 million in repairs for it to continue housing students in kindergarten through sixth grade. The review showed Roosevelt to be over capacity with 350 students, crumbling infrastructure, and in need of handicap accessibility and more space (Daniel, 2009a).

Around the same time, a higher-than-average percentage of minority and low-income students, some 20 percent above the district average, led state officials to label Roosevelt "racially and socio-economically isolated" (Daniel, 2009a)—a hint at future elements of debates about the role neighborhood schools can play in a city in which its neighborhoods maintain stark socioeconomic differences.

The end of the original Roosevelt—one that served students in its neighborhood—was a shock to many parents, and its death was almost certain from the moment school officials announced their plans. A new school was proposed, and parents were told that their students would be dispersed between that new school and other schools in the community. Within weeks of initial news reports that officials might shutter the school, parents joined to oppose replacing Roosevelt with one in the Western subdivision of Miller-Orchard. One parent was quoted in the *Press-Citizen* as saying that closing Roosevelt was "the equivalent of taking an inner-city school and moving it to the suburbs. It marginalizes us" (Daniel, 2009b).

Public meetings to discuss the closure attracted, on average, about 150 parents and community members to speak out against the proposal. Most of this coverage focused on district officials and parents: some residents worried their children would no longer experience short commutes to school; others were concerned about the safety of moving too many students from Roosevelt into other, already crowded, schools; while others spoke of not wanting to lose Roosevelt as an historic fixture. (This debate continues in 2014.)

The core of most early concerns, though, seemed to surround finding solutions to racial and economic inequalities in the community that stop Southeast Side students from spilling out into the rest of the city or that would stop some of the Roosevelt students from being in schools with Southeast Siders. The Roosevelt closing, after all, would require a smaller form of redistricting to move these students elsewhere, and, rightfully so, the closing served as an initial step for more widespread school boundary changes.

Because news coverage of the Roosevelt closing occurred during a period of racial tension surrounding the Southeast Side and would later serve as one of the several issues that I would use to conduct a news analysis for this project, I spoke with local journalists then to gather their perceptions about how the school closing fit within the larger Southeast Side discussion.

In the summer of 2010, Jeff Charis-Carlson, the opinion page editor at the *Press-Citizen*, told me that the overlap of schools and the Southeast Side revolved around low test scores in the Southeastern neighborhood and particularly the "urban migrants coming into the Iowa City area from schools that are less academically rigorous or more dangerous," Charis-Carlson said. How these students adapt to their new environment—or how they are perceived to adapt—Charis-Carlson said, places upon the students dominant beliefs about inner-city youth as being violent and, in Iowa City, threatening.

"When they arrive in town, (the children) don't know the 'unwritten rules' of social decorum or how to get along in schools," he said. "What's acceptable in a large, urban metropolitan area where there's a lot more anonymity that's afforded to the average person and what's acceptable in Iowa City are very different, because people are watching them." Discussions of closing schools and altering which students attend which schools brings about concerns of how the local educational system will balance two of its seemingly competing functions—creating equality and reducing an educational "achievement gap" among newly arriving students that, if not harnessed, could deplete learning among all students (Jencks and Phillips, 1998).

The "achievement gap," while focused on the interest and performance of students within schools, has become a talking point for ideologies focused on widening racial and class barriers as a means by which to ignore larger structural and institutional racism. Standardized testing, for instance, which provides data-as-evidence for implementing racist institutional policies within education (such as the school-to-prison pipeline) uses fear and intimidation of "failure" that's inherent in any "bad test results" as a means to "motivate" both students and teachers (Chilcott and Guggenheim, 2010). Yet while testing is supposed to measure everyone on the same topics in the same testing conditions at the same time and in the same manner to achieve a form of equality, testing becomes a rhetorical move to reveal both efforts to equalize (or standardize) means of measuring learning and as an attempt to "measure" the achievement gap (for overview, see Ravitch, 2010).

In turn, the achievement gap—and those that the gap celebrates and those it demonizes—influences public treatments of youth and residents of particular neighborhoods: "performing" students are said to have strong families, a dedication to education, and safe streets while those who "underperform" come from bad homes, are lazy, live among social disorder, or suffer from deficiencies because they share classrooms and resources with less motivated and capable students. Indeed, neighborhood segregation, unequal economic distribution across geographies and races, and policies that punish minority students at greater rates than non-minorities have led some educators to conclude that, by and large, black students arrive to school already less prepared than their white counterparts. As a broad discussion, debate about the achievement gap, however, has been co-opted by data that support cultural reasons for differences and ignore structural influences that start some students off in life later or slower than others.

Public documents such as the *Moynihan Report*, the *Coleman Report*, No Child Left Behind data, and *The Bell Curve* have resulted in a score of public debates and perceptions that are focused on cultural explanations and blame the victims of structural oppression. What we are left with, then, are dominant perceptions, including some that contradict others, that include: (1) whites learn more—and better—than blacks do in school, (2) black students are opposed to white teachers and education in general, as education is perceived within "their community" to be unimportant, (3) black parents and communities urge black students away from school by endorsing poor classroom behavior and hindering the desire of black students to learn, and (4) testing that determines a student's academic status (intellect) and tracks the student's progression in school are fair, unbiased, and the most equal method of measuring student achievement, their personal interest in education, and the ability of schools to adequately educate.

Yet few of the dominant perceptions regarding education—particularly regarding black education—focus on an established history of how education represents power and resistance in many black communities. Just like Nell, whose story started this chapter, educational institutions persist in presenting barriers for black learning by applying dominant perceptions of black youth as being counter to positive elements of schools.

Though much education existed in secret while blacks were in the bonds of slavery, more overt efforts to educate themselves spread from plantations during Reconstruction. With few resources, blacks themselves paid for much of their own schooling—building structures, funding teachers, and by providing whatever means necessary for their children to be schooled. While whites largely controlled much of what blacks could learn and which teachers and administrators would conduct the lessons, former southern slaves built their own school buildings and sent their children to school (Anderson, 1988).

If these stories of black education were shared in history books, celebrated by all educators, and used as examples of dedication and commitment to both community and education, then they might alter how dominant culture explains educational disparities. Instead, news discourse about neighborhood schools in Iowa City continue to report on the usual suspects when it comes to schools—dramatic stories from government officials about pending danger from darkening classrooms, tales about the necessity of having police in schools, and language related to school disorder across the nation that surrounds vague language of disorder, such as "'insubordination,' 'disobedience,' 'inappropriate language or behavior,' 'verbal assault,' 'offensive language,' or 'gang-related activity'" (Kim, Losen and Hewitt, 2010, p. 86).

Indeed, few teachers and experts on education other than school board members and district administrators still appear in news articles about what is best for neighborhoods and local education. Surprisingly, the school-related discourse rarely overtly discusses the Southeast Side, though that place is at the center of the real issues regarding local schools in that parents are concerned how students from that neighborhood will negatively influence students across the city.

For example, stories about parents leading efforts to keep Roosevelt open in 2010—culminating with community members donning "We Are Roosevelt" tee-shirts to board meetings—became more about the process of how a decision to close Roosevelt would happen than about the closing itself. When Roosevelt finally closed in 2011, it was called a "jewel of the city" and a "microcosm of global society" (Crews, 2012). The school reopened the next year as Theodore Roosevelt Education Center, an "individual needs" school that works with students with behavioral problems.

Still, debate over closing Roosevelt as a neighborhood school revealed several conflicts in the community, including a distrust of public institutions to make decisions that were best for the public, subtle racism in discourse about the purpose of schools and how they represent people in neighborhoods throughout the city, and the role of the news to serve as an independent forum to address community needs. Finally, the Roosevelt debate opened the doors to seeing schools as being directly influenced by the types of people who live in the neighborhoods that the schools serve, particularly students that come from low-income families and who might undermine the ability of the school to best serve all students. Such a discussion became more apparent later in 2009 and 2010 when the school district began its full-fledged redistricting effort.

Redistricting: School Boundaries as Racial Lines

As in its coverage of Roosevelt in which news media turned to the nostalgia of the old school and the loud voices coming from the community at the time of the debate to save it, news stories about redistricting focused on the process, not the people—revealing the power of the connection between the news institution and other formal institutions within a community, such as a school board or city council. Redistricting served as another issue in the news that contributed to my analysis for this book in that journalists discussed neighborhood schools with the same kind of nostalgia as was applied to the city overall in other debates about how new arrivals from Chicago were altering a local sense of community. In discussions about both Roosevelt and redistricting, then, the Southeast Side became a place that represented change that was seemingly, and for some reason designed, to destroy the traditional ways of living—and schooling—in Iowa City.

Newspapers continually used the efforts of parents and other community members to broaden the conversation over the closure of Roosevelt and redistricting and focused not on creating schools for the city's future that will almost surely continue to diversify, but on how to form schools that would keep things the same in terms of the community's dominant cultural values. Duncan Stewart, a long-time Iowa City resident and a guest columnist for the *Press-Citizen*'s Writer's Group, told me in the summer of 2010 that the closing of Roosevelt and discussion about school redistricting revealed how "the racial thing has really come to a head in the last couple years." Those who voice concerns about changing school boundaries are, in effect, commenting about the Southeast Side, its racial demographics, and fears associated with people living there, Stewart told me.

"To see your neighborhood change quite dramatically and have the prototypical 'other' come in, most people are resistant to change," he said. "If your neighbors are playing loud rap music or if they look threating because it's a cultural thing to stand together on the corner and talk late into the night ... whether you agree with the implicit threat they see in the change is another thing, but I think it's a mistake to deny that things have changed."

Stewart—who'd written about local and national politics from the perspective of a self-proclaimed liberal Iowa City townie for the *Press-Citizen*—said that despite the influence redistricting would have on neighborhood schools, it was a topic so connected to controversy about race that he "stayed away from" writing about the process. "I don't think there's a middle ground on race," he told me. "It's easier to bash George Bush or the war in Iraq than to talk about racial issues in your own back yard."

Emotional elements surrounding debates on race in Iowa City made statistical data about schools that much more important for journalists and officials as some kind of "objective" characterization of the Southeast Side, neighborhood schools, and pending changes to the community. In compliance with the No Child Left Behind legislation, the Iowa City school district compiled data on its students and schools, and in correspondence between the Iowa City School Board and the Iowa City City Council, specifically identified data on poverty in Iowa City's schools.

In correspondence with local governmental agencies, the school district defined poverty within the schools as the number of students who received free and reduced lunches during the 2003–2004 academic year. Such data from Iowa's Department of Education, the Census, and the school district itself, revealed specific geographies with the highest numbers of students receiving free and reduced lunch.

Indeed, an analysis of DOE data from the 2009–2010 and 2005–2006 school years shows the further South one gets in the school district, the more diverse the schools become based on socioeconomic status and race, specifically in the representation of blacks in the schools. More precisely, percentages of poverty ranged from 1 percent at Shimek Elementary on the city's far North Side and those schools which had more than 40 percent of children in poverty, including Roosevelt Elementary in the city's Southwestern Side (40 percent), and Mann Elementary, just north of downtown (44 percent).

Two of the schools with the highest levels of students receiving free or reduced lunches were in or near the Southeast Side of the city, attending Mark Twain Elementary (57 percent) and Grant Wood Elementary (43 percent). Grant Wood, Mark Twain, and Roosevelt scored at least 20 points below schools in other geographic areas of the district, such as Hoover and Penn, in the percent of fourth grade students found to be proficient in the time period of 2006 to 2008.

But, as most of this book has argued, data alone can't explain all social and cultural elements of neighborhoods and communities, despite the wishes of officials, journalists, and experts (for review, see Zuberi and Bonilla-Silva, 2008). Instead, how schools define race, poverty, and academic achievement is based on rhetoric of its own. For example, *socioeconomic status* (SES), a complex understanding of racial, ethnic, and economic factors, is also an essential—yet complicated—characteristic of the district. Furthermore, that the city and region are home to universities may also skew the understanding of who makes up the workforce and the overall community by attracting formally educated and highly paid faculty, a transient student population, and a service-sector workforce.

With this understanding, it's difficult, then, to meaningfully quantify the influences that shape these communities and create the diverse student body that is entering the schools within a single district. Nevertheless, visiting the wide macro-level demographics of this district sets the stage to understanding the multiple complex socio-cultural elements that community leaders and members may face when discussing complex political and social issues, such as equality in the schools.

Additionally, data that emerge from racial categorization and that are used as primary sources for interpreting social conditions and have been discussed in this project further white supremacy by serving as a veil for racialized explanations of the world that benefit whites. Indeed, as Alexander (2010) writes, data help explain the world in simplistic language that allow the public to ignore "that racism manifests itself not only in individual attitudes and stereotypes, but also in the basic structure of society" (p. 179), and that these structures are based on narratives rooted in racist versions of history. She writes that

> [i]t is far more convenient to imagine that a majority of young African American men in urban areas freely choose a life of crime than to accept the real possibility that their lives were structured in a way that virtually guaranteed their early admission into a system from which they can never escape [p. 179].

Furthermore, the social construction of race is not clearly recognizable in quantitative data. Race is an individual definition, and racial categorization and its meaning to the individual is lost in the collection and interpretation of solely demographic data (Omi and Winant, 1994). Also included in the conversation of school boundaries was the idea of neighborhood schools, though a consistent definition of what that term means to this district and what it looks like within the idea of demographics is unclear.

Demographic categorization—and particularly the ambiguous definitions of "race," "neighborhood schools," and even the idea of diversity itself—is one understanding of the confusing and complex framework through which one can note the diversity of communities within the community. Categorizing students based on race and neighborhoods based on school performance serves as a rhetorical distraction from creating "the other" by adding another layer of controversy at an institutional level that matched a level of authority and officials, a process that occurred during coverage of both city school issues and Southeast Side violence in 2009 and 2010.

Themes of socioeconomic and racial diversity that have emerged in the public conversation about the closing of Roosevelt remains alive and well to frame the rhetoric throughout the public process of redistricting. Roosevelt's disparities identified by the Iowa Department of Education—that the school had a high level of minority and low-income students—also began an evaluation of student populations elsewhere in the district.

That these sets of coverage occurred simultaneously and in similar ways embedded narratives of "the inner city" and normative explanations of school data without looking at history, economic and structural inequalities, or including the personal stories of those who were being written about. In this way, then, news coverage and public discourse about Iowa City schools represents the role of color blindness in modern society and shows how ignoring race in discussions that very much have to do with race was a common element of press coverage about the city's Southeast Side.

Conclusion

In this chapter, I have attempted to complicate otherwise simple stories about the role of schools in our nation—and in our neighborhoods—particularly in terms of Iowa City's Southeast Side. Much of the coverage of city schools focused on the deterioration of the community as a whole. The very reasons for Roosevelt's closing and for redistricting, then, were related to the same influx of new residents to Iowa City—particularly those from Chicago—who bring learning challenges and their low-income households that present an added pressure for local schools to maintain an equal education for all students.

In turn, coverage of schools, which very much focused on maintaining or improving city neighborhoods directly, contributed to news place-making in that the Southeast Side and its schools served as an ideograph to frame the fear and concern related to redistricting the changing community. Indeed, that the news coverage avoided overt discussion about race relations in the city and instead focused on Manoff's (1986) *shadow texts*—such as "SES," "free and reduced lunch" and "failing schools" to reveal an intentionality of how the press shape public discourse. Moreover, this language and these stories about the importance of local control over education, the value of neighborhood schools, and the purpose of redistricting work on the back of history and embedded ideologies based in racial tensions.

In this conclusion, I argue that the rhetoric about local schools—and, in fact, the very school issues in Iowa City at the time—was based in elements of white supremacy, particularly the elements of control that were rooted in placing the interests and futures of whites above non-whites. To a degree, the ways in which the press covered these issues revolved around a form of what educators call *oppositional culture* (Ogbu, 2004)—the belief that blacks oppose (and therefore don't deserve) education, in part because achieving in school is a form of "acting white" (Tyson, Darity and Castellino, 2005). Oppositional culture further suggests that in an attempt to "act black" and oppose education, these students are disruptive in school, fail to learn and, most importantly, impede the educations of others—in this case, white students.

Here, I'm not as interested in debating the merits of oppositional culture as much as I wish to present the ways in which the concept is applied as a cultural truism that then simplifies people's understandings of how students interact with teachers, educational structures, and how the public misplaces explanations for student performance.

Oppositional culture is presented within education as the sole answer that relates to a pathological cultural (and sometimes biological) explanation for social ills of a community—and of a student. Let it be made clear, then: the answers to questions of performance, perceived behavior, parental and community influences on children, public perceptions informed by personal experiences and media exposure, the role of teachers and the forces of testing combine within a complex set of issues that may not be simply explained by returning to issues of pathology and culture (see discussion in Lewis, 1963/1998; Wilson, 1997).

The veracity of oppositional culture has been scrutinized (for discussion, see Ainsworth-Darnell and Downey, 1998; Diamond, Lewis and Gordon, 2007; Farkas, Lleras and Maczuga, 2002), yet oppositional culture supporters turn to test scores that show urban blacks are performing well below whites as evidence to apply their notions of "black culture" and accompanying sociological meanings to show an "achievement gap." However, these supporters haven't adequately addressed the cultural and social constructions of standardized tests themselves, which further complicate the understanding of individuals' academic abilities and interests based, in part, on race (Santelices and Wilson, 2010). Other scholarship—including ethnographic research –further explores potential meanings behind not just testing, but that deals with other challenges within schools and students' lives (for example, see Harris, 2006; MacLeod, 1995; Maly, 2005).

Yet it's our commitment to cultural (not institutional) answers to social and individual problems that influences discourse and debate about social conditions. Sociological methods have revealed that cultural explanations rooted in nativist ideology dominate a hegemonic structure used to reinforce itself throughout sectors of society, including education, as discussed in Chapters 6 and 7.

These forms of cultural determinism—which both appear to rely on cultural narratives that say blacks are largely deviant, dangerous, ghettoized, etc. (Fairclough, 2008; Hirsch, 2002; Skogan, 1990; Wilson, 1997; 2009)—position education as being for whites and not for blacks. Harkening back to attempts at the country's quest for separate-but-equal schools, this dynamic creates a tense educational environment in which blacks have been suggested to perform below their white peers.

Perhaps more than anything, the research about our schools that applies most to the case of Iowa City and how the public and news media talk about education is the work that looks at white culture's expectations of minority students. Such research is particularly strong in terms of the teacher/student relationship. Indeed, it's been suggested that teacher perception of students based upon race and class influence student performance (Downey and Pribesh, 2004), and while oppositional culture does include the teacher as a dynamic figure within the conflict between herself and the student, the student is suggested to have opposition to the teacher, not vice versa. Still, there's no clear consensus or conclusion for a silver-bullet status of oppositional culture. Conversations with students and teachers, community members and parents, reveal the complexity of social phenomena and individual decision-making that the press misses in its overarching story about bad neighborhoods, such as the Southeast Side.

In this discussion, school news in local press was shown to have performed a geographic and ideological function. Rhetoric assigned to school performance and the students, parents, and neighborhoods that funneled into the schools was similarly hostile toward notions of expanding educational opportunities to all people in Iowa City. Additionally, had the school news carried the same level of overt racialized discourse as did coverage of the Southeast Side, the school news would have been revealed as serving a particular rhetorical function. Instead, its hegemonic subtleness that further contributes to my argument of how news place-making is a complex and intentional tool that shapes notions of places and people—even when the reports are suggested to be about completely different stories.

Conclusion

On the Role of News, Place and Being Human

A one-way bus ticket from Chicago to Iowa City costs about $30. Five hours and a couple of stops later, someone from the Windy City can arrive at a stretch of sidewalk outside Iowa City's bus depot. That's a pretty cheap and convenient way out of the ghetto. The only problem is that the ticket lands someone in a place where they aren't welcome.

In this Conclusion, I summarize the major themes associated with how local press discourses characterized the Southeast Side as a black, inner-city ghetto. I then surmise as to the reasons why. In this discussion, I present place as being a racial identifier and further explicate my notion of news place-making. Next, I provide practical changes journalists could make in covering neighborhoods, communities, and geographies to address how dominant ideologies and journalistic practices characterize place in the news. I end the chapter with a brief discussion on the future of the Southeast Side and future areas of research on news place-making, which I've identified throughout this project.

How and Why Place Appears in News

As I've argued throughout this book, news media—in collaboration with local policymakers—disinvested in the abilities and rights of those from the Southeast Side in order to complicate the most popular articulations of local city life, particularly in terms of their own neighborhood. In effect, public discourse about community policies regarding neighborhoods, schools, and maintaining the city's traditional values via news media duplicated already complicated racial relationships in the city. Beyond discourse surrounding the city's rapid and radical demographic changes, news constructions of the Southeast Side explained cultural and social changes in that geography through dominant perceptions of danger and deviance of places *other than* the Southeast Side— the ghettos of Chicago. Such action led to several tangible outcomes.

First, by characterizing the Southeast Side as an urban place more similar to stereotypical presentations of other places and inherently different from Iowa City (simply because black people lived in those neighborhoods), local news media separated the Southeast Side from the rest of the community. This separation, then, normalized a difference between the Southeast Side and other neighborhoods, dividing a sense of community throughout the city and allowing those areas outside of the Southeast Side to remain ideologically distant.

Second, news coverage that focused on "outside" sources to explain social conditions "inside" the Southeast Side confused perceptions of who can claim "the right" to define city spaces, their neighborhoods, and their people. This extension of authority by journalists as dominant community storytellers to official sources resulted in the avoidance of residents who are authorities on their own neighborhoods.

Third, place-making served as a fundamental ideological function of the press to explain everyday life, to discuss issues of race, and to embed culturally dominant understandings of white supremacy. Lastly, the ideological power of the Southeast-Side-as-place, itself, became so strongly connected to its black residents that place meanings were affixed to people who even looked like they were "from the Southeast Side." In other words, black folk and places where black folk appeared in Iowa City, such as the Los Cocos restaurant and the city's downtown bus stop, spaces that were discussed earlier in the book, became understood via the fluidity of racialized place. The bus stop was no longer a bus stop, but a sign of the Southeast Side; Los Cocos was no longer a restaurant or club, but a black hangout.

The Southeast Side as a racialized place was also constructed by news about other local places, such as the city's downtown, and news about other violence in the city. In 2008, for instance, a white father murdered his wife and four children in a McMansion on Iowa City's East Side. Police reports indicate that the father beat his family with a baseball bat or another blunt object (KCRG, 2009). He then killed himself by driving his van into concrete on the Interstate. The father of his adopted children, who were aged three to ten, was said to be a family man and community steward. He had also been charged with embezzling more than $550,000 from a local bank where he was an executive.

Yet, despite the heinous crime, news media never hosted a conversation about the effects of bank fraud (i.e., don't do it), about values associated with adoption (i.e., "people who adopt..."), about being white (i.e., "white people..."), or about living in a wealthy subdivision (i.e., "that place is...").

There are several reasons why this brutal murder in a wealthy subdivision of America's Heartland received different treatment in news media than the killing of a white landlord by a black man on the city's Southeast Side. First, one could argue that the family's murder was an isolated event. But so are crimes dealing with drugs, assault, and general mischief—at least throughout all of Iowa City. Overall, it's unusual for murders in Iowa City and Johnson County as a whole (which includes several cities and towns)—there have been fewer than 10 murders between 2008 and 2014 and it was rare for incidents of other major crimes to exceed double digits (Hermiston, 2013). Second, only one person was accused of murdering of an entire family, whereas in the Southeast Side, several people were believed to be involved in stories of general disorder.

Third, the family man was a long-time Iowa resident with roots in the community and a wide family and social circle. On the other hand, "people from Chicago" who settle in the Southeast Side are just that—they are not *from here*, they are not *of us*, this is not *their community*, and they will (hopefully) go away. Lastly, of course, one could argue that news treated these events differently because the father was white and Southeast Siders (at least according to news reports) are black. Could it be that simple?

Consider that it might be. After all, most people in Iowa City probably don't think that much about the Southeast Side or the other areas of the city that are less desirable every day unless the places emerge in public discussion connected to some news event or crime in that neighborhood and particularly among its black residents. People who either don't think about the Southeast Side or would say they don't know anything about that neighborhood (including where it is) but *who do* know or *who have heard* it is a black neighborhood are among those I call *intentionally ignorant*.

In law, this concept may be considered *willful blindness* in which a person avoids learning certain information to avoid liability, and my conceptualization is similar. In fact, as I've discussed throughout this book, several of the local journalists and city officials—including police officers—said that they avoid areas or show no interest in parts of the city that they do not need to enter or that they already believe they "know about"; in almost all of the mental maps of Iowa City by officials and journalists, the Southeast Side was either empty, said to be devious or unimportant—even though those participants regularly interacted with news, data, and discussion about the Southeast Side in their jobs.

Of course, residents also had blank spaces on their maps and told me that they knew even less about the wider geographies of Iowa City than people who were more integrated in the broader community, and said much of the city wasn't important to their daily lives. However, I'm much more concerned with the responsibility that dominant storytellers in the city have to experience a space in order to represent its complexities in media, since they are the ones, after all, charged with influencing dominant understandings of social issues and spaces.

Understanding how media characterize place—and how media producers experience those places both ideologically and in person—becomes even more important in a time when mainstream media further extend their use of geotechnologies and cross more geographic divides, all the while operating within an age of color blindness in which place is increasingly being used as a racial identifier.

Place as Racial Identifier?

Journalists are often taught to not identify an individual's race in a news story unless race is crucial to the story and are encouraged by journalistic standards to avoid writing stories that highlight race for no reason. Take this fake example: "Police say a dark-skinned black man broke into the bank at 1 a.m. and took $50,000." The argument goes that journalists would be less likely to write "a white man broke into the bank," because "white" is rarely used as an identifiable feature. In our fake bank robbery story here, for instance, mentioning race would be an accepted journalistic practice only if it was among the robber's multiple other identifiers. Try: "Police say the man appeared to be black, tall, wearing a red shirt and a black baseball cap. He also had a scar on his right cheek."

Journalists seem to agree that stories that identify only those suspects with clear racial features by perceived race (and mainly those with dark skin) further polarizes society. (As an aside, next time you hear news stories that say alleged perpetrators of crimes that occur at night "appear to have dark skin," remember that anyone's skin appears darker at night.) Through the lens of news place-making that centers geography as an ideological feature of news discourse, I argue that proper names of places, such as Chicago, can also hold its own racialized meaning and that, in some cases, geographic locations have become a new racial identifier.

Consider this 2011 headline from *The Gazette* and its corresponding television station, KCRG: "Chicago Man Accused of Coralville Robbery Now Behind Bars" (KCRG, 2011). Combine the headline with the story's opening sentence: "Johnson County Sheriff's Office reports indicate that a 21-year-old

Chicago man accused of participating in an armed robbery at 708 18th Avenue, Coralville, in 2009 is now behind bars at the Johnson County Jail." What does it matter that the man is from Chicago?

Before answering, also consider that (1) news articles about affordable housing, city council candidates, and crime South of Iowa City's Highway 6 are full of reader comments that affordable housing options have attracted droves of poor, deviant blacks from Chicago, thereby transplanting the "ghetto" from one place (Chicago) to another (Iowa City); (2) a story about a reported shooting on the city's "Southeast Side" in May 2011 reveals the connection people are making between violence and Chicago (Pennington, 2011). As one reader commented on the story to another user:

> ... you have to admit there's increasing crime in the cr/ic (Cedar Rapids/Iowa City) corridor and it just soo [*sic*] happens many of the criminals are black and formally [*sic*] or currently from Chicago. I wish it wasn't so but its [*sic*] true. Find statistics that state otherwise and I will shut up.

And another, (3):

> ... people bellyache about "Chicago" as a code for "black." And, living in Iowa City/Coralville, you can't throw dirty dishwater out a window and not hit a FIB (nice translation: "Foolish Illinois Buffoon") who's attending Iowa on Mommy and Daddy's dime. No one gripes about white Chicago-land suburbanites... [parenthesis in original].

In news and other public discourses about issues of race and place in Iowa City, it seems fairly clear that "Chicago" holds more meaning than just a geographic location. Indeed, as Figure C.1 indicates, I have used research on meanings associated with major places that have been called upon in the construction of the Southeast Side, including Chicago, and mythologies of Africa that have informed mainstream, dominant ideologies in the U.S. associated with media coverage of blacks, where they live in the U.S., and what they do in life (Abel, 2010; Ewen and Ewen, 2008) to help answer our question from above.

Indeed, if it's true that "Chicago" holds a negative connotation about local blacks among the general public, as I believe it does—and as several journalists, officials, and residents have revealed for this project (see Chapters 5 and 6)—then what responsibility do journalists have in reporting the news via such a code? Richard Pratt, a content editor at thegazette.com, who I talked to about the use of "Chicago" in headlines, says journalists have no responsibility in this respect. Printing geographic locations in website headlines, he said, is more about identifying location, not cultural position. "We're not attempting to characterize newsmakers from being from urban area or bringing any specific problems to the community," Pratt told me in 2011.

Instead, the website, Pratt said, is "more likely to score more highly if

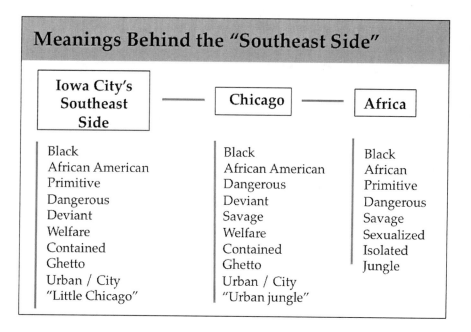

FIGURE C.1. Previous research and popular discourses reveal rhetorical foundations for building the "Southeast Side."

people are looking for news" based on location and keywords, and any interpretation of what location may mean (such as the notion of "Chicago," as "black, "The Inner City," the spot of crime) is made by the reader—not journalists.

But when does a reporter and her news outlet need to evaluate the cultural meanings within words—especially about space and place—in terms of what those codes may say about where we live and those we live with? Journalists I spoke with for this project argued that perceptions about location didn't matter in how they covered the Southeast Side. Journalists acknowledged the coverage of the Southeast Side and the "Chicago migration" had been brewing for years, building the same narrative that they ascribed to Iowa City's Southeastern neighborhood in 2009 and 2010.

For instance, this very study could have traced a history of urban narratives in Iowa that extends further back than recent events. Indeed, a *Des Moines Register* article from 2004 details a now-familiar narrative about life in Chicago and quotes Zaida Cruz, a black, unmarried mother who moved "from the trauma of ghetto life" to Iowa about finding food stamps and health insurance for her children that's "covered by a federal program" (Rood, 2004). The story, part of a series on efforts by the state to "lure highwage, highly educated workers to Iowa," however, also attacks "[m]ost newcomers [who] have been like Cruz: poor and looking for opportunities."

The *Register*'s story continues by presenting Iowa's potential for helping cure residents from the ills of the inner city ghetto:

> Were it not for desperation, Zaida Cruz might have stayed indefinitely in the only neighborhood she had known, on Chicago's rough west side. But last year, the former movietheater worker [*sic*] had no job, no home and no way to protect her family.
>
> With $7 in her pocket and three children under the age of 6, Cruz boarded a Greyhound bus bound for Iowa City. The former gang member told herself she would stay long enough to get back on her feet, then head home.

Cruz, who was 24 at the time, is quoted as saying, "When you come to Iowa and see all the good things out here, you think of Chicago and you wonder: Man, how did I live like that?" It's the nostalgia of Iowa's Midwestern ways of life that drew Cruz in, a nod to the wholesome Heartland:

> Gangs, who made homicides and beatings everyday events in her neighborhood, afforded Cruz another way of making money: dealing drugs. Cruz's longtime boyfriend, the father of her children, also sold drugs and wound up behind bars.
>
> "People have to eat; people have to survive," Cruz said. "Where I came from, people ... can't provide for their families, so what's the next step? Selling drugs."

So how do we get journalists to think that location should matter more in how they report the news? Answers to this question elude me. Journalists seem so stuck in their routines and so dedicated to "how we do things" that quite frankly, my approaches to getting them to acknowledge that they might be contributing to social disorder through their racialized reporting would be counterproductive. The question I am more prepared to answer is, "What should journalists do about their reporting that seems to embed the news with racialized meanings, particularly in terms of how they cover place?" To that question, I have several thoughts.

First, I should say that scholars often present recommendations for how journalists should operate, including ideas about improving neighborhood and hyper-local journalism, increasing citizen journalism, enhancing social media to involve the public, and conducting reporting from within particular spaces as a means to embed journalists in the geographies they cover. I will not be making those recommendations as a journalist, nor as a scholar, in part, because those recommendations would seem to have little influence upon the institutionalized influences that have been revealed as having the most impact in *this case* of news place-making.

Instead, I offer a short list of other recommendations that, if implemented, might make some major changes to how journalists work and what they report:

- Journalists should recognize the cultural power of news place-making.
- Journalists should incorporate alternative sources to coverage to begin addressing inequalities in news storytelling that traditionally and consistently places blame on racial and ethnic minorities (Ettema and Peer, 1996; Holt, 2013; Gutsche, 2013).
- Journalists should maintain a focus on social justice reporting to uncover injustices in communities—perhaps even within media itself—and uphold the very tenants of journalism that have attracted many of us to the field in the first place: the ability to provide an independent and open source of information and self-governance (Kovach and Rosenstiel, 2007; Meiklejohn, 1965).
- Journalists should stop talking so much to officials, should question officials' motives and facts on even everyday news items, should confirm officials' and other journalists' explanations about social conditions, and should construct standards of balance between covering the news based on information from officials and residents (Holt and Major, 2010; Naughton, 2013).
- Journalists should stop covering government meetings, reporting directly on police reports and press releases, and consider spending this extra time reporting on stories about the community from the level of the worker, the resident, those who aren't in a spot of "official" power (Bannister and Kearns, 2013; Williamson and Scicchitano, 2013).

Whether or not journalists consider these recommendations, the public should, at the very least, request members of the media respond as to why these recommendations would not work as a means to address inequalities in news coverage. In the end, it's not enough to rely on media to manage itself; the public must make demands on how media cover communities to force local institutions to meet the needs and desires of those our institutions serve.

On Being Human in Iowa

While this study captures a snapshot during a time of cultural change within Iowa City, the dominant news narratives identified in coverage of the Southeast Side are part of an enduring pattern of race and class inequalities in America. Iowa's cultural history and meanings also serve as a starting point for illustrating the importance of capturing moments of change. At a time when our nation is seeing a diminishing white population (in numbers, not in power) and a meshing of communities among all geographies, it's necessary to critically evaluate our past and to frame today in ways that will challenge future revisionists who wish to white-wash history.

WELCOME TO IOWA. Interstate billboards that read "The People of Iowa Welcome You" greet drivers at each of the state's borders. Signs such as this one on the Illinois border advertise Iowa as "Fields of Opportunity." Some new arrivals, however, question the degree to which they are really welcome. Photograph by Andre Brock.

Iowa, then, might have been a surprising place to discuss these changes, but its rural, "homegrown," über–Americanized environment and history makes Iowa the best place for us to acknowledge our current actions as a nation so as to not allow ourselves to forget tomorrow the tragedies we employ today through notions of color blindness in "post-racial" America. Through this book, I have attempted to continue the vein of scholarship that argues modern day racism is a process dedicated to positioning whites as a dominant force and that today's racism is perhaps less overt than in the past, but even more deadly.

It seems that by the time we come to understand any day's modern racism, we are on to the next form of it. Switching up dominant ideas of what racism is and how it operates every time we get close to tearing it apart, revealing its details and shutting it down, cultural leaders find ways of staying ahead, altering institutions, policies, and dominant beliefs to keep us silent and confused, a process Raymond Williams (1977) calls *incorporation*. In Iowa City's case, incorporation appears in a minor change to a bus line that carries kids home, but that doesn't deal with larger issues of inequality in transportation, housing, classroom conflict, and outrageous police action.

Iowa City's is a complicated story, and what concerns me the most is how the story will end. In other words, will Iowa City ever be able to escape from the myths that have divided its residents, both by skin color and geography? Some efforts have attempted to create calm and inclusion in Iowa City, using art as activism. Middle and high school art teachers have led group and public projects to paint and install—even temporarily—art designed to create discourse. Murals led by local artist Daniel Kinney have appeared in the Wetherby Park shelter, inside the Broadway Street Neighborhood Center. Separately, a cluster of Southeast Junior High School students also gathered in 2011 to create a heart shape for an aerial photograph to celebrate diversity.

Issues related to the Southeast Side gained even more attention in 2011 when more than 600 people turned out to a public screening of *Black American Gothic*, a documentary that featured local voices in the Chicago-to-Iowa City migration. Following the film, screened at the local Landlocked Film Festival, about 100 people met in small groups throughout the downtown to discuss *Black American Gothic* and the racial issues it addressed.

In 2012, the stories and words of Southeast Side residents appeared in a unique way that tried to complicate dominant explanations of how Iowa City was changing—*Mayberry*, a play based on one of its main characters, a white redhead puppet by the same name, and her journey to understand the city's changing culture. In the play, Mayberry is a perfect Iowan: she's innocent, honest, humble, and cheery—but not *too cheery*. Like all characters in the play, her dialogue came from interviews producers had conducted with Iowa City residents that focused on color blindness, banishment, and hatred.

Perhaps more than any of the discourse presented in *Mayberry*, the voices of white longtime Iowa Citians said the most about how the city is challenged by its recent changes. One character—a white farmer and long-time Iowan named Schrader [*sic*]—tells the audience that his people are about the land, the soil, and uphold the dominant traditions of Iowa as being a wholesome, hardworking place.

He wears jeans, a green John Deere baseball cap and carries a pail he uses to feed cattle when he delivers his monologue:

> I'll accept anyone into this community... if they are willing to give back. A community is not every man for himself. It's not separate parts of town and to each their own. A community is every man for each other. It's not leave them alone and let them do their own thing. You do that with guests. With people visiting, not staying. My family built this house—if we're talking about Iowa City—so if you're staying help me put out the sheets. Help me make the bed. Otherwise

MAYBERRY. The 2012 play *Mayberry* focused on stories of newly arrived blacks to Iowa City, segregation on the Southeast Side, and the city's challenge to adapt to change. Photograph by Alicia Kramme.

have a nice visit. You're a visitor. And well, you're gonna be treated as such [Lewis, 2012, p. 28].

Other narratives in the play presented the veiled racism that appears in discourse about Chicago migrants. For instance, Moira—one of the play's white liberals who tells the audience she has "an Obama bumpersticker"— discusses, before she moves off stage that:

[A] town can't just be given over. And as much as we think no one owns a town, well, we know that's not true. Highway 6 owns this town. If you live on one side of the Highway you're one kind of Iowa City-ian [*sic*], on the other side you're another. In the eyes of others. Of course. But the people moving in ... share a lot of the same former addresses the Robert Taylor Homes, the Cabrini-Green Homes... [p. 13].

But *Mayberry* is more about the conversations and perceptions of people who aren't welcome in Iowa City, or in the state as a whole, and who have a right to feel that way, said the play's writer and director, Sean Christopher Lewis. "The changing dynamics of this state is one of the major reasons we started this theater company," Lewis told a reporter in 2012 (Nollen, 2012).

"We kept seeing how West Liberty and Columbus Junction [two cities near Iowa City that have seen an increase in their Latino population] are changing. What's happening in Iowa City is not different from what's happening in Des Moines with displaced populations. We just found it really fascinating."

Lewis and his team spent a year in Iowa City, interviewing new and old residents, white and black, and working with high school students who, Lewis said, were open and honest about their experiences in the city. Lewis and his wife, Jennifer Fawcett, also moved to the Southeast Side as they prepared for the play, creating characters based, in part, on their neighbors, students, local activists, and city officials.

Perhaps more than anything, though, wide audiences seemed to be drawn to the play for its black voices—those that seemed to be presented as representing all black folk in Iowa City and that addressed the Chicago migration. Here's J. Dope, a black man in a red hoodie, talking about what's discussed as a mass exodus of black folk from Chicago. "Fuck Chicago," he says:

> All the papers up there brag about crime going down—well, of course! A quarter of your population lives in Madison, Wisconsin. A quarter live in Iowa City. A quarter live in the Quad Cities ... that's not change. That's re-arranging the deck chairs. It's throwing your trash on someone else's lawn [p. 21].

Dope's comments obviously occurred prior to the 2012 increase of violence in Chicago, but the details of the city's crime isn't his point: Dope is one of several characters that reveal the frustration on the parts of new arrivals to Iowa City in how whites view and frame blacks—even those who were born and lived in Iowa City their whole lives—as being other-than-Iowan. Yet, it isn't like the play is the first time these ideas have been presented to the community.

Ironically, if Lewis had set *Mayberry*'s script next to public documents and reports on the quality of life in Iowa City and the Southeast Side from over the last 10 years, he'd (unfortunately) never have had to conduct a single interview for the play. Quotes from Southeast Side residents that they need more sidewalks to move about the city, more time to cross between streams of speeding traffic on Highway 6 so that they can become better integrated with the community, improved access to the city's stores and its public services, and the ability to shape dominant media narratives about their neighborhood appear in a stack of local studies as far back as 1999 (Averill, Gates, Hartman and Wellner, 1999; Bailey, Law, Mason, Phillips, 2011; CRJ, 2013; Spears and Landsman, 2004; Spence, Lawson and Visser, 2010). Take these examples from one of the reports (Bailey, Law, Mason, Phillips, 2011):

- "When it's dark it doesn't feel safe because of a lack of streetlights" (p. 28).

- "More buses are needed—transportation without a vehicle is a hindrance" (p. 28).
- [There are] "no Sunday buses—takes forever to get across town—need a shortcut route" (p. 72).
- "People don't know how to drive... sometimes you try to run across [Highway 6], but police complain that you're jaywalking" (p. 27).
- "If kids have been in trouble before, the police will see them and circle around... it makes (them) uncomfortable. They're trying to change, they're supposed to feel safe and secure, not feel tortured. You can't make a move [without them tracking you]" (p. 28, parenthesis and brackets in original).

Where were these comments in news coverage? Why didn't more stories with these kinds of concerns appear? These residents' thoughts would certainly supplement other news stories about inequalities in and around Iowa City, including 2013 news coverage that non-whites accounted for roughly half of the county's jail population, though they make up only 14 percent of county residents.[1] But local press failed to report on the cultural reasons for this discrepancy or even to discuss the influence of such policing on the local community. Instead, journalists turned to local officials, reporting that "local leaders Monday committed to assembling a committee to study ways to address minority overpopulation in the jail" and vowed to "curb that disparity" (Sullivan, 2013). The *Press-Citizen* quoted one city council member as saying that the committee "would focus attention on it, ask ... what the causes of that are, what can be done to alter those arrest rates... There's something wrong or at least on the face of it there appears there may be something wrong in the process."

Project Limitation and Suggestions for Future Research

My hope is that this project, in some form, furthers future work on understanding the construction of news. To that end, several limitations regarding this project should be considered. First, as with any study, it's difficult to ascribe the findings identified here to all journalists and their construction of all places. Therefore, future research should continue to explore how news media shape place and identify how dominant ideologies and power appear in media representations of place. Such research may expose researchers to more complex and nuanced portions of the news place-making process.

Second, I recognize that many interviews for this project were conducted between 2011 and 2014 and my textual analysis focused on news in 2009 and 2010. Had I conducted all interviews in 2009 and 2010, this may have been a very different study in that the responses about place-making would have been more immediate to the news as it appeared. However, for this project I was more concerned with perceptions on the lasting perception of place that was constructed by news media in 2009 and 2010. Still, future research might consider exploring the immediacy of local news coverage in how notions of place complicate explanations of social conditions.

Third, the mental mapping work in this study focused on three sets of participants—journalists, officials, and Southeast Side residents. Save for a couple of interviews, I didn't focus much of this project on long-term residents, youth, college students, or other community members. While these other groups may have provided expanded explanations of place-making, I considered black residents who rely on the Broadway Street Neighborhood Center to be the most vulnerable and stigmatized, affected by negative characterizations of the Southeast Side. Widening the pool of participants to include more sectors of the community, however, may contribute to a broader examination of news place-making and may deepen what otherwise may be considered an oversimplification of place-making in that it focuses on subsets of larger communities of officials, journalists, and Southeast Side residents.

Fourth, this project focuses on place-making of the Southeast Side as a local issue, specific to two or three neighborhoods in one city. Future research on local news place-making may consider the degree to which the inquiry should include perceptions of place from a regional level—particularly if mobility is a factor, such as it was in this case. Indeed, mental maps by journalists and officials who contributed to this study show their interest in cities neighboring Iowa City, with several noting routes they take to cities such as North Liberty, West Branch, and Cedar Rapids. It was also common for participants, including Southeast Side residents, to include the Coralville shopping mall as though it were part of Iowa City itself. Furthermore, the migration from Chicago to Iowa City has expanded to a migration into other cities around Iowa City, making the movement a regional one. Expanding future research to explore regional influences, therefore, might reveal added explanations and descriptions of place-making.

Lastly, future research on news place-making should consider implementing the methodology of mental maps through a feminist lens (as I have lightly attempted here) as a means to make such inquiry a chance to explain, rather than just describe, people's experiences with the power of place. Feminist ethnography, a subfield that focused on issues of power and inequality among women and minorities takes multiple forms—fiction, ethnography, and field notes—though always with consistent acknowledgement of the researcher/participant relationship. It is especially important to the feminist ethnographer that they realize the inherent dangers in "speaking for others."

In these projects, the researcher must recognize her role, her *perceived* role, her entitlement to enter and exit communities and people's lives, to write, ultimately, what she desires, to interpret as she wishes, and be "prepared to be the resented Other to the 'objects' of our study" (Wolf, 1992, p. 13). While this book may not constitute a "true ethnography," it is these approaches through which I presented the counter-stories to Iowa City's Southeast Side and present what some previous scholars call "vindicationism" (Harrison and Harrison, 1999), in which the researcher explores oppression through the desire to undermine racist cultural and structural elements of society.

Mental mapping also gets to the notion of participant involvement, in that the methodology provides an opportunity for participants to offer a deeper understanding of their maps and their stories. Asking people to recreate place in a map and express that map to a researcher attempts to bridge what ethnographers have struggled with—the idea of writing from "here" about people who are "there" (Denzin, 1997; Lewin, 2006; Soja, 2010). Scholars who use this methodology are also able to spur social action by "listening to voices" (Cloke, et al., 2004, p. 30) of those who are being studied. Combined with the textual analysis of news stories, mental mapping provides an analysis of media production and reception that emerges from an interaction of various texts and stories (Bauman, 2004).

My hope is that this project has been successful in reaching a depth of understanding based upon these methods, and as a form of media anthropology, I hope that such an approach can continue to be used as a means to bridge connections between universities, the communities they serve, and those in our institutions that shape our lives—for better or worse—including the press.

Epilogue

Beyond the Southeast Side: News Place-Making Elsewhere

Cairo, Illinois, is built on sand.

Placed in the middle of the confluence of the Ohio and Mississippi Rivers, 60 percent of Cairo's 3,600 residents are black and more than 30 percent live in poverty. The city—pronounced (KAY-roe)—is surrounded by farmland, small towns, and white neighbors. For decades, the rivers have been eating at the riverbanks, pushing against levees. Within its borders, the people of Cairo have been pushing back—keeping water at bay—but finding that the regional economy and racism might ruin the city before the rivers ever do.

Cairo was to be a true river town: a space for business, transportation, tourism, expansion, and recreation. The city's sliver of land is lined by water. At the top is Future City, Illinois, a high school, a port for docked barges and boats along the Ohio River at its east, and slight rapids of the Big Muddy to the west. Highway 51 takes us through the city's main stretch along Washington Avenue that runs parallel to Rev. Martin Luther King Avenue a couple of blocks over. Cairo's southern tip ends at the city-owned land that's gated off when waters rise, a space named after Camp Defiance, a Civil War fortification.

A bustling river town in the 1920s, Cairo's early history represents America's mobility, its resolve, and its ability to recreate natural space into something. Indeed, while initial plans to start the city failed in 1818 (it turns out that it costs a lot of money and support to build a city), Cairo came back in the 1830s and has been around ever since—despite its troubles (Lantz, 1972; Seng, 1982).

The Ohio River had served as the boundary between Jim Crow and the "free" North, a divide that shaped the city's future and has contributed to tensions about what it has become today. Wilkerson (2010) writes about what Cairo was like at the height of the nation's more formalized racial tension. "For a time in the 1920s," she writes, "the ride to Chicago was interrupted after the train crossed the Ohio River into Cairo, as if the train were passing from Poland into the old Soviet Union during the Cold War" (p. 200). As segregated train cars entered the North at Cairo, riders were quickly forced to integrate with the white community in a part of the country where integration might not have been easy, but was at least possible.

But Cairo's possibilities were always questionable—its fate at the mercy of both people and nature. Flood waters of 2008 represented yet another swat at the city. Levees were constructed around the city in the early 1800s, reinforced during the Civil War, and blown by explosives in 1937 to empty out a surging river. That saved Cairo then, but for generations, people have continued to say this town is dying. Some argue it's already dead. Plywood and boards cover rows of downtown buildings. Homes throughout the city are locked and sit empty. Some city streets are more deserted than a river island—one with ready access to water, trees, and open land—should be. Beyond the city and the rivers, farmland stretches deep into the Midwest, and beyond those, the cities of Nashville and St. Louis. Cairo, then, is an enigma that stands out within an area of the country surrounded by a majority of white communities. In early 2011, the city was in danger.

By late April of that year, the rivers at Cairo rose to the highest marks since 1937. Immediately, debate emerged about what to do with the water that stretched through thousands of levees, past islands, and over dams that control the flow, protect homes, create a wildlife refuge, and provide environment for river towns and communities. The levees can protect the city against water up to 64 feet. They are Cairo's only hope.

When waters reached record heights that spring, the surge was already approaching reaches that were a foot above the 1934 level of 60.5 feet. There was no question that the levees would need to be breached to release the pressure (Yount, 2011). The real question, then, for local politicians and the U.S. Army Corp of Engineers, which maintains levees up and down the rivers, was: "Where should the water go—into Illinois or into Missouri?" If the levees were blown on the Missouri side, some 130,000 acres of farmland and 100 homes would be submerged. Chances for successful crops this year and next, perhaps, would be destroyed, and houses may float away. The other option was to blow the levees on the Illinois side, pushing waves of water into Cairo that when settled could be 15 feet high.

As news media had started covering the 2011 flooding of both rivers,

Cairo was just another town mentioned in news stories—until an April 26 press conference, when Cairo became something else; it became a comment on larger, national narratives about race and our cities. At the press conference, Missouri's Republican House Speaker Steve Tilley, sitting in a light-colored suit, focused his comments on concerns about potentially flooding farmland (Stewart, 2011). He was one of the louder voices to save the Missouri farmland—whatever the cost.

"Would you rather have Missouri farmland flooded or Cairo underwater?" a reporter asked Tilley during the press conference.

"Cairo," Tilley said. He didn't blink. "I've been there," he said as reporters chuckled. "Trust me: Cairo."

Smiling, Tilley eyed the gaggle of reporters.

He asked one, "Have you been to Cairo?"

"Yes," replied Rudi Keller, a columnist for the *Columbia Daily Tribune*. "OK, you know what I'm saying, then."

But just what was Tilley *really* saying about Cairo? And how did the reporters "know" what he was saying? How and why was Cairo worth losing?

After political debates between the Attorneys General of Missouri and Illinois, a media frenzy and a full mandatory evacuation of Cairo, the night sky on May 2 erupted in flames as a clay levee at Birds Point, Missouri, was blown. Flashes of fire pushed into the sky after tons of liquid explosives that had been sitting on barges in the Mississippi for days were set and sparked, forming an 11,000-foot hole. Water rushed through.

Certainly, the environmental, agricultural, and economic effect of the rivers burping up millions of gallons of floodwater is in and of itself an important conversation to have. The Mississippi River, for all of its beauty, does unfortunately carry with it deludes of chemicals and toxins that enter the river through farmland runoff. After initial waters flooded thousands of acres of farmland once Birds Point was blown, Missouri officials said insurance costs to cover a year's worth of lost crops for farmers would exceed $300 million. At the same time, farmers whose fields had flooded were initiating lawsuits against the U.S. Army Corp of Engineers for breaching levees.

But conversation around Cairo, its people, future, and *how decisions were made* about sparing "African-American lives over white-owned land"[1] from floodwaters in 2011 is an opportunity to explore the role of race within our smaller communities, rural America, and the way in which cultural narratives and stories we tell about race continue to operate. What happened to Cairo, its promise and its potential as a river town, and what meanings are embedded in a weeks-long debate in the press—one ultimately involving the U.S. Supreme Court—about whether Cairo could be lost?

In this Epilogue, I step away from Iowa City and its Southeast Side to apply news place-making to a historically black Midwestern city—Cairo, Illinois. I present this case as one in which journalists operated within a second level of interpretive community, speaking the same language as their official sources, maintaining an understanding within white institutions about a city that carried a cultural history journalists chose to ignore when covering an official's comments to let Cairo drown. I then place Cairo in a context of discourse about other changing cities in the U.S. and end by returning to the importance of race in how we construct dominant understandings of race and place in the press and schools.

Building Cairo, Racial Tensions and "Little Egypt"

Starting in 1850, the Illinois Central Railroad that connected Chicago to Cairo and to the Deep South and the West through waterways and the expansion of railroads into the plains. As the railway extended from Cairo into Louisiana, Mississippi, and Tennessee, it took with it the banned *Chicago Defender* newspaper, bootlegging into the South its pro-black messages. Later, following World War I, the railroad would provide an escape for blacks wishing to move out of the Jim Crow South.

Cairo had been a port of supply for Northern troops during the Civil War. At the same time, as neighboring counties pushed blacks out—or created laws that excluded them from settling in some communities altogether—Cairo became a haven for blacks from the South. Through the next century, Cairo sat below what historian Charles Colby called the "Dead Line," a space in Illinois that stretched from right below McClure, across to Ullin, Karnak and over to Rosiclare in the southernmost tip of the state, above which blacks were not allowed to live (Loewen, 2005).

Along with the constant influx of African Americans into Cairo, racial tensions in the city and surrounding areas made Cairo one of the many U.S. cities struggling with increased racial integration and recovery following the war. In 1909, racial tensions in Cairo peaked. William James, a black man, was hanged, burnt, and decapitated for being accused of rape after he was hunted into the woods by a white civilian mob that followed the sheriff and captured him.

Herman Lantz's 1972 history of Cairo, *A Community in Search of Itself*, details James' murder, which epitomizes Americans' dominant narrative of lynching:

> A trainload of Cairoites appeared and took the prisoner from the sheriff; they brought the prisoner back to the city and tried to hang him, but the rope broke;

so they shot him, set his body on fire, and mutilated it. They then beheaded the body and planted the head on a stake [p. 76].

Though the numbers are not exhaustive and lynching has been a tool for social dominance and oppression for centuries, between 1882 and 1959, some 4,733 persons had been lynched in the U.S., according to the Tuskegee Institute. Lynching of blacks at the hands of white civilians in particular became a naturalized means of maintaining social order and control within white communities across the country (Hirsch, 2002). Photographs of lynching became so everyday, so commonplace, that they made their way into whites' family photo albums (Abel, 2010).

James' lynching—and the events that led to the lynching—followed traditional patterns associated with white justice; yet, it marks a moment in the history of Cairo that signaled growing pains which would follow Cairo into the 21st Century. In the 1960s, for instance, Cairo became a site of racial resistance, including rioting of blacks against oppression and a boycott by blacks of white-owned businesses in the city (for history, see Seng, 1982).

By 1920, Cairo had a population peak at around 15,200. Cairo's waterways and strategic placement into the West had become a pivotal part of what would soon be demarcated as "Little Egypt," the southernmost tip of Illinois. Stories of how "Little Egypt" emerged as a space revolve around stories including a "common sense" explanation that the region included cities named after Egyptian places, people, or concepts, such as Cairo, Goshen, Karnak, and Thebes (Allen, 2010). The idea of "Little Egypt" would be used to create regional tourism and to stop—or slow—economic decline as the Rust Belt around the Great Lakes continued to attract workers from across the country.

Yet, it's unclear to what degree the branding of "Little Egypt" has shaped—or saved—Cairo and other small communities. Really there is little that branding can do to save a community that's always in a battle to save its very foundation—especially when media support only the dominant and "novel" elements of the community, not its core values and its storied histories: 1937, when Cairo officials blew the city's levees to reduce the stress and strain and prevent catastrophe; the 1950s, when Cairo had lost more than 3,000 people since the 1920s; 1970, when the population declined to roughly 6,000 and then to about 3,600 in 2000; scenes of residents surging together to save the city during floods and racial violence of the 20th century; 2011, when the city ordered a mass evacuation due to swelling rivers and the U.S. Supreme Court intervened to ensure the city—then encompassing a deserted downtown and a population still around 3,000—was once again saved (Gauen, 2011; Munz, 2011).

To some, Cairo and its racial histories and current struggles may seem to have come out of nowhere. The 2008 election of Barack Obama as America's first non-white president fueled conversation about the nation's "post-racial" status. A New Great Migration had also been occurring as thousands of blacks return to Southern states from the North. Before the first Great Migration (1915–1970), in which blacks turned to the highly industrializing North for work and a sense of freedom from generations of overt oppression, more than 90 percent of blacks who lived below the Mason-Dixon Line spread to the West and the North in droves that ultimately equaled some six million blacks (Wilkerson, 2010); by 2010, less than 60 percent of the country's black population lived in the South (Tavernise and Gebeloff, 2011).

Hurricane Katrina in 2005 forced thousands of blacks from New Orleans (the actual numbers are unknown, though estimates place the figure around 140,000). The population of New Orleans shrank by 29 percent (Robertson, 2011). News reports of census data in early 2011 showed that at the time, "the city has roughly 24,000 fewer white residents than it did 10 years ago, though the proportion of the white population has grown to 30 percent" (Robertson, 2011), revealing racialized changes to a city that once claimed a black heritage.

Debate about the destruction of Cairo is a smaller version of other U.S. cities, including Newark, New Jersey; Chicago; Kansas City, Missouri; Los Angeles; and Washington, D.C., that are among a growing list of American cities strained by economic challenges and demographic shifts that have forced cities to stop public service, forced the poor out into the suburbs, and closed schools. Places like Cairo, despite how poorly they match the realities of these other cities in terms of location, size, and demographics, carry with them the dominant narratives set by the other city spaces. Newark, for instance, was the focus of Sundance Channel's documentary *Brick City*, featuring Democrat superstar Corey Booker. Focused on the work of local activists, politicians, and businesses leaders, the film shows a city trying to save itself.

Yet, an *Esquire* magazine article in 2008 revealed the depth of racism, institutions and economic decline that have turned the city into a playground for what the article calls "zombies" and "Zulus" (Raab, 2008). In the piece, author Scott Raab stretches back to the race riots of the 1960s that plagued many U.S. cities, including Newark, and says, simply, that little has changed. Newark, he argues, has yet to recover from the tensions and the construction of a "city yoked for forty brutal years to a self-devouring paradigm of racist thought and cannibal violence." He continues:

> What remained of Newark after the riots—after the last loyal holdouts, too, left town, and after the political clout shifted from the Italians to the blacks, and after the blacks now running the city proved to be as uncaring, incompetent, and corrupt as the Italians; each Newark mayor over the last forty years has

ended his public career as a convicted criminal—was a toxic brew of hopeless rage, rancid pride, and bitter need.

Esquire's article fueled a strong response from Mayor Booker, who was especially critical of Raab's assessment that Newark is "racked by decades of ruin, a town known only for murder, blight and feckless negritude" (Booker, 2008). Yet it is those cultural narratives of African American cities that we return to in order to easily understand social and cultural unrest, disorder, and conflict.

In her analysis of British news coverage surrounding "riots" more than 30 years ago in London, Liverpool, and Manchester (discussed previously in this book), Burgess (1985) reveals that *where the events happened* shaped how news media explained the events—and their causes. That the news media constructed the setting of social unrest as occurring within an urban environment, capitalizing on social perceptions of city space as especially dangerous and devious, Burgess writes, newspapers performed "an ideological role in which a myth is being perpetuated of *The Inner City* as an alien place, separate and isolated, located outside white, middle-class values and environments" (Burgess, p. 193; italics in original).

Burgess' attention to geography and place in terms of how news media and the public discuss social issues continues to occur in public and news discourses about America's urban environments. In this case, the scene that was set by the news media replaced the media's need to focus on the racial and economic tension that led to the violence. It's within similar dialogue—that which focuses on racial cases for economic upheaval and social disorder—that American cities, such as Detroit, have come to epitomize the country's economic challenges that started in 2007 and continue today. Not only is Detroit widely recognized for its large black population, but also as Motor City, home to the automobile industry and mass production that was blamed for the economic recession of the late 2000s.

In 2011, rap star and Detroit-area native, Eminem, responded to attacks on Detroit as being a mecca of financial poison, by appearing in a moving two-minute Super Bowl commercial for Chrysler. In what was titled "Imported from Detroit," which focuses upon the city's history, its work ethic, its potential, and its "luxury," the commercial was just as much about the city as it is the Chrysler 200 it touted. The male narrator's deep voice played over the recognizable interlude to Eminem's popular song "Lose Yourself," tells a tale of a recovering Detroit, a "story" that's "probably not the one you've been reading about in the papers, the one written by folks who've never even been here," as the commercial states. In the voiceover, in fact, the narrator suggests that the luxury in the product they are pimping "is as much about *where it's from* as who it's for" (my emphasis).

A collection of documentaries, books, and newswork has focused on the "decline" and "demise of Detroit." In 2009, *Time* magazine bought and converted a house in Detroit to use as a hub for its Assignment Detroit Project, a collection of news articles, blogs, videos and photographs to detail the city's decline and potential for revitalization. The project lasted for one year when, the next fall, the magazine moved out.

The list of similar work surrounding Detroit continues to grow. The 2010 BBC documentary "Requiem for Detroit" (a play on the 2000 film *Requiem of a Dream*, which focuses on the decline of its four main characters) focused on the decline of an industrial city and its reclamation by the natural environment. Andrew Moore's *Detroit Disassembled*, published in 2010, also provides striking images of this urban exploration throughout much-abandoned Motor City and came to represent a genre of "ruin porn" that celebrates the art of decline but also ignores the social and economic inequalities inherent in such forms of decay.

And in 2013, rebellious, but honest, journalist Charlie LeDuff wrote *Detroit: An American Autopsy*. Detroit's fall from urban grace has been depicted in entertainment media, as well, including ABC's cop show, *Detroit 1-8-7*, a title that refers to the code for murder. However, as Nancy Franklin in *The New Yorker* points out, 1-8-7 is a code for murder in California, not Michigan (Franklin, 2010). But a code from one place was picked up and assigned to another—with the intent of carrying the same message—in the case of Cairo and its people as well: a black population in the middle of the Midwest held the same value as an inner-city ghetto.

Conclusion: Place Through the Lens of Placelessness

It may be easy to understand what Representative Tilley and dozens of other government officials and residents of both Missouri and Illinois meant when they selected flooding Cairo over farmland. It's easy to know what Rep. Tilley meant when he said, "Have you been there? ... Then you know what I am saying, then."

Even if none of us had set foot in or near Cairo, Illinois, we could make a pretty good guess what he meant. Either by reading the newspaper, driving across the deserted urban and rural landscapes of the country (perhaps including some of our own hometowns), or watching popular cable television representations of Baltimore in *The Wire* or about New Orleans in *Treme* and in Spike Lee's documentaries *When the Levees Broke* and *If God Is Willing and Da Creek Don't Rise*, then we've all been to a "Cairo."

And, at least, we all know what Tilley meant: Cairo wasn't worth saving. Maybe the critics of Cairo were right—maybe the town hasn't been worth saving for generations. Similar arguments have been made about other changing spaces within the U.S.—that it is best to abandon public housing projects, such as Cabrini-Green and the Robert Taylor Homes in Chicago. But, in each of these cases, these abandoned (or almost-abandoned) places exist, as publically defined, through imagination and authoritative claims from authoritative people and institutions—the same kind of ideological emptiness and ideological gaps that people have from a lack of experience or deep understanding of place that are then filled with commentary and coverage from, among other sources, the news about *ideas of place* and of *placelessness* (Relph, 1976; Seamon and Sowers, 2008). As Burgess (1985) writes: "Events take place but often the geography of the news remains an unquestioned backcloth to those events" (p. 192).

Indeed, what's missing in storytelling and conversations about our changing neighborhoods, cities, and regions—as both a brief history of Cairo and the previous chapters that focused on the complexities of Iowa City's Southeast Side demonstrate—are the historically informed narratives about race, crime, and space. When the debate about whether to save Cairo (a city of tradition, history, and African American culture) or farmland (farmland that acted as a reproduction of marketplace, economy, and Whiteness) what we see is a recreation and a reconstruction of a past ignored by politicians, the press, and the people of "Little Egypt" and Missouri, alike. In fact, news of Cairo's black history as an indicator of the city's significance did not appear as the focus of news stories about the 2011 crisis until a story appeared online from the Black Entertainment Network (Jones, 2011). That's pretty telling about the role and purpose of mainstream (white) media—and who works in it.

Each day, my students in Iowa (and now in Miami) tell me that race relations in America are better than at any time before: people can drink from the same water fountain, they say. Ride the same buses, they say. They can even (*and do*) date each other. These college students (white, black, Hispanic, alike) push back—hard, sometimes—at the suggestion that their parents (no matter what race) would likely not love them dating a person of another race, particularly if these are white parents with white children.

OK, I'm forced to tell them, maybe they're right about some of those "changes." Indeed, at my university in Miami, Hispanic students represent around 80 percent of the student body. In Miami–Dade County, for instance, more than 64 percent of the 2.5 million residents identify as being of Hispanic or Latino origin, and an added 16 percent of the population consider themselves to be only white. Here, 19 percent of the population considers themselves black, 51 percent of the population was born outside of the U.S., and 72 percent speak a language other than English at home. Miami is a true global city (for history, see Portes and Stepick, 1993); still, there is resistance in talking about racism and, especially, the role of whiteness in U.S. society.

Because, here in South Florida, English/Anglo whites don't appear to be in positions of power when stacked against Cuban, Venezuelan, and other international groups that hold economic and political clout, it's especially challenging in an environment such as this to express how white supremacy continues to hold its grasp on popular culture, economic systems, racial classification, consumerism, the legal system, national politics, and dominant expectations and purposes of public education.

But then I ask them about Rosa Parks, often an icon of how the U.S. Civil Rights movement started—and "succeeded." I ask: What was her job? How old was she? Why did she sit down on the bus? Students almost always get the story "wrong." (I put wrong in quotation marks, because they usually tell the Parks story as they were taught—or as they have been conditioned to remember it—and it is *that story, that history* that is flawed). Parks wasn't a feeble old woman, as many of these students seem to remember from their elementary school teachings, and, she wasn't just tired from a day at the factory and just needed to sit down, damn the consequences.

Instead, Parks was a 42-year-old textile worker *who was also* an active local NAACP worker at the time of her disobedience (Theoharis, 2013). She was a rebel, pure and simple, and she showed it when she fought (for at least the second time) this same bus driver and the bus system. There are other elements of this story that are untold, too, such as details surrounding the complex social makeup of the bus seating, but the main problem in Parks' narrative lives in that Parks tends to be taught (and remembered) as being old, tired, and brave (the last is surely true).

If history books and popular remembrances via the press and entertainment showed Parks as she was—young, black, organized, intentional, and brave—she would represent a black movement as it was at the time: young, black, organized, intentional, and brave. In short, her act would represent a threat against a system of white-enforced injustice rather than a fight against a list of issues such as age, long workdays, and blatant racism that cloud the institutional and cultural oppression that she was really up against.

Had my students read that Parks' organized disobedience was a function of black power, a mission by a host of black leaders against white supremacy, dominant and legitimate history would ascribe more power to subversive groups, alternative explanations of life, and, most importantly, the experience, power, and agency of non-whites. However, if that were the case, Parks would be cast as crazy, she would likely never be spoken of again, and her face would surely not have been placed on a U.S. stamp as it was in 2013 (Hicks, 2013).

With barriers to understanding the power of race, and ideology that's so engrained and so well maintained that we all seem to "know" what we are talking about when we say "ghetto," "black"—and, in some cases "Southeast Side," "Chicago," and "Cairo"—the only way to make change is to address these issues, saying things that are uncomfortable to hear to implicate the social and cultural institutions that contribute to covert, racialized discourse—including the press.

Notes

Preface

1. Kowinksi (1985) writes that public spaces exist even within the spaces that are privately owned. Shopping malls and grocery stores, for instance, have long been seen as public gathering spots. For this project, I also consider streets, parks, schools, government buildings, and coffee shops to be, in varying degrees, public spaces.

2. A good source for information about health disparities based upon race and place can be found in a documentary series and its website, unnaturalcauses.org.

Introduction

1. In 2011, police also found another young black man, believed to be an accomplice, hunkered down in Texas. Much more about the Versypt trial can be found in news articles on local newspaper websites.

2. As discussed in the Preface, the majority of this book relies on data up to 2010 to reflect the issues of news place-making related to the Southeast Side at a particular time of immense news coverage. More and updated data specific to Iowa City can be found in the "Local Discussions Related to Disproportionate Minority Contact," March 2013, presented by the Iowa Department of Human Rights, Division of Criminal and Juvenile Justice Planning; "Racial Equity in Johnson County," The Coalition for Racial Justice, July 2013.

Chapter One

1. There is great debate about whether journalists are professionals, and whether journalism is a trade, craft, or art. Largely because journalists (at least in the U.S.) do not require a certificate or license as do other "professions," controversy remains in both the industry and scholarship about how to explore the standards and organizational elements of American journalism (Zelizer, 2004).

Chapter Two

1. Mapping via GIS provided data for several published papers by members of the research team.

2. A similar account of this writing appeared on my blog, What News Is, robertgutsche jr.com/blog.

3. It's especially ironic that blacks are far more likely to have heart disease and to die of heart disease than other racial and ethnic groups in the U.S. While blacks are more susceptible

to this kind of disease, and the coverage of the walking event would never lead one to believe so, all the while, a good number of Iowa City's blacks—and a host of other skin colors, too—were outside, being active, and enjoying their community.

Chapter Three

1. I apply this level of detail to provide readers the ability to examine my own inquiry through a systematic and rigorous evaluation of news as a cultural and authoritative text.

2. *The Daily Iowan* takes a publication hiatus for several weeks in the summer and other breaks that align with the university's schedule.

3. Much of my understanding about *The Press-Citizen*'s Writer's Group comes from interviews I conducted with several group meetings and the newspaper editor who oversaw their columns in 2010.

4. Even though letters to the editor and reader columns are not produced by professional journalists, these texts are still relevant, because newsworkers select which submissions to publish, and because such contributions have the potential to influence news coverage (Nielsen, 2010).

5. Whereas previous readings had been done in groups based upon news publication (for example, I read all *Daily Iowan* stories at once before reading another newspaper's coverage), I read texts in groups based upon the event or topic. While previous readings gave me an understanding of how particular news organizations were covering the events and topics, I wanted an understanding of how journalists as a group (an interpretive community) characterized the same places, events, and topics. The third reading was performed based upon chronology.

Chapter Four

1. This information comes from personal conversations with the woman in the photograph and Shelter House's executive director within a couple of weeks of the photograph's publication.

Chapter Five

1. In my initial study, Michael's name was assigned the pseudonym Ulrich, but I found that name too distracting for this project.

2. Interviews were conducted specifically for my dissertation at the University of Iowa School of Journalism and Mass Communication and built upon hundreds of other conversations between 2009 and 2013 specific to rhetoric surrounding the Southeast Side. I attempt to indicate throughout this project when and where interviews occurred to help place participants' comments in perspective.

3. My mental mapping protocol asked participants to "draw a map of Iowa City as you know it to be. You will only have this sheet of paper to draw your map. Consider drawing roads, people's homes, schools or whatever you think is important. Draw where you go in the city and what you do. Write in the map your thoughts about specific spaces. What do these places mean to you?" I allowed participants to begin drawing for a few moments and then asked to them describe the maps as they were drawing them. General questions that guided the semi-structured interviews included: Where do you live on this map? Tell me about specific features of the map. How long have you lived in Iowa City? Tell me your thoughts about the neighborhoods on this map. What do you think about the different parts of town? How do you find media coverage of these neighborhoods and the different parts of town?

4. In compliance with the University of Iowa's Institutional Review Board (IRB), I emailed the journalists to measure their interest in participating in the study and to inform them of the process. Participants selected the location for their interviews, often choosing to meet in coffee shops or at the Moeller Media Research Lab in the University of Iowa's Adler Journalism

Building. Each interview was conducted within one week of the initial email, and all interviews were completed within a one-month period. Once we met, I again explained the study to each participant and answered questions about the project. With IRB approval, participants were not required to sign an informed consent form: My initial email to them indicated that their affirmative email response to participate would serve as acceptance of informed consent.

5. Interviews lasted between 45 and 60 minutes, and each participant agreed to have their interview audio recorded. My initial email to journalists said that they would not be given confidentiality so that I could refer to specific news stories that they had published, thereby identifying them by name. However, several participants said that they would only participate if they were assigned a pseudonym to protect their confidentiality. Therefore, all journalists were given pseudonyms, and I promised not to connect their pseudonyms with specific news stories.

6. Those who chose not to participate in this study said that they were concerned about confidentiality and the controversy about issues pertaining to the Southeast Side.

7. As with journalists, officials and community leaders were informed that their affirmative response to participate in the study waived the need for a signed informed consent document. Participants selected the location for the interview. Two met in coffee shops; the remainder met in their offices or in the Moeller Research Lab. Each interview lasted between 45 and 60 minutes and was audio recorded with the participants' permission. Participants were assigned a pseudonym to protect their confidentiality, although none requested such protection.

8. The City of Iowa City does recognize a Southeast Neighborhood Association; however, this space is North of Highway 6 and further East of the locations participants identified as the "Southeast Side."

9. It's ironic that an apartment complex in Iowa City's Southeast Side, which tends to house large numbers of racial and ethnic minorities (particularly blacks) would be called an "enclave," a term that also carries a negative connotation as a "ghetto."

10. As I introduced myself, and again as we began the interview, I told clients that they were free to decline to participate in the study. I read an informed consent form with each client before they agreed to participate. If they wished to participate, I informed them of their choice to consent during our initial meeting or at a later date.

11. Per IRB permissions, participants were not required to sign a consent form in order to participate. I was concerned that asking participants who are often marginalized in this community to sign a form would undercut trust between us. Instead, reading the informed consent forms to them, answering their questions about the project, allowing them to select pseudonyms, and allowing participants to end their involvement with the project at any time provided more protection than a traditional informed consent process. Participants were also asked to take an informed consent form with them after the interview. Originally, I planned to record my sessions with residents, with their permission, but after several residents said they did not want their interviews recorded, I set aside that plan and relied on notes taken during the interviews supplemented by field notes completed immediately following each interview. Interviews lasted between 45 and 60 minutes.

12. None of *The Daily Iowan* reporters I spoke with were aware that their newspaper was provided for free on the city's public buses and that many Southeast Side residents who use the bus read the college paper for their information about the city. In fact, residents I spoke with told me that they were more familiar with community news, places, and people because of *The Daily Iowan*.

13. I experimented with the mental mapping method with five acquaintances prior to using the method with study participants. This helped me test what approach, directions, and questions might arise in the field and allowed me to be more clear with participants about the project and its methods.

Chapter Six

1. Little reporting appears in *The Daily Iowan* that is not connected directly to the university campus and downtown, journalists told me. However, *The Daily Iowan* did report on the murder of a white landlord in the Southeast Side, the opening of a new police station there, and elementary school redistricting. Thirty-one of the 82 news stories analyzed in Chapter 4 came from *The Daily Iowan*. Additionally, *Daily Iowan* staffers say that these stories were presented as newsworthy by professional papers, *The Gazette* and *The Iowa City Press-Citizen*, and that *The Daily Iowan* needed to cover them to remain competitive.

2. I consider neighborhood associations and their representatives to be officials. Neighborhood associations are, after all, groups recognized and endorsed by the city government, acting as a liaison between residents and city officials. The neighborhood center is funded by the county and assigned roles in daycare and guiding residents to governmental resources. Neighborhood association members and neighborhood center staff were news sources in coverage of the Southeast Side in 2009 and 2010. Furthermore, these sources were the "boots on the ground" who brought a recognizable level of authority and legitimacy to the stories.

Chapter Seven

1. While U.S. Census block group and tract level data are not specific enough to provide further details of who lives where in this geography, trailer parks in and around Iowa City tend to be largely white and Hispanic.

Conclusion

1. Data also appear in "Local Discussion Related to Disproportionate Minority Contact," a report published in March 2013 by the Iowa Department of Human Rights Division of Criminal and Juvenile Justice Planning.

Epilogue

1. These words appeared in a story headlined "A levee blast saves an Historic Black Illinois Town" by Joyce Jones on the Black Entertainment Television website on May 4, 2011. The story was one of the few in the initial weeks of coverage of Cairo that overtly spoke to the city's past—and the present day.

References

Abel, E. (2010). *Signs of the times: The visual politics of Jim Crow.* Berkeley, Los Angeles and London: University of California Press.

Abu-Lughod, J. L. (2007). *Race, space, and riots in Chicago, New York, and Los Angeles.* New York: Oxford University Press.

Ainsworth-Darnell, J. W., and Downey, D. B. (1998). Assessing the oppositional culture explanation for racial/ethnic differences in school performance. *American Sociological Review, 63*(4), 536–553.

Alexander, M. (2010). *The new Jim Crow: Mass incarceration in the age of colorblindness.* New York: The New Press.

Allen, J. W. (2010). *Legends and lord of Southern Illinois.* Carbondale, IL: Southern Illinois University Press.

Anderson, J. D. (1988). *The education of Blacks in the South, 1860–1935.* Chapel Hill and London: The University of North Carolina Press.

Attoh, K. A. (2011). What *kind* of right is the right to the city? *Progress in Human Geography, 35,* 669–685.

Averill, S., Gates, J., Hartman, K., and Wellner, K. (1999). *Strengthening neighborhoods through equity planning: The Broadway-Crosspark Study.* Iowa City, IA: University of Iowa, School of Urban and Regional Planning.

Bailey, J., Law K., Mason, S., and Phillips, R. (2011). *Broadway-Crosspark neighborhood quality of life study.* Iowa City, IA: University of Iowa, School of Urban and Regional Planning.

Bal, M. (2009). *Narratology.* Toronto, Buffalo, and London: University of Toronto Press.

Ball-Rokeach, S. J., Kim, Y. C., and Matei, S. (2001). Storytelling neighborhood: Paths to belonging in diverse urban environments. *Communication Research, 28*(4), 392–428.

Balousek, M. (1995). *Wisconsin heroes.* Oregon, WI: Waubesa Press.

Bannister, J., and Kearns, A. (2013). The function and foundations of urban tolerance: Encountering and engaging with difference in the city. *Urban studies.* doi: 10.1177/0042098013477705.

Bannow, T. (2013, March 7). Crime alarms Casey's lawyer. *The Iowa City Press-Citizen.*

Bantz, C. R. (1985). News organizations: Conflict as a crafted cultural norm. *Communication, 8,* 225–244.

Bantz, C. R., McCorkle, S., and Baade, R. C. (1980). The news factory. *Communication Research, 7*(1), 45–68.

Barnett, B. (2006). Medea in the media: Narrative and myth in the newspaper coverage of women who kill their children. *Journalism, 7*(4), 411–432.

Barnett, B. (2013). Toward authenticity: Using feminist theory to construct journalistic narratives of maternal violence. *Feminist Media Studies, 13*(3), 505–524.

Bauman, R. (2004). *The world of others' words: Cross-cultural perspectives on intertextuality.* Malden, MA: Blackwell.

Beauregard, R. A. (2003). *Voices of decline: The postwar fate of U.S. cities.* New York and London: Routledge.

Beckett, K., and Herbert, S. (2009). *Banished: The new social control in urban America.* New York: Oxford University Press.

Belz, A. (2009, September 20). Exuberance of youth, liquor a heady brew. *The Gazette.*

Ben-Porath, E. N., and Shaker, L. K. (2010). News images, race, and attribution in the wake of Hurricane Katrina. *Journal of Communication, 60*, 466–490.

Berger, M. A. (2011). *Seeing through race: A reinterpretation of civil rights photography.* Berkeley and Los Angeles: University of California Press.

Berkowitz, D. (1997). *Social meanings of news: A text reader.* Thousand Oaks, CA: Sage.

Berkowitz, D. (2011). *Cultural meanings of news: A text reader.* Thousand Oaks, CA: Sage.

Berkowitz, D., and TerKeurst, J. V. (1999). Community as interpretive community: Rethinking the journalist-source relationship. *Journal of Communication, Summer*, 125–136.

Bettelheim, B. (2010). *The uses of enchantment. The meaning and importance of fairy tales.* New York: Vintage Books.

Bialek, N. (2007, August 23). Remembering the struggle. Retrieved from http://bayview now.com.

Bird, S., and Dardenne, R. (1997). Myth, chronicle and story: Exploring the narrative qualities of news. In Berkowitz, D. (Ed.), *Social meanings of news* (pp. 333–350). Thousand Oaks, CA: Sage Publications.

Bird, S. E. (2002). It makes sense to us: Cultural identity in local legends of place. *Journal of Contemporary Ethnography, 31*(5), 519–547.

Blaeser, K. (1997). On mapping and urban Shamans. In Penn, W. S. (Ed.), *As we are now: Mixblood essays on race and identity* (pp. 115–125). Berkeley and Los Angeles: University of California Press.

Blank-Libra, J. (2004). Choosing sources: How the press perpetuated the myth of the single mother on welfare. In Heider, D. (Ed.), *Class and news* (pp. 25–43). Lanham, MD: Rowman and Littlefield.

Bloom, S. (2011). Observations from 20 years of Iowa life. Retrieved from http://www.theatlantic.com/politics/archive/2011/12/observations-from-20-years-of-iowa-life/249401.

Bohner, G., Bless, H., Scharz, N., and Strack, F. (1988). What triggers causal attribution?: The impact of valence and subjective probability. *European Journal of Social Psychology, 18*, 335–345.

Bonilla-Silva, E. (2010). *Racism without racists: Color-blind racism and racial inequality in contemporary America.* Lanham, MD: Rowman and Littlefield.

Booker, C. (2008, July). Cory Booker's angry letter to *Esquire. Esquire.*

Borowski, G. (2006, December 7). A hint of trouble, then tragedy. *Milwaukee Journal Sentinel.*

Bourdieu, P., and Passeron, J. (2000). *Reproduction in education, society and culture.* London, Thousand Oaks, CA and New Delhi: Sage.

Breed, W. (1955). Social control in the newsroom: A functional analysis. *Social Forces, 33*, 326–355.

Burd, G. (1977). The selling of the Sunbelt: Civic boosterism in the media. In Perry, D. C., and Watkins, A. J. (Eds.), *The Rise of Sunbelt Cities, 14*, 129–149. Sage Publications.

Burgess, J. A. (1985). News from nowhere: The press, the riots and the myth of the inner city.

In Burgess, J. A., and Gold, J. R. (Eds.), *Geography, the media and popular culture* (pp. 192–229). London and Sydney: Croom Helm.

Campbell, C. P. (1995). *Race, myth and the news*. Thousand Oaks, CA: Sage.

Carey, J. W. (2009). *Communication as culture*. New York: Routledge.

Carlson, M. (2006). War journalism and the "KIA Journalist": The cases of David Bloom and Michael K elly. *Critical Studies in Media Communication, 23*(2), 91–111.

Carlson, M. (2012). "Where once stood titans": Second-order paradigm repair and the vanishing U.S. newspaper. *Journalism, 13*(3), 267–283.

Cecil, M. (2002). Bad apples: Paradigm overhaul and the CNN/Time "Tailwind" story. *Journal of Communication Inquiry, 26*(46), 46–58.

Chaichian, M. A. (2006). *White racism on the western urban frontier: Dynamics of race and class in Dubuque, Iowa (1800–2000)*. Trenton, NJ: Africa World Press.

Chilcott, L (Producer), and Guggenheim, D. (Director). (2010). *Waiting for Superman* [Motion picture].

Chiricos, T., and Eschholz, S. (2002). The racial and ethnic typification of crime and the criminal typification of race and ethnicity in local television news. *Journal of Research in Crime and Delinquency, 39,* 400–420.

Cloke, P., Cook, I., Crang, P., Goodwin, M., Painter, J., and Philo, C. (2004). *Practicing human geography*. Thousand Oaks, CA: Sage.

Coleman, C. (1995). Science, technology and risk coverage of a community conflict. *Media, Culture and Society, 17,* 65–79.

Collins, D., and Coleman, T. (2008). Social geographies of education: Looking within, and beyond, school boundaries. *Geography Compass, 2*(1), 281–299.

Collins, P. H. (2009). *Another kind of public education: Race, schools, the media, and democratic possibilities*. Boston: Beacon Press.

Coman, M. (2005). Cultural Anthropology and mass media. In Rothenbuhler, E. W. and Coman, M. (Eds.), *Media Anthropology*. (pp. 46–58). Thousand Oaks, CA: Sage.

Conzemuis, M. H. (2009, September 11) Is isolation what the city wants? *The Iowa City Press-Citizen*.

Conzemius, M. H. (2010, July 13). Perpetrators of urban decay. *The Iowa City Press-Citizen*.

Corbett, S. (2001, April). The lost boys of Sudan: The long, long, long road to Fargo. *The New York Times Magazine*.

Coyle, J., and Lindlof, T. (1988). Exploring the universe of science fiction: Interpretive communities and reader genres. Paper presented at the International Communications Association conference. New Orleans, May.

Crews, A. L. (2012, May 26). "It became the jewel of the city." *The Iowa City Press-Citizen*.

CRJ. (2013). *Racial equity in Iowa City and Johnson County*. Iowa City, IA: The Coalition for Racial Justice.

Curry, T. J. (2013, May 24). When black news disappears: White holds on black intellectuals' minds and misinforming the black public. Retrieved from http://truth-out.org/opinion/item/16567-when-black-news-disappears-white-holds-on-black-intellectuals-minds-and-misinforming-the-black-public.

Daily Iowan. (2009, September 30). Questions still remain in Deng death. *The Daily Iowan*.

Daniel, R. (2009, August 8). Number of homeless steady in area, nation. *The Iowa City Press-Citizen*.

Daniel, R. (2009a, January 28). Plan calls to replace Roosevelt. *The Iowa City Press-Citizen*.

Daniel, R. (2009b, February 11). Parents upset about replacing Roosevelt. *The Iowa City Press-Citizen*.

Darden, J., and Kamel, S. (2000). Black residential segregation in the city and suburbs of Detroit: Does socioeconomic status matter? *Journal of Urban Affairs, 22*(1), 1–13.

Darnton, R. (1975). Writing news and telling stories. *Daedalus, 104*(2), 175–194.

Davies, D. R. (2001). *The press and race: Mississippi journalists confront a movement.* Jackson, MS: University of Mississippi Press.

de Certeau, M. (1984). *The practice of everyday life.* Berkeley and Los Angeles: University of California Press.

Deggans, E. (2012). *Race-baiter: How the media wields dangerous words to divide a nation.* New York: Palgrave Macmillan.

Degh, L. (1972). Folk narrative. In Dorson, R. M. (Ed.), *Folklore and folklife* (pp. 53–83). Chicago: University of Chicago Press.

Delpit, L. (2006). *Other people's children: Cultural conflict in the classroom.* New York: Norton.

Denzin, N. K. (1997). *Interpretive ethnography: Ethnographic practices for the 21st Century.* Thousand Oaks, CA: Sage.

Deuze, M. (2005). What is journalism? Professional identity and ideology of journalists reconsidered. *Journalism, 6*(4), 442–464.

Diamond, J. B., Lewis, A. E., and Gordon, L. (2007). Race and school achievement in a desegregated suburb: reconsidering the oppositional culture explanation. *International Journal of Qualitative Studies in Education, 20*(6), 655–679.

Donohue, G. A., Olien, C. N., and Tichenor, P. J. (1989). Structure and constraints on community newspaper gatekeeping. *Journalism Quarterly, 66,* 807–812.

Downey, D. B., and Pribesh, S. (2004). When race matters: Teachers' evaluations of students' classroom behavior. *Sociology of Education, 77,* 267–82.

Downey, D. B., von Hippel, P. T., and Broh, B. A. (2004). Are schools the great equalizer? Cognitive inequality during the summer months and the school year. *American Sociological Review, 69*(5), 613–35.

Du Bois, W. E. B. (1989). The Souls of Black Folk. 1903. Rpt. *Du Bois: Selected Writings.*

Durham, F. (2008). Media ritual in catastrophic times: The Populist turn in television coverage of Hurricane Katrina. *Journalism, 9*(1), 95–116.

Earnest, N. (2011, January 21). Police, community happy with Southeast substation. *The Daily Iowan.*

Eckstein, B. (2006). *Sustaining New Orleans: Literature, local memory, and the fate of a city.* New York and London: Routledge.

Edy, J., and Dardanova, M. (2006). Reporting through the lens of the past: From *Challenger* to *Columbia. Journalism, 7*(2), 131–151.

Eggers, D. (2007). *What is what.* New York: Vintage Books.

Elliott, B. (2009, November 6). City needs orientation program. *The Iowa City Press-Citizen.*

English, T. J. (2011). *The savage city: Race, murder, and a generation on the edge.* New York: HarperCollins.

Entman, R. M., and Rojecki, A. (2001). *The black image in the white mind: Media and race in America.* Chicago and London: The University of Chicago Press.

Entrikin, J. N. (1991). *The characterization of place.* Worchester, MA: Clark University Press.

Ettema, J. S. (2005). Crafting cultural resonance: Imaginative power in everyday journalism. *Journalism, 6*(2), 131–152.

Ettema, J. S., and Peer, L. (1996). Good news from a bad neighborhood: Toward an alternative to the discourse of urban pathology. *Journalism and Mass Communication Quarterly, 73*(4), 835–856.

Ettema, J. S., Whitney, D. C., and Wackman, D. B. (1987). Professional mass communicators. In Berkowitz, D. (Ed.), *Social meanings of news* (pp. 31–45). Thousand Oaks, CA: Sage.

Ewen, S., and Ewen, E. (2008). *Typecasting: On the arts and sciences of human inequality.* New York, NY: Seven Stories Press.

Fairclough, A. (2008). *Race and democracy: The civil rights struggle in Louisiana, 1915–1972.* Athens: University of Georgia Press.

Farkas, G., Lleras, C., and Maczuga, S. (2002). Does oppositional culture exist in minority and poverty peer groups? *American Sociological Review, 67*(1), 148–155.

Filak, V. F., and Pritchard, R. S. (2007). News (un)scripted: An analysis of support and blame in the wake of two fatal shootings. *Journalism, 8*(66), 66–82.

Fish, S. (1980). *Is there a text in this class?* Cambridge, MA: Harvard University Press.

Forman, M. (2002). *The hood comes first: Race, space, and place in rap and hip-hop music.* Middletown, CT: Wesleyan University Press.

Forman, M., and Neal, M. A. (2004). *That's the joint! The hip-hop studies reader.* New York and London: Routledge.

Frank, R. (2003). "These crowded circumstances": When pack journalists bash pack journalism. *Journalism, 4*(4), 441–458.

Franklin, N. (2010, October). Watching the detectives. *New Yorker.*

Fraser, J. C., Burns, A. B., Bazuin, J. T., and Oakley, D. A. (2013). Hope VI, colonization, and the production of difference. *Urban Affairs Review, 49*(4), 525–556.

Fry, K. (2003). *Constructing the heartland: Television news and natural disaster.* Cresskill, NJ: Hampton Press.

Fry, W. H., and Liaw, K. (2005). *Interstate migration of Hispanics, Asians and Blacks: Cultural constraints and middle class flight.* Population Studies Center, University of Michigan Institute for Social Research.

Galesburg. (2008). *A call to action: Poverty in Knox County, Illinois.* Galesburg Area Chamber of Commerce.

Gallagher, C. A. (2008). "The end of racism" as the doxa: New strategies for researching race. In Zuberi, T. and Bonilla-Silva, E. (Eds.), *White logic, white methods: Racism and methodology* (pp. 163–178). Lanham, MD: Rowman and Littlefield.

Gallegos, R. (2009, August 16). Neighbors fight back. *The Iowa City Press-Citizen.*

Gandy, O., and Baron, J. (1998). Inequality: It's all in the way you look at it. *Communication Research, 25*, 505–527.

Gans, H. (2004). *Deciding what's news: A study of CBS Evening News, NBC Nightly News, Newsweek and Time.* Evanston, IL: Northwestern University Press.

Gans, H. (2011). Multiperspectival news revisited: Journalism and representative democracy. *Journalism, 12*(3), 3–13.

Garland, S. (2009). *Gangs in Garden City: How immigration, segregation, and youth violence are changing America's suburbs.* New York: Nation Books.

Gauen, P. (2011, May 5). Saving Cairo meant choosing between catastrophes. *St. Louis Post-Dispatch.*

Geertz, C. (1973). *The interpretation of cultures.* New York: BasicBooks.

Gilliam, F. D., Jr. (1999). The "Welfare Queen" experiment: How viewers react to images of African-American mothers on welfare. *Nieman Reports, 53*(2).

Goetz, E. G. (2003). *Clearing the way: Deconcentrating the poor in urban America.* Washington, D.C.: The Urban Institute Press.

Goetz, E. G. (2013). *New Deal Ruins: Race, economic justice, and public housing policy.* Ithaca, NY and London: Cornell University Press.

Goodman, J. (1994). *Stories of Scottsboro.* New York: Vintage.

Gould, P., and White, R. (1974). *Mental maps.* London and New York: Routledge.

Graham, H. D. (1967). *Crisis in print: Desegregation and the press in Tennessee.* Nashville: Vanderbilt University Press.

Gravengaard, G., and Rimestad, L. (2012). Elimination of ideas and professional socialisation: Lessons learned at newsroom meetings. *Journalism Practice, 6*(4), 465–481.

Gruber-Miller, S. (2013, Sept. 15). Iowa's opportunity gap. *The Gazette.*

Gruber-Miller, S., and Hennigan, G. (2013, Oct. 13). Homes remain elusive for some Iowans. *The Gazette.*

Gruber-Miller, S., and Hennigan, G. (2013a, Sept. 29). Grade rates for blacks, Latinos not keeping up. *The Gazette.*

Gruber-Miller, S., and Pigee, J. (2013, Oct. 6). Disparity remains in minority jailings. *The Gazette.*

Gruber-Miller, S., and Sutter, J. (2013, Sept. 22). Low-end jobs, low pay contribute to minority poverty in Iowa. *The Gazette.*

Gutsche, R. E., Jr. (2011). Building boundaries: A case study of the use of news photographs and cultural narrative in the coverage of local crime and in the creation of urban space. *Visual Communication Quarterly, 18*(3), 140–154.

Gutsche, R. E., Jr. (2011a). Missing the scoop: Exploring the cultural and sociological influences of news production upon college student journalists. In Franklin, B. and Mensing, D. (Eds.), *Journalism education, training and employment* (pp. 63–77). New York and London: Routledge.

Gutsche R. E., Jr., (2012). "This ain't the ghetto": Diaspora, discourse, and dealing with "Iowa Nice," *Poroi, 8*(2).

Gutsche, R. E., Jr. (2013). There's no place like home: Storytelling of war in Afghanistan and street crime "at home" in the *Omaha World Herald. Journalism Practice,* doi: 10.1080/17512786.2013.778602.

Gutsche, R. E., Jr. (in-press). News place-making: Applying "mental mapping" to explore the journalistic interpretive community. *Visual Communication.*

Gutsche, R. E., Jr., and Salkin, E. R. (2011). News stories: An exploration of independence within post-secondary journalism. *Journalism Practice, 5*(2), 193–209.

Gutsche, R. E., Jr., and Salkin, E. R. (2013). "It's better than blaming a dead young man": Creating mythical archetypes in local coverage of the Mississippi River drownings. *Journalism, 14*(1), 61–77.

Hall, A. and Mosiman, D. (2005, April 10). Allied Drive: One year later, *Wisconsin State Journal.*

Hall, S. (1980). Encoding and decoding in television discourse. In Hall, S., Hobson, D., Loew, A., and Willis, P. (Eds.), *Culture, media, language* (pp. 128–138). London: Hutchinson.

Hallin, D. C. (1986). Cartography, community, and the Cold War. In Manoff, R. K. and Schudson, M. (Eds.), *Reading the news.* (pp. 109–145). New York: Pantheon.

Handley, R. L. (2008). Israeli image repair: Recasting the deviant actor to retell the story. *Journal of Communication Inquiry, 32*(2), 140–154.

Harris, A. L. (2006). "I (don't) hate school": Revisiting oppositional culture theory of Blacks' resistance to schooling. *Social Forces, 85*(2), 797–834.

Harrison, I., and Harrison, F. (1999). *African American pioneers in anthropology.* Urbana and Chicago: University of Illinois Press.

Harry, J. C. (2004). "Trailer Park Trash": News, ideology, and depictions of the American underclass. In Heider, D. (Ed.) *Class and news* (pp. 213–229). Oxford: Rowan and Littlefield.

Harvey, D. (2003). *Paris, capital of modernity.* New York: Routledge.

Harvey, D. (2009). *Social justice and the city.* Athens, GA: The University of Georgia Press.

Heider, D. (2000). *White news: Why local news programs don't cover people of color.* Mahwah, NJ: Lawrence Erlbaum Associates.

Heldt, D. (2009, May 22). I.C. residents share their concerns in wake of brawls. *The Gazette.*

Hennigan, G. (2009, September 17). I.C. officials concerned over rise in crime. *The Gazette.*

Hennigan, G. (2009a, September 4). I.C. Council will consider curfew, loitering ordinances. *The Gazette.*

Hennigan, G. (2010, August 1). Bad reputation. *The Gazette.*

Hennigan, G. (2010b, July 29). Johnson County looks to make properties safe. *The Gazette.*

Herman, E. S., and Chomsky, N. (2008). *Manufacturing consent: The political economy of mass media.* London: The Bodley Head.

Hermiston, L. (2009, July 31). Public helps police find man's family. *The Iowa City Press-Citizen.*

Hermiston, L. (2009a, August 1). Police look for men who fired gun. *The Iowa City Press-Citizen.*

Hermiston, L. (2009b, August 7). Police investigate 2nd report of gunshots. *The Iowa City Press-Citizen.*

Hermiston, L. (2009c, May 22). Raised voices, ideas fill meeting. *The Iowa City Press-Citizen.*

Hermiston, L. (2009d, August 8). Experts: Refugees' pasts can haunt them in U.S. *The Iowa City Press-Citizen.*

Hermiston, L. (2010, February 12). 17-year-old charged in Broadway murder. *The Iowa City Press-Citizen.*

Hermiston, L. (2010a, July 26). Gang activity not new to Iowa City. *The Iowa City Press-Citizen.*

Hermiston, L. (2010b, July 17). Regency residents: Now what? *The Iowa City Press Citizen.*

Hermiston, L. (2013, March 29). Crime levels decreasing in surrounding areas. *The Iowa City Press-Citizen.*

Hicks, J. (2013, February 4). Rosa Parks postage stamp is released. *The Washington Post.*

Hindman, E. B. (2003). The princess and the paparazzi: Blame, responsibility, and the media's role in the death of Diana. *Journalism and Mass Communication Quarterly, 80*(3), 666–688.

Hines, H. (2013, Oct. 31). District addressing special ed concerns. *The Iowa City Press-Citizen.*

Hines, H. (2013a, Oct. 10). School officials divided on diversity policy. *The Iowa City Press-Citizen.*

Hirsch, A. R. (1998). *Making the second ghetto: Race and housing in Chicago 1940–1960.* Chicago and London: The University of Chicago Press.

Hirsch, J. S. (2002). *Riot and remembrance: The Tulsa Race War and its legacy.* Boston and New York: Houghton Mifflin.

Holland, M. M. (2012). Only here for the day: The social integration of minority students at a majority white high school. *Sociology of Education, 85*(2), 101–120.

Holt, L. F. (2013). Writing the wrong: Can counter-stereotypes offset negative media messages about African Americans? *Journalism and Mass Communication Quarterly, 90*(1), 108–125.

Holt, L. F., and Major, L. H. (2010). Frame and blame: An analysis of how national and local newspapers framed the Jena Six controversy. *Journalism and Mass Communication Quarterly, 87*(3/4), 582–597.

Hough, G. A. (1994). *Newswriting.* Independence, KY: Houghton Mifflin.

Hu, L. (2013). Changing job access of the poor: Effects of spatial and socioeconomic transformations in Chicago, 1990–2010. *Urban Studies,* doi: 10.1177/0042098013492229.

Hunt, M. O., Hunt, L. L., and Falk, W. W. (2012). "Call to home?" Race, region, and migration to the U.S. South, 1970–2000. *Sociological Forum, 27*(1), 117–141.

Hymes, D. H. (1980). Functions of speech. In Hymes, D. H. (Ed.), *Language in education* (pp. 1–18). Washington, D.C.: Center for Applied Linguistics.

Ispa-Landa, S. (2013). Gender, race, and justifications for group exclusion: Urban black students bussed to affluent suburban schools. *Sociology of Education, 86*(3), 218–233.

Iyengar, S. (1991). *Is anyone responsible? How television frames political issues.* Chicago: University of Chicago Press.

Jencks, C., and Phillips, M. (1998). *Black-White test score gap.* Washington, D.C.: Brookings Institution Press.

Johnson, K. L. (2007). Writing deeper maps: Mapmaking, local indigenous knowledges, and literary nationalism in native women's writing. *Studies in American Indian Literature, 19*(4), 103–120.

Jones, J. (2011, May 3). A levee blast saves an historic Black Illinois town. Retrieved from http://www.bet.com/news/national/2011/05/04/a-levee-blast-saves-an-historic-black-illinois-town.html.

Kaniss, P. (1997). *Making local news.* Chicago and London: The University of Chicago Press.

Katz, M. B. (1989). *The undeserving poor: From the war on poverty to the war on welfare.* New York: Pantheon.

Katz, M. B. (2012). *Why don't American cities burn?* Philadelphia, PA: University of Pennsylvania Press.

KCRG. (2009, March 24). One year ago: Sueppel murders. KCRG. Retrieved from http://www.kcrg.com/news/local/41754802.html.

KCRG. (2011, July 18). Chicago man accused of Coralville robbery now behind bars. KCRG. Retrieved from http://www.kcrg.com/news/local/Chicago-Man-Accused-of-Coralville-Robbery-Now-Behind-Bars-125734583.html.

Keene, D. E., Padilla, M. B., and Geronimus, A. T. (2010). Leaving Chicago for Iowa's "Fields of Opportunity": Community dispossession, rootlessness, and the quest somewhere to "be OK." *Human Organization, 69*(3), 275–284.

Keppler, C. (2009, May 14). Neighborhood anxious after riots in I.C. *The Gazette*.

KGAN. (2012, February 1). Steps to prevent bus stop problems in downtown Iowa City. KGAN. Retrieved from http://www.cbs2iowa.com/shared/newsroom/top_stories/videos/kgan_vid_9773.shtml.

Khalek, R. (2013, May 31). Racist school closings in Washington, D.C. Retrieved from http://truth-out.org/news/item/16672-racist-school-closings-in-washington-dc.

Kieran, M. (1997). *Media ethnics: A philosophical approach*. Westport, CT: Praeger Publishers.

Kim, C. Y., Losen, D. J., and Hewitt, D. T. (2010). *The school-to-prison pipeline: Structuring legal reform*. New York and London: New York University Press.

King, G. (1996). *Mapping reality: An exploration of cultural cartographies*. New York: St. Martin's Press.

Kneebone, E., and Berube, A. (2013). *Confronting suburban poverty in America*. Washington, D.C.: The Brookings Institution.

Kneebone, J. T. (1985). *Southern liberal journalists and the issue of race, 1920–1944*. Chapel Hill: University of North Carolina Press.

Kotlowitz, A. (1992). *There are no children here: The story of two boys growing up in the other America*. New York: Anchor.

Kovach, B. and Rosenstiel, T. (2007). *The elements of journalism: What newspapers should know and the public should expect*. New York: Three Rivers Press.

Kowinski, W. S. (1985). *The malling of America: An inside look at the great consumer paradise*. New York: William and Morrow Company.

Kozol, J. (1991). *Savage inequalities: Children in America's schools*. New York: Harper Perennial.

Kozol, J. (2005). *The shame of the nation: The restoration of Apartheid schooling in America*. New York: Three Rivers Press.

Krivo, L., Peterson, R., and Kuhl, D. (2009). Segregation, racial structure, and neighborhood violent crime. *American Journal of Sociology, 114*(6), 1765–1802.

Ladd, F. (1967). A note on "the world across the street." *Harvard Graduate School Education Association Bulletin, 12*, 47–48.

Lantz, H. R. (1972). *A community in search of itself: A case history of Cairo, Illinois*. Carbondale, IL and Edwardsville, IL: Southern Illinois University Press.

Lefebvre, H. (1991). *The production of space*. Malden, MA: Blackwell.

Lewin, E. (2006). *Feminist Anthropology: A reader*. Malden, MA: Blackwell.

Lewis, O. (1963/1998). The culture of poverty. *Society, January/February*, 7–9.

Lewis, S. C. (2012). *Mayberry*. Iowa City, IA: Working Group Theatre.

Lindlof, T., and Taylor, B. (2010). *Qualitative communication research methods*. Thousand Oaks, CA: Sage.

Lipsitz, G. (2006). *The possessive investment in whiteness: How white people profit from identity politics*. Philadelphia, PA: Temple University Press.

Loewen, J. W. (2005). *Sundown towns: A hidden dimension of American racism*. New York: Touchstone.

Lule, J. (2001). *Daily news, eternal stories: The mythological role of journalism.* New York and London: The Guilford Press.

Lule, J. (2004). War and its metaphors: News language and the prelude to war in Iraq, 2003. *Journalism Studies, 5*(2), 179–190.

Lynch, K. (1980). *Managing the sense of a region.* Cambridge, MA: The MIT Press.

MacLeod, J. (1995). *Ain't no makin' it: Aspirations and attainment in a low-income neighborhood.* Boulder, San Francisco and Oxford: Westview Press.

Maly, M. T. (2005). *Beyond segregation: Multiracial and multiethnic neighborhoods in the United States.* Temple University Press.

Manning, P. (2001). *News and news sources: A critical introduction.* Thousand Oaks, CA: Sage.

Manoff, R. K. (1986). Writing the news (by telling the "story"). In Manoff, R. K. and Schudson, M. (Eds.), *Reading the news* (pp. 197–229). New York: Pantheon.

Marable, M. (2011). *Malcolm X: A life reinvented.* New York: Penguin Books.

Masquelier, A. (2006). Why Katrina's victims aren't *refugees*: Musing on a "dirty" word. *American Anthropologist, 108*(4), 735–743.

Massey, D. S., and Denton, N. A. (1993). *American apartheid: Segregation and the making of the underclass.* Cambridge, MA: Harvard University Press.

Massey, D. S., Rothwell, J., and Domina, T. (2009). The changing bases of segregation in the United States. *The ANNALS of the American Academy of Political and Social Science, 626,* 74–90.

Matei, S., Ball-Rokeach, S. J., and Qui, J. L. (2001). Fear and misperception of Los Angeles urban space: A spatial-statistical study of communication-shaped mental maps. *Communication Research, 28*(4), 429–463.

McChesney, R. (2013). *Digital disconnect: How capitalism is turning the internet against democracy.* New York: The New Press.

McGee, M. C. (1980). The "ideograph": A link between rhetoric and ideology. *Quarterly Journal of Speech, 66,* 1–16.

Meiklejohn, A. (1965). *Political freedom: The Constitutional powers of the people.* New York: Oxford University Press.

Meyers, M. (2004). African American women and violence: Gender, race, and class in the news. *Critical Studies in Media Communication, 21*(2), 95–118.

Miller, V. (2013, March 8). Reports: Minorities overrepresented in Johnson County justice system. *The Gazette.*

Mitra, R. (2010). Resisting the spectacle of pride: Queer Indian bloggers and interpretive communities. *Journal of Broadcasting and Electronic Media, 54*(1), 163–178.

Monmonier, M. (1996). *How to lie with maps.* Chicago, IL: The University of Chicago Press.

Munz, M. (2011, May 2). Corps set to break levee near Cairo, Ill. *St. Louis Post-Dispatch.*

Mutel, C. F. (2010). *A Watershed year: Anatomy of the Iowa floods of 2008.* Iowa City: University of Iowa Press.

Naughton, L. (2013). Geographical narratives of social capital: telling different stories about the socio-economy with context, space, place, power and agency. *Progress in Human Geography,* doi: 10.1177/0309132513488731.

Neiger, M., Meyers, O., and Zandberg, E. (2011). *On media memory: Collective memory in a new media age.* Hampshire, UK: Palgrave MacMillan.

Nielsen, R. K. (2010). Participation through letters to the editor: Circulation, considerations, and genres in the letters institution. *Journalism, 11*(1), 21–35.

Noguera, P. A. (2008). *The trouble with black boys... and other reflections on race, equity, and the future of public education.* San Francisco: Jossey-Bass.

Nollen, D. (2012, April 23). "Mayberry": Bold Hancher-commissioned play looks at race relations in Iowa City. Retrieved from http://hooplanow.com/2012/04/23/mayberry-bold-hancher-commissioned-play-looks-at-race-relations-in-iowa-city.

NPR. (2010, July 12). Nashville schools see racial disparities in suspensions. National Public Radio. Retrieved from http://www.npr.org/templates/story/story.php?storyId=128466 061.

Ogbu, J. (2004). Collective identity and the burden of "acting White" in Black history, community, and education. *The Urban Review, 36,* 1–35.

O'Leary, J. (2009, August 27). Los Cocos to close temporarily. *The Iowa City Press-Citizen.*

O'Leary, J. (2009a, August 10). Police charge man with attempted murder. *The Iowa City Press-Citizen.*

O'Leary, J. (2009b, August 27). Residents' views mixed on proposed curfew. *The Iowa City Press-Citizen.*

O'Leary, J. (2009c, August 19). Residents ask city council to take action. *The Iowa City Press-Citizen.*

Omi, M. and Winant, H. (1994). *Racial formation in the United States: From the 1960s to the 1990s.* New York and London: Routledge.

O'Reilly, S. (2010, July 9). Myths about Iowa City crime don't fit the facts. *The Iowa City Press-Citizen.*

Parisi, P. (1998). *The New York Times* looks at one block in Harlem: Narratives of race in journalism. *Critical Studies in Mass Communication, 15,* 236–254.

Payne, C. M. (2008). *So much reform, so little change: The persistence of failure in urban schools.* Cambridge, MA: Harvard Education Press.

Pennington, E. (2011, May 16). Iowa City police investigating gunshot. *The Gazette.*

Petrus, J. (2009, August 16). Iowa City neighborhood upset about crime. *The Gazette.*

Portes, A. and Stepick A. (1993). *City on the Edge: The Transformation of Miami.* Berkeley and Los Angeles: University of California Press.

Press-Citizen. (2009, September 9). Curfew raises more concerns than solutions. *The Iowa City Press-Citizen.*

Press-Citizen. (2013, Sept. 29). Iowa city police investigating two armed robberies and a stabbing. *Iowa City Press-Citizen.*

Raab, S. (2008, July). The battle of Newark, starring Cory Booker. *Esquire.*

Ravitch, D. (2010, November 11). The myth of charter schools. *New York Review of Books.* Retrieved from http://www.nybooks.com/articles/archives/2010/nov/11/myth- charter-schools.

Reese, S. D. (1990). The news paradigm and the ideology of objectivity: A socialist at the *Wall Street Journal. Critical Studies in Mass Communication, 7,* 390–409.

Reese, S. D. (2001). Understanding the global journalist: A hierarchy-of-influences approach. *Journalism Studies, 2*(2), 173–187.

Reich, Z. (2011). Source credibility and journalism: Between visceral and discretional judgment. *Journalism Practice, 5*(1), 51–67.

Relph, E. (1976). *Place and placelessness.* London: Pion.

Rhatigan, C. (2009, May 19). Police discuss controlling recent violence. *The Iowa City Press-Citizen.*

Rich, M. (2012, September 20). Segregation prominent in schools, study finds. *The New York Times.*

Riegert, K., and Olsson, E. (2007). The importance of ritual in crisis journalism. *Journalism Practice, 1*(2), 143–158.

Roberts, G. and Klibanoff, H. (2006). *The race beat: The press, the civil rights struggle, and the awakening of a nation.* New York: Knopf.

Robertson, C. (2011, February 3). Smaller New Orleans after Katrina, Census shows. *The New York Times.*

Robinson, S. (2007). "Someone's gotta be in control here": The institutionalization of online news and the creation of a shared journalistic authority. *Journalism Practice, 1*(3), 305–321.

Robinson, S., and DeShano, C. (2011). "Anyone can know": Citizen journalism and the interpretive community of the mainstream press. *Journalism, 12*(8), 963–982.

Robinson, W. (2010). *Disintegration: The splintering of black America.* New York: Doubleday.

Rood, L. (2004, February 1). Job-hungry newcomers look for hope in Iowa, *The Des Moines Register.*

Rood, L. (2010, July 11). Trapped. *The Des Moines Register.*

Rood, L. (2010a, July 12). Trailer dwellers have few rights. *The Des Moines Register.*

Rood, L. (2010b, July 27). Evictions fly amid missing money. *The Des Moines Register.*

Rood, L. (2010c, July 11). Couple: We don't have a choice. *The Des Moines Register.*

Roth, G. (2009, June 1). Council has introduced a culture of violence. *The Iowa City Press-Citizen.*

Round, P. H. (2008). *The impossible land: Story and place in California's Imperial Valley.* Albuquerque, NM: University of New Mexico Press.

Rozin, P., and Royzman, E. B. (2001). Negativity bias, negativity dominance, and contagion. *Personality and Social Psychology Review, 5*(4), 296–320.

Said, E. W. (1979). *Orientalism.* New York: Vintage.

Santelices, M. V., and Wilson, M. (2010). Unfair treatment?: The case of *Freedle,* the SAT, and the standardization approach to differential item functioning. *Harvard Educational Review, 80*(1), 106–134.

Saulny, S. (2010, March 11). Board's decision to close 28 Kansas City schools follows years of inaction. *The New York Times.*

Schettler, E. (2010, July 30). Regency issues more evictions. *The Iowa City Press-Citizen.*

Schettler, E. (2010a, August 24). Iowa AG: Regency needs to change. *The Iowa City Press-Citizen.*

Schettler, E. (2010b, September 1). Mobile-home task force says progress being made. *The Iowa City Press-Citizen.*

Schettler, E. (2010c, September 9). Board talks housing code issues. *The Iowa City Press-Citizen.*

Schmidt, M. (2013, August 8). Police investigating taxi robberies in Iowa City. *Iowa City Press-Citizen.*

Schram, S. F., Fording, R. C., and Soss, J. (2011). Neoliberal paternalism: Race and the new poverty governance. In Jung, M., Costa Vargas, J. H., and Bonilla-Silva, E. (Eds.), *State of White Supremacy: Racism, governance, and the United States* (pp. 130–157). Stanford: Stanford University Press.

Schudson, M. (2003). *The Sociology of news.* New York: W.W. Norton and Co.

Schudson, M. (2005). News as stories. In Rothenbuhler, E. W. and Coman, M. (Eds.), *Media Anthropology* (pp. 121–128). Thousand Oaks, CA: Sage.

Schultz, I. (2007). The journalistic gut feeling: Journalistic doxa, new habitus and orthodox news values. *Journalism Practice, 1*(2), 190–207.

Seamon, D., and Sowers, J. (2008). Place and placelessness, Edward Relph. In Hubbard, P., Kitchin, R., and Valentine, G. (Eds.), *Key Texts in Human Geography,* (pp. 43–51). London: Sage.

Seng, M. P. (1982). The Cairo experience: Civil rights litigation in a racial powder keg. *The. Or. L. Rev., 61,* 285.

Shah, H. (2009). Legitimizing neglect: Race and rationality in conservative news commentary about Hurricane Katrina. *Howard Journal of Communications, 20*(1), 1–17.

Shoemaker, P. J., and Reese, S. D. (1996). *Mediating the message: Theories of influence on mass media content.* White Plains, NY: Longman.

Shoemaker, P. J., and Vos, T. P. (2009). *Gatekeeping theory.* New York and London: Routledge.

Shurson, A. (2009, July 24). Tough crowd. *The Gazette.*

Shurson, A. (2009a, August 21). 3 charged in connection with shots. *The Gazette.*

Sillars, M. O. (1991). *Messages, meanings, and culture: Approaches to communication criticism.* New York: HarperCollins.

Singer, J. B. (2007). Contested autonomy: Professional and popular claims on journalistic norms. *Journalism Studies, 8*(1), 79–95.

Skogan, W. G. (1990). *Disorder and decline.* Berkeley, CA: University of California Press.

Skovsgaard, M., Albæ, E., Bro, P., and de Vreese, C. (2013). A reality check: How journalists' role perceptions impact their implementation of the objectivity norm. *Journalism, 14*(1), 22–42.

Soja, E. W. (2010). *Seeking spatial justice.* Minneapolis, MN: University of Minnesota Press.

Soloski, J. (1989). News reporting and professionalism: Some constraints on the reporting of the news. *Media, Culture and Society, 11,* 207–228.

Sotirovic, M. (2003). How individuals explain social problems: The influences of media use. *Journal of Communication, March,* 122–137.

Spears, J. A., and Landsman, M. J. (2004). Broadway Neighborhood Community Assessment. University of Iowa School of Social Work. National Center for Family Centered Practice.

Spence, M., Lawson, B., and Visser, B. (2010). *The transformation of Iowa City's Southeast Side. Project on the Rhetoric of Inquiry.* University of Iowa.

Stabile, C. (2006). *White victims, black villains: Gender, race, and crime news in U.S. culture.* New York and London: Routledge.

State Data Center. (2012). *African-Americans in Iowa: 2012.* The State Data Center of Iowa and the Iowa Commission on the Status of African-Americans.

Stewart, B. (2011, April 29). Missouri speaker enrages Cairo. *Southern Illinoisan.*

Stocking, S. H., and Gross, P. H. (1989). *How do journalists think?* Bloomington, IN: ERIC Clearinghouse on Reading and Communication Skills.

Sullivan, A. (2012, May 10). City officials re-examine bus route following downtown bus stop fights. *The Iowa City Press-Citizen.*

Sullivan, A. (2013, April 29). Officials vow to address minorities in jail. *Iowa City Press-Citizen.*

Tavernise, S., and Gebeloff, R. (2011, March 24). Many U.S. Blacks moving to South, reversing trend. *The New York Times.*

Telles, E., Sawyer, M., and Rivera-Salgado (2011). *Just neighbors?: Research on African American and Latino relations in the United States.* New York: Russell Sage Foundation.

Theoharis, J. (2013). *The rebellious life of Mrs. Rosa Parks.* Boston: Beacon Press.

Thompson, J. B. (1990). *Ideology and modern culture: Critical social theory in the era of Mass Communication.* Oxford: Polity Press.

Time. (1967, September). Milwaukee: Groppi's army. *Time.*

Touré. (2011). *Who's afraid of post-blackness? What it means to be black now.* New York: Free Press.

Tuchman, G. (1973). Making news by doing work: Routinizing the unexpected. *American Journal of Sociology, 79*(1), 110–131.

Tyson, K., Darity, W., and Castellino, D. (2005). It's not a "black thing": Understanding the burden of acting white and other dilemmas of high achievement. *American Sociological Review, 70*(4), 582–605.

Valentine, D. (2009, September 2). No go zone. *The Daily Iowan.*

Venkatesh, S. A. (2000). *American project: The rise and fall of a modern ghetto.* Cambridge and London: Harvard University Press.

Venkatesh, S. A. (2006). *Off the books: The underground economy of the urban poor.* Cambridge and London: Harvard University Press.

Wallace, A. (2008). Things like that don't happen here: Crime, place and real estate in the news. *Crime Media Culture, 4*(3), 395–409.

White, D. M. (1950). The "Gate Keeper": A case study in the selection of news. *Journalism Quarterly, 27,* 383–396.

Wilkerson, I. (2010). *The Warmth of Other Suns: The Epic Story of America's Great Migration*. New York: Vintage.

Williams, R. (1976). *The country and the city*. New York: Oxford University Press.

Williams, R. (1977). *Marxism and literature*. New York: Oxford University Press.

Williamson, A. R., and Scicchitano, M. J. (2013). Dimensions of public meeting participation: Evidence from Florida's Truth-in-Millage Act. *Urban Affairs Review*, doi: 10.1177/107808 7413480463.

Wilson, W. J. (1997). *When work disappears: The world of the new urban poor*. New York: Alfred A. Knopf.

Wilson, W. J. (2009). *More than just race: Being black and poor in the inner city*. New York: W. W. Norton and Company.

Wolf, M. (1992). *A thrice told tale: Feminism, postmodernism and ethnographic responsibility*. Stanford, CA: Stanford University Press.

Wood, D. (2010). *The power of maps*. New York: The Guilford Press.

Yaccino, S. (2013, May 21). Chicago school closing may leave some communities without old lifelines. *The New York Times*.

Yanich, D. (2005). Location, location, location: Urban and suburban crime on local TV news." *Journal of urban affairs, 23*(3–4), p. 221–241.

Yount, B. (2011, April 28). Worst feared for Cairo floods. *Daily American*.

Zelizer, B. (1993). Journalists as interpretive communities. *Critical Studies in Mass Communication, 10*, 219–237.

Zelizer, B. (2004). *Taking journalism seriously: News and the academy*. Thousand Oaks, CA: Sage.

Zilbermints, R. (2009, April 15). Violence tests police. *The Daily Iowan*.

Zilbermints, R. (2009a, May 14). Fight central. *The Daily Iowan*.

Zuberi, T., and Bonilla-Silva, E. (2008). *White logic, white methods: Racism and methodology*. Lanham, MD: Rowman and Littlefield.

Index

Numbers in *bold italics* indicate pages with photographs.